Hanging In

Hanging In

WHAT
YOU
SHOULD
KNOW
ABOUT
PSYCHOTHERAPY

HARVEY R.
GREENBERG,
M.D.

FOUR WINDS PRESS   NEW YORK

LIBRARY OF CONGRESS
CATALOGING IN PUBLICATION DATA

Greenberg, Harvey R.
  Hanging in.

  Bibliography: p. 259
  Includes index.
  Summary: Discusses common emotional problems of adolescence
which can be helped by psychotherapy and gives practical advice on
getting the kind of professional help that is needed.
    1. Adolescent psychotherapy—Juvenile literature. 2. Adolescent
psychology—Juvenile literature. [1. Psychotherapy. 2. Psychology.
3. Emotional problems. 4. Adolescence] I. Title.
RJ503.G73   1982   616.89′14   82-70408
ISBN 0-590-07483-0

Published by Four Winds Press
A Division of Scholastic Inc., New York, N.Y.
Copyright © 1982 by Harvey R. Greenberg, M.D.
All rights reserved
Printed in the United States of America
Library of Congress Catalog Card Number: 82-70408
1   2   3   4   5   86   85   84   83   82

To Dr. Edward J. Hornick…
fragile token of durable affection

Table of Contents

A Word from the Author

This book is about the common emotional problems of adolescence and getting professional help for them. It describes what psychotherapy is and how different forms of psychotherapy work. It is written in simple, everyday language.

Like an encyclopedia, *Hanging In* covers a lot of territory and is not meant to be read all at once. Please feel free to "sample" the book. If you want to find out about one particular psychological problem, or one kind of psychotherapy, just read the chapters containing the information that interests you.

Hanging In

1 | *"If Only . . ."*

Besides practicing psychotherapy with teen-agers, I also treat adults. They're used to seeing young people in my office, and down through the years, I've heard them say things like:

If only I hadn't been so scared or stubborn when I was young, maybe I could have gotten help, and I wouldn't be in such a jam now!

If only someone had told me about psychotherapy, maybe I would have straightened myself out then, instead of waiting so long, and hurting so much.

If only my parents had realized I wasn't just going through "growing pains." *If only* my family hadn't tried to kid themselves that my troubles would disappear when I got older. *If only* they had forced me to go for help, even though I said I didn't want it, perhaps I wouldn't be seeing you now.

Of course, it's always easier to look backward and say what would have helped. The fact is, an adult patient might *not* accept psychological help if he or she were suddenly changed back into a teen-ager. Yet, I've found there's a lot of sad truth in these "if onlys." For many of my older clients, there's no doubt that therapy in their teens would have helped them find a better direction in life, or simply would have made getting through their adolescent years more bearable, thus making a happier adulthood more possible. That's why I decided to write a book that would answer the most important questions young people have about emotional problems and psychotherapy. If *Hanging In* can correct any "weird," scary, or misinformed notions you have that stand in the way of getting the help you may need, perhaps you won't have to end up saying "if only" to some psychotherapist years from now!

This is not meant to be a self-help book like *How to Be Your Own Best Friend*. *Hanging In* is meant for adolescents who've *already* gone as far as they can on their own, and are now thinking of turning to someone else for help. *Hanging In* isn't a psychology textbook either. You won't learn how to diagnose yourself or how to become the neighborhood "shrink," although you might get sound advice on helping a troubled friend or relative find professional assistance.

Basically this book is a practical guide to what psychotherapy is about, when and why it is needed, how it works, and how to go about getting it. First I will describe the complicated process of adolescent physical and psychological growth. Then I'll show why adolescents often do *not* get their emotional difficulties treated. I'll discuss the typical symptoms and situations that bring teen-agers into therapy, and give you some pointers on how to recognize whether you should consult a psychotherapist. I'll tell you about the different kinds of professionals who practice psychotherapy, and how to know a good therapist from a "dud." I'll describe the very special relationship between psychotherapist and patient and how it develops from the first visit to the last as the adventure of psychotherapy unfolds. You'll learn how a psychotherapist will deal with your parents, family members, and other adults outside your home. You'll find out what you are supposed to get from therapy, and how to tell when you aren't getting it and should go elsewhere.

Hanging In chiefly concerns the most common form of psychological treatment—individual outpatient psychotherapy. In this form you solve your problems with a therapist in a clinic or private office, while continuing to live your regular life at home. I'll also discuss other popular treatment methods such as group, family, and behavioral therapy, which may be combined with individual therapy or used alone. You will find chapters on medication, hospitalization, and other placements which are sometimes necessary when adolescents must leave their families (temporarily or permanently) because of their problems or their family's difficulties.

Before going any further, I want to let you know that even if you are having emotional troubles, as an adolescent you possess a great gift—a tremendously strong, natural drive for positive change. I have always enjoyed working with adolescents because of their basic energy, enthusiasm, and desire to heal their wounds so they can get back to the exciting business of growing up. With your enormous possibilities for growth, you can probably make better use of psychotherapy, if you do need it, than many adults.

2 Formal Adolescent Growth— The Vital Balance and Its Disturbances

Physical and Psychological Growth

A beautiful passage in the Bible says that for every time there is a season—a time to live, a time to die, a time to sow, and a time to reap. Life can be thought of as one great process of increase and decrease, of growth and death, containing within itself many smaller processes and rhythms.

Every life stage from childhood to old age has its own natural way of unfolding. When you become emotionally troubled, it often means that some process of development, of going on to the next step, has been interrupted. Instead, you have taken a wrong and hurtful path. Psychotherapy helps you remove the blocks placed in the path of your orderly, healthy development, so that you can go freely in whatever direction your natural talents point. In order to see if your adolescence has taken a wrong turn, it will be useful to know a little about the physical and emotional changes of ordinary adolescence. Let's start with the changes that take place in your body during your teens.

Growth during adolescence is brought about by the increasing amount of substances in the blood called *hormones*. They are manufactured by organs called *endocrine glands*, including the *pituitary*, *thyroid*, *adrenal*, and *sex* glands (the *testes* in a boy, the *ovaries* in a girl). It is thought that the pituitary gland is the "master" regulator and coordinator of all gland activity.

Youngsters vary as to when they undergo the physical changes of adolescence, and in how long it takes them to complete these changes. Some may show the first signs of *puberty* (the medical name for adolescence) as early as age ten or eleven, while others may not show any signs until their mid-teens. The first sign of puberty in a boy is usually the increase in the size of the testes (or testicles) at about age twelve. The penis then enlarges in length and width, and overall growth continues quickly. Body hair first appears in a boy's genital (or pubic) area about age eleven or twelve, in a typical "diamond" shape. More hair then grows under the armpits and on the chest and face (the hair present from childhood on the arms and legs also thickens). The boy's voice deepens when he is about fourteen; he is then usually able to have his first *ejaculation* of sperm, which indicates that the testicles are fully mature. The boy is now physically able to make a girl pregnant, although emotionally, he's far from ready! By mid-adolescence, age fifteen to sixteen, most boys show the muscular male body build, with broad shoulders and a tapering waist. The *primary sex characteristics* (penis and testicles) and *secondary sex characteristics* (male hair distribution, voice, body build) are fully developed by age seventeen; a bit more growth in height and weight may continue slowly for several years.

Budding of the breasts is the girl's earliest physical sign of puberty, starting as early as age ten. Hair first appears in the pubic area, then under the armpits. Hair on the arms and legs also thickens, but not as much as the boy's. There is little, if any, facial hair growth. Female pubic hair has a typical triangular shape. The labia (outer and inner lips surrounding the vagina, the female birth canal) increase in size, while the breasts enlarge throughout early adolescence. *Menstruation* (a girl's "period") first occurs at about age thirteen to fourteen, a sign of the maturity of the girl's inner sex organs, the ovaries and the womb (or uterus). For unknown reasons, many adolescent girls throughout the world have started menstruating earlier during the past forty years; thus it's not unusual for some girls to begin menstruation at age eleven to twelve. The girl is now physically ready to become pregnant, or will be within a year or so, although she is no more emotionally prepared for pregnancy than the boy! The girl's voice doesn't deepen like a boy's, but develops a richer, more adult tone quality. By about fifteen, the adolescent girl usually has the typical feminine body build, with narrow shoulders and wider hips. She has more fat beneath the skin, and less muscle bulk than a boy. Primary sex characteristics (breasts, vagina, and labia) and secondary sex characteristics (female hair distribution, voice tone, body build) are fully developed in most girls by age seventeen, and a regular monthly pattern of menstruation will be present by then. Growth in height and weight may continue for several years at a much slower rate. A girl's physical changes often begin one to two years earlier than a boy's, and maximum height and weight is likely to be reached earlier, too.

The power of the adolescent mind increases with physical growth. Thinking becomes more logical. The teen-ager is both more curious and better able to reason things out. Creativity blooms, too; it's during adolescence that serious artistic, scientific, and mathematical talent first make an appearance. Often teen-agers with average talent show some interest in literature, music, or art.

The emotional changes of adolescence begin roughly at the same time the body starts to mature, but it takes much longer for most youngsters in our culture to grow up emotionally than physically. While your body has undergone most of its development from child to young adult by your late teens, you're likely not to be fully mature psychologically until your early twenties or even later.

The chief psychological tasks you must face during early adolescence include adjusting to your rapidly changing body and all the exciting new feelings that come with a new physique. You also must begin to let go of the childhood dependency you've had upon your parents and family. This is never easy. You're caught in a typical adolescent dilemma—your body is changing tremendously, stretching out in wonderful, scary ways. You feel the first stirrings of sexual need, sense new power and strength, and hear the distant call of approaching adulthood. But at the same time you still have "childish" feelings of wanting to be taken care of, protected, told what to do.

Often as a result of this situation, you become panicky over the inner push toward adulthood by growing even more childlike, dependent, and demanding toward your parents. Then you may suddenly do an about-face and become resentful about still being dependent. It's common at this stage to blame your parents for "holding on," treating you like a baby, not giving you enough freedom, when in fact it may be *you* who can't get untangled from your own wish to hold on.

Experts believe the typical psychological process of early adolescence is *mourning*, or *grief*. Teen-agers often say they feel blue, lonely, and sad for no reason. There's nothing unusual about these feelings, and every good reason to have them. Much of this sadness stems from feeling so keenly the loss of the security of childhood. You really are growing *up*, and being able to look your parents squarely in the eye, you also see their weaknesses and failings much more clearly. Most adolescents don't like what they see at first. It's very disappointing but necessary to discover that your parents and other grown-ups aren't perfect. Then you really can start to take responsibility for your own life, without any false belief that some magically powerful person will always show up to make everything all right, the way your mother seemed to take hurt away with a smile, a kiss, or a cookie when you were young.

The most painful realization of all about grown-ups is that they won't live forever. This carries with it the awareness that you, too, must die some day. You now start to feel the *reality* of death. Perhaps you don't worry about it consciously, but nevertheless the awareness is there. This sad knowledge contains a disguised blessing. It actually extends your horizons, allowing you to have a much broader and deeper emotional life. Temporarily you may feel quite bitter toward your parents for not being bigger than life size. But these resentful feelings pass, as you recognize that we all share a common fate, common strengths and weaknesses, and common powers and limits.

Your need to know that you can be a person in your own right, your natural emotional and physical growth, your disappointment with your parents—these all combine to make young adolescents reach outside their family and form important new relationships with peers and adults. You will seek these new relationships as strongly as a river flows toward the sea, with individuals and groups, in school, clubs, teams, and in many different settings and organizations.

Your involvement outside the family is likely to take up a great deal of time and exclude your family. Outsiders are now often idealized, given all that special power and goodness your parents once seemed to have! Some of your relationships may have a fickle quality. You praise a friend or a "crush" to the skies, only to drop him or her like a hot potato and move on to a new idol. The previous idol then can seem stupid and "square."

Parents often grow confused and hurt by all these changes, as they watch their lovable little child turn into a stranger living under their roof. It's hard for them to understand that you are putting distance between your family and yourself in an effort to stand on your own two feet.

By age seventeen to eighteen, if everything goes well, you will have managed to work out the issue of dependency so that you can have a good social life away from home and better relations in your home. You don't have to bend over backward to show how little you need your family. You now see your parents and other grown-ups more as they really are. Relationships outside your family also have become more clear, less idealized, loyal and deeper, based on the reality of who the other person is. Now you can give to and take from others more meaningfully, and you are ready to fall in love—not the "puppy love" or crush of your early teens, but a much more serious, important relationship.

A keen sense of right and wrong, a concern for social, moral, and religious issues also ripens in later adolescence. You grow more concerned with making the world a better place to live in, and may get involved with "causes." You wonder abut the existence of God and the meaning of life. You start to wrestle with the realities of finding a secure place in the adult world, asking yourself what sort of work you want to do, what sort of person you want to marry, what kind of parent you want to be. You may have asked these questions before, but never as seriously. Now you begin to answer them, using beliefs and values you have learned from others inside and outside your family, adding your own valuable ideas. Gradually, as a blacksmith hammers a piece of iron into the proper shape, you forge an *identity*, a sense of self that is uniquely your own.

This process of identity formation continues into young adulthood. It is mostly completed by the late twenties, and yet in another sense, the task should never be totally finished if you are to remain emotionally healthy. You should be open to growth and change every day you are alive. Truly happy individuals, I think, always have some of the adolescent's eagerness for change, no matter how old they may be!

▌ *The "Vital Balance" and Your Emotional Life*

Every human being has to undergo the normal process of adolescent emotional and physical growth I've just described. But certainly not everyone develops psychological difficulties during their teens. Why is it that, exposed to the same kind or amount of stress, some people become troubled, and others don't? At *any* stage of life, your mental health depends on a *vital balance* of many inter-related factors.* These include:

(1) *Constitution and physical health.* Being born with a healthy makeup, and then continuing to enjoy good physical health is important for mental health. *Constitution* is every person's basic psychological and physical equipment for coping with life. Each of us is born with a unique set of rhythms and ways of reacting to our surroundings. If you watch fifty babies in a nursery, you'll see fifty highly individual ways of reacting. Some infants are slow to respond to light or noise, while others respond quickly and easily get upset. Experts have shown that your basic activity patterns often remain with you throughout life and are very important in determining how you handle emotional stress. It's not yet entirely clear where constitutional patterns, healthy or unhealthy, come from. Heredity, body chemistry, your mother's state of health and nourishment during pregnancy, and the kind of birth you had all play a part in forming your constitutional makeup.

The ancient Romans had a saying: *Mens sana in corpore sano.* That means: "A sound mind in a healthy body." Physical illness always makes it hard to feel well emotionally, but we know that future emotional well-being is particularly threatened by long illnesses in childhood, especially illnesses that continue on into adolescence, and keep you bedridden, away from normal contact with others your age.

(2) *Stable family life and good relationships.* Being raised in wholesome family surroundings is also important. The family should meet the emotional needs of its members, while encouraging their healthy growth outside the family. Meaningful, loving relationships with friends, your parents, or with your spouse and children (if you've formed your own family) are necessary. Loving rela-

---

*The idea of the *vital balance* was discussed by a noted American psychiatrist, Dr. Karl Menninger.

tionships, at the proper time of life, include sexual activity, enjoyed without guilt or fear.

(3) Work. You need work that's both interesting and rewarding enough to give you freedom from physical want. For a child, adolescent, and many young adults in our society, schooling takes the place of work and should be just as satisfying.

(4) Spiritual, creative, and recreational satisfaction. You need opportunities to develop your spiritual or religious beliefs; to enjoy play, whether play means hitting a baseball, catching a fish, or going for a walk; to be creative, based on your natural talents, such as writing a poem or playing an instrument; or to enjoy someone else's creativity, at a theater, a movie, or a museum.

(5) Society. You need to grow up and live in a healthy society, under a government that rules wisely, responds well to changing times, and allows each person to realize his or her special abilities.

Your emotional health probably would be guaranteed if you could be born with a strong constitution, have perfect health, grow up in a perfectly happy family, find a completely satisfying job that pays well, make a perfectly happy marriage, have wonderful friendships, and live, work, and play, free to follow your personal beliefs, in a perfect society. Of course this perfection doesn't exist, except in fairy tales or at the movies. We don't live in the best of all possible worlds. Even with our advanced knowledge, children are still born with crippling diseases. Although we are the richest people in the world, many of our citizens still suffer from poverty, malnutrition, discrimination—all conditions that breed emotional illness. And even people favored with good health and plenty of wealth can be scarred emotionally from being raised in families filled with problems. Because so many ingredients enter into the vital balance, because there is so much that can go wrong in our lives, no one is ever going to be totally free of stress or suffering. The vital balance should be seen as an ideal, certainly one worth striving for, but one that very few of us are ever likely to reach. What you can hope for is a *reasonably* good level of health or satisfaction in each area of the vital balance.

A good way of thinking about an emotional problem is to know that it always reflects some kind of disturbance within the vital balance. The disturbance may be brand-new, troubling someone who has previously done quite well. Or it may be the latest episode in a life filled with trouble. The disturbance may begin or involve one area of the vital balance or many. It may develop quickly or slowly. It may be caused chiefly by outside stresses, such as an accident or a business failure. But if a poor constitution, or early childhood problems have made an individual very sensitive to stress, even minor difficulties—getting a poor grade, being yelled at by a traffic policeman—can trigger off an emotional reaction that is much more explosive than the outside stress deserves.

How you react to the typical stresses of every stage of life depends upon your overall state of balance at that time, which also is dependent on the state of balance you bring into that stage. And your state of balance within each life stage probably will affect how well or poorly your following life stages are handled. The expected difficult situations of a life stage will be dealt with properly by someone who is pretty much "in balance," but the same stress may create emotional difficulties for someone who is already "off balance." Thus a child's first day in school can be extremely rough if that child has already been prevented from relating well to other children by its poor family relationships. A man about to retire may grow very troubled, if there is little at home that's important to him, now that his work is done.

At times in your growth when you have to undergo great physical and emotional changes, you are much more likely to get caught off balance, and possibly to develop psychological "hang-ups." Adolescence is one of the most stressful stages of growth, because it does involve the enormous changes already described. If you become troubled at this time, the psychotherapist can help you discover and correct areas of disturbance, or help you make better use of areas of strength already within your balance.

Signs, Symptoms, Situations

People go to a medical doctor because of a sign or a symptom, something they can see, like a rash, or something they can feel, like a pain in the chest, that indicates the body isn't working right. Aside from the obvious discomfort it causes, a symptom may be a distress signal sent out by the body to show it is in trouble.

The signal may be very strong –a high fever, serious weight loss—so that it is clear the patient is very ill. Occasionally, however, a sign or symptom is like the tip of an iceberg: It isn't that troublesome, the patient may not appear ill, but there's a lot of trouble lurking "below the water line"—for instance, when a painless lump in a woman's breast turns out to be cancer.

Like your body, your mind sends out messages when you are troubled, when your vital balance is disturbed, in the form of signs and symptoms. These indicators of psychological distress may not be as obvious as a rash or fever, or they may be painfully evident. When a "tip-of-the-iceberg" situation exists, there often will be weeks or months before a big emotional blowup when mild early-warning symptoms appear: trouble falling asleep, slight loss of appetite. You may disregard these warnings, but family and friends may notice them.

Severe psychological suffering isn't always directly related to how troubled you really are. It's common for teen-agers to tell me they are terribly disturbed, going crazy, falling apart, but for me to discover they are quite strong psychologically. Scared by their symptoms, they become so fearful they can't make use of their natural strength.

Like the doctor who treats your body, the psychotherapist tries to decode the distress signals you are sending to yourself. The medical doctor discovers from a symptom which part of the body isn't working properly—the circulation, lungs, or digestive system. The healer of the mind discovers how psychological symptoms or troubled behavior point to difficulties in your outside world and your inner, emotional world.

The medical doctor decodes physical distress signals by taking a careful history, performing a physical examination, and ordering studies such as blood tests and X rays. The doctor is then able to learn the cause of your illness and know what treatment to give. In order to figure out a method of treatment, the psychotherapist relies for the most part on what you say about your problems, as well as what can be directly observed about your appearance, speech, and behavior. While there are psychological tests that you can take (see Chapter 13), a psychotherapist's chief tools—emotional X rays, so to speak—are his or her training, sensitivity, and ability to create an atmosphere in which distressed people can feel free to reveal their troubles.

Now I am going to tell you about the most typical psychological signs, symptoms, and situations that bring adolescents to a psychotherapist. If you have been hurting emotionally and don't know what's the matter, I hope you'll get some useful basic information from these descriptions. It's possible that, like so many individuals with problems, you've been living in fear that something terribly mysterious has been happening to you, and *only* to you. The truth is that plenty of other youngsters have had exactly the same problems and have overcome them. Just naming a problem won't magically make it go away. But even knowing a little about what is bothering you is an important first step out of darkness.

One word of caution: If you do recognize a symptom or problem you're having, don't jump to conclusions about how sick you are. Don't think you've got a bad case of everything! *Only a trained professional can make the final judgment about the exact nature of your condition, about how mild or serious it is, and about what kind of treatment you need.*

3 | *Anxiety and Depression*

Anxiety and Related Problems

Imagine you are starting to cross a street with a green traffic light. Halfway down the block, a car is speeding toward you. The driver doesn't look as though he's going to stop, so you start to run back to the corner. But he's going so fast you're not sure you'll be able to get out of the way. Let's freeze the action and take a look at your emotional state the instant you know you are in danger. A raw feeling grips your gut; your heart races, your mouth is dry, your hands are clammy with sweat, your legs are weak, your knees shaky. You must move, and move *fast*—but you feel paralyzed.

        Next imagine you're taking a chemistry examination. You've studied hard, but aren't really sure you understand the topics. You're worried about failing.

Let's say you come from a family where poor grades might be met with anger and disappointment. Your sister always brought home high marks, always got along with your parents. *She* never was yelled at the way they pick on you. She's still racking up the A's in college, while you're limping along, barely pulling a C average, working hard at your books with no time for fun. As you sit down and pick up your pencil, all your worries about failure come rushing at you like a speeding car. A horrible feeling grips your stomach. Your heart starts racing, your mouth grows dry, your legs are weak. You have to get moving on the test—but you feel completely paralyzed.

These situations both have produced the *same* emotional response. What is the difference? In the first there is an actual threat to life and limb. If you don't get out of the driver's way, you'll be hit, hurt, maybe even killed. There's no physical threat in the second situation. If you fail the exam, they might chew you out at home, you might fail the course, or even, if the course was important enough, fail school. These are all unpleasant events, but they aren't going to kill you. Yet you reacted as if the test was as dangerous as the speeding car!

You've experienced *fear* in the first situation, and *anxiety* in the second. With fear there is a real danger. With anxiety there's no real danger, but because of inner conflict, it feels as if there were. I've known youngsters who have worked doubly hard in school because failing an exam seemed as great a shock as being physically injured. The possible loss of their parents' love or the possible shame of becoming a school dropout seemed as disastrous as being crippled or killed. In fact a person may deal better with a threat to the body than to his or her self-respect. When I was in the army, I saw men who hadn't flinched from the horrors of combat suffer terrible anxiety because of personal problems.

Just as fear may be mild or severe, depending upon the seriousness of the outside threat, anxiety ranges from mild to severe, depending upon how seriously you feel your self-respect or emotional balance is threatened. Anxiety, in one form or another, is probably the most common problem a psychotherapist treats. Anyone can become anxious, and everyone does, sooner or later. Experts believe a certain amount of anxiety is needed to help us get organized and move toward our goals. If you feel slightly nervous about your parents' reaction to your low grades, your anxiety may be one factor among others, such as ambition and a natural desire to learn, that makes you study a little harder. But with too much anxiety you get swamped, and it is difficult, even impossible, to get organized.

With anxiety you can feel continuously on edge and jittery, or you may experience anxiety in waves, panicky "attacks" lasting a few minutes to several hours. Usually it's hard to pin down a cause for your discomfort. People with anxiety attacks will say: "I don't know why I get so scared, I have nothing to worry about or be afraid of." But this only means you are unaware of or *unconscious* of what's triggering off the anxiety. Everyone has consciously denied one thing or another that's unpleasant. You get a bad report card, and have to show it to your parents. You bring it home, put it in your desk, then forget about it altogether. For the time being you've denied that the report card exists, yet in the back of your mind you do know it's there and that you'll have to "face the music" eventually. Psychologists have found that your mind can put something threatening or unpleasant aside, burying a problem without your ever having been conscious that it was there in the first place. Anxiety, and other unpleasant feelings, can be signals to you that a problem is still there, despite your unconscious efforts to make believe it isn't.

Anxiety may be related to an obvious conflict in your everyday life. It also may be traced back to deeply buried feelings that you are ashamed or afraid of, related to early family life, especially angry and sexual feelings. As children we've all had wishes to be the only kid at home. We want brothers and sisters to go away or die, or hope a parent who has yelled at us will fall down and break a leg. It's been shown that little children aren't as innocent about sex as grown-ups would like to think and are quite able to have sexual feelings toward the people they live with. A little boy wants to have babies with his mother, a little girl with her father. Brothers and sisters often "play doctor" with each other to explore the exciting, mysterious world of sexuality. Everyone has had such childhood desires; it is surprising how many people carry tremendous unconscious shame about them into adolescence and adulthood. An example:

A seventeen-year-old boy always got involved with girls who were already involved with other boys. Finally a girl actually left her boyfriend for him. His previous crush evaporated. He began having bad anxiety attacks, first during dates with her, then even when he thought about her. I learned he had had a very strong attachment to his mother as a child. His father was a traveling salesman who spent weeks away from home. When he was gone, the mother grew very lonely and turned to her son for the affection she missed. Sometimes she would take him into bed. Although nothing happened sexually, the boy still felt very stimulated, without quite knowing why. When the father came home, the mother showered her attention on him again, making the boy feel jealous and angry. Although he consciously forgot about these early experiences, his painful relationships with girls who "belonged" to other boys were really based on his jealous love for the mother who kept "rejecting" him. And when a girl said she would leave her boyfriend for him, he became terribly guilty and anxious, because this present-day victory was like defeating his father for his mother's love.

Some anxious teen-agers also have been anxious throughout childhood without any one particular conflict being responsible, leading experts to believe that this kind of anxiety may be part of a person's constitution. Anxious children are likely to be shy and timid, have more than the usual share of fear of strangers, the dark, or animals. They may have been anxious infants, easily startled by sounds or light, crying a lot, sleeping and eating poorly.

Anxiety often causes uncomfortable physical symptoms that sometimes mask emotional distress: rapid heart beat and pulse, palpitations (your heart feels as though it is pounding, or skipping beats); rapid, shallow breathing, difficulty catching your breath, tightness in your chest; loss of appetite, nausea (feeling like throwing up), diarrhea (frequent loose bowel movements), belching and abdominal pain (from swallowing a lot of air); dryness of your mouth; sweating of your palms, coldness and numbness of your hands and feet; dizziness; urinating frequently. Anxiety also may show up as tension. You feel that the muscles of your arms, legs, neck, or back are knotted up. Tension often leads to headaches and backaches that don't respond easily to painkillers.

During the day anxiety can make it difficult for you to concentrate, read a book, pay attention to what a teacher is saying, or to what's going on in a TV program. In the evening anxiety may make it difficult to fall asleep or stay asleep. You may awaken terrified, with your heart racing, from an anxiety attack during sleep. Nighttime attacks are often associated with vivid dreams or nightmares. Anxiety can make you look distracted; your expression is worried, and you are likely to behave irritably toward others.

Severe *pure* or *free-floating anxiety* (called free-floating because you can't pin down the reason for it) is one of the most painful feelings you can have. People have told me they'd rather endure physical illness than this raw emotional pain. Pure anxiety seems to be easily switched or exchanged for other symptoms that are at least easier to live with. We don't really know how or why this switching occurs. You don't consciously choose a substitute symptom for anxiety the way you'd pick out the best apple at a grocery store. There's evidence that you tend to use the same style or substitute for dealing with anxiety your parents have used, either by imitation or inheritance. Recent research has shown that complex disturbances in brain and blood chemistry may be a strong factor in some anxiety problems.

Other forms anxiety takes, besides the free-floating type, include:

▌ *Hypochondriasis.*
In this condition you focus your anxiety entirely upon your body. You become convinced something is very wrong or about to go wrong physically. You begin to watch the way your body functions the way an airport controller watches a radar screen,

taking your pulse and temperature frequently, worrying about the least little ache or pain. People with severe hypochondriasis often wander from one doctor to another, seeking relief without ever finding it. They are frequently criticized for making up physical problems or exaggerating minor ones. This is ignorant and unkind. With hypochondriasis you aren't putting on an act or consciously trying to get attention. You sincerely believe that your ailments are real and serious.

Just as you can have mild anxiety without being very troubled, you can have all sorts of mild physical complaints during adolescence without there being anything wrong with your body. These "growing pains," as they are popularly called, represent a kind of normal hypochondriasis, reflecting your anxious feelings about your body going through so many changes so quickly. But there are always a few youngsters who grow so upset by their physical changes (as well as other psychological stresses) that they develop constant, severe feelings of hypochondria requiring professional help.

Conversion Reaction.

This anxiety symptom is also known as *conversion hysteria*. Its main cause is thought to be the switching or conversion of anxiety (about an unconscious or barely conscious conflict) into an "illustration" of the conflict by using a part or function of the body. A good example is a fifteen-year-old girl who had an extremely troubled relationship with her mother. She grew very angry one evening when her mother screamed at her father during dinner because of his table manners. This was the last straw; her eyes fell on a carving knife, and hardly being aware of it, she thought: "I'd like to pick up that knife and cut her throat. Then maybe Dad and I could live in peace!" The thought of killing her mother made her terribly anxious and terribly guilty. Suddenly her hand grew weak and numb, then her whole arm was paralyzed. Her anxiety had been quickly *converted* into the paralysis, as if her mind had said: "To make sure you will never hurt your mother, to punish you for having such evil ideas, you won't move a muscle in that arm."

Other reasons for conversion symptoms may be a concern with a body part because of earlier illness or accident, or an unconscious wish to escape from a difficult life situation into the security of being taken care of as a sick person (a wish that also can be present in many other psychological problems). Whatever the cause, one is usually *completely* unaware of it. Unfortunately, like someone with hypochondriasis, a person with conversion is often criticized for putting on an act to get sympathy. While he or she may indeed want sympathy, the symptom is not made up, and the problems it causes are as real as in a physical illness. With an arm paralyzed from conversion, you don't pick up a tennis racket when the doctor's back is turned!

At the turn of the century, severe conversion symptoms were quite common in adults. For unknown reasons this pattern has now changed. Milder cases with a brief period of symptoms are seen today, more often by the pediatrician (child doctor) than the psychotherapist, and usually in girls in their early teens. Conversion symptoms seem to take place with the beginning of menstruation, possibly because it has stirred up anxious, unacceptable sexual thoughts.

Phobias.

With a *phobia*, your anxiety attaches itself to some object or situation which then makes you extremely afraid. A phobia may involve something realistically scary, but more often there's nothing about the object or situation that deserves any fear. One phobic boy I knew panicked whenever he saw a butterfly!

Some experts think the phobic object illustrates a deep, unconscious conflict. Others believe the unconscious cause of the phobia doesn't matter so much as the typical vicious cycle of behavior you get trapped in. Something scares you, you take steps to avoid it, feel better, and thus learn to continue an avoiding-behavior pattern. More fear is piled on top of your original fear as your avoidance continues, and a phobia that may have been quite small is now blown up to bigger than life size. It is also thought that some phobias at least partly stem from disturbed body chemistry.

Just about anything you can imagine may become targeted for a phobia. Common phobic objects are dogs, cats, bugs (especially spiders), and snakes. Common phobic situations include high places; closed-in spaces like an elevator or subway; open, exposed, or crowded places like a football stadium or a restaurant. Most people will stick to one phobic object or situation, but in severe cases phobias spread, taking in more and more of the person's life. A fear of riding buses may spread to every form of transportation, public or private, then to a fear of going outside the house at all.

Fear of school is the phobia treated most often by an adolescent psychotherapist. With school phobia, you suffer terror just at the thought of leaving home for classes. You find yourself complaining about physical problems so you can stay at home, especially on Monday mornings. Stomachaches and sore throats are popular excuses. You may give yourself realistic reasons to explain away your avoidance: Other kids make fun of you, teachers have it in for you.

School phobia *isn't* playing hooky. If hooky is your problem, chances are you're not scared; instead you feel bored, turned off by school, and would rather hang around somewhere else with your friends or by yourself. With a school phobia, you don't hang out. Instead you make a beeline straight for home, because kids with school phobia typically are very dependent upon their families, particularly their mothers (their mothers also tend to have trouble letting go of them). Severe school phobia is likely to be an iceberg situation. Avoidance of school is a signal that you are so strongly involved with people in your home that good relationships with people outside haven't developed properly.

Obsessions and Compulsions.

With symptoms called *obsessions* and *compulsions*, anxiety is channeled into thoughts or acts which are repeated over and over again, like magic rituals or spells. It's thought that these repetitious activities both express and deny—at the same time—those troublesome aggressive or sexual wishes that seem involved in so many emotional problems.

In an obsession a thought keeps popping into your mind that you recognize is "silly," "strange," or "outlandish," but you still can't shake it off.

A fourteen-year-old boy had obsessional thoughts about touching older women on the bus. He tried to reassure himself that his touching thoughts were ridiculous, that he would never be crazy enough to do such a thing; besides he wasn't even attracted to them so there was no good reason to touch them. Yet a few minutes later he'd be off thinking about touching again, and run through the entire painful process of reassuring himself. The thoughts of touching and the reassurances were repeated until he was emotionally exhausted. This obsession developed just as his sexual feelings were maturing. Without being too conscious of it, he was growing sexually aroused by his attractive eighteen-year-old sister, whose room was directly across the hall, and whom he occasionally glimpsed undressed. The uncomfortable sexual desire toward her reached his conscious mind through his obsession. Reassuring himself that it was silly to even think of touching older women who didn't excite him was a way of indirectly reassuring himself that he would never act on his sexual desire for his sister.

In a compulsion, an uncomfortable, unconscious, or barely conscious wish is worked out through performing some action repeatedly. It, too, is thought of as "silly," but is just as hard to stop.

A sixteen-year-old girl had to wash her hands six times before going to bed. It was shortly after getting into bed that she would want to masturbate, which she was very ashamed about, since she came from a very religious background that condemned masturbation. Her compulsive handwashing had become a substitute for masturbation. She was using her hands in a more acceptable activity, performing a "cleaned-up" version of the deed she felt so badly about! Another girl I treated, who was very angry at her critical and insensitive father, developed the "weird" notion that he would die unless she touched the furniture in her room in a certain order. In this way she magically protected him from her "hateful" thoughts.

Obsessions and compulsive rituals frequently occur together. If you have one or two of them, and they don't particularly limit your life, you may not even think about getting help. Indeed most of us have a few mild obsessions or compulsions without realizing it, pet superstitions about not walking under ladders, or avoiding black cats. However, in very severe obsessional states, symptoms grow like weeds, taking up more of your time, so that you can become withdrawn from your usual activities. Once in the grip of these symptoms, you often have a strong feeling that something dreadful will happen if your routines are stopped. You know they are ridiculous, but you have to continue on with them anyway. You may be worried that you are going crazy because you have such strange notions. Actually it is rare for someone with these problems to lose control, "flip out," or require hospitalization. Worrying about insanity can in itself be an obsession, rather than a concern for a real problem.

The most common obsessional thoughts involve worrying about doing some outrageous, destructive, unsocial, or criminal act, such as shouting out dirty words in a crowded theater or shoving someone in front of a subway train. I've never known anyone bothered by these thoughts who actually carried them out! Common compulsions include counting rituals, handwashing, checking to see if lights are out or doors are closed, arranging objects in an exact fashion . . . the list is endless.

Obsessive and compulsive difficulties often bring adolescents into psychotherapy. Studies show that 50 to 60 percent of these problems begin before the twenties.

Depersonalization.

Depersonalization makes you feel as if you are looking at yourself from a point "outside," often a great distance away. We have an observing part of the mind that keeps us from losing our "cool," from being swamped by our emotions, letting us exercise good sense by standing back from what's happening. Ordinarily you aren't aware of your inner "observer," but with depersonalization it's as if the observer has taken over completely, making you feel terribly removed from yourself. One patient told me: "It's like being on the ceiling and looking at myself far below . . . my hands and feet looked distant, almost as if they didn't belong to me."

Depersonalization often occurs when you are trying to distance yourself from a situation or conflict that is making you feel overwhelmed. Moments of depersonalization are common in adolescence, with all the stress you're dealing with. But frequent, long-lasting attacks are *not* common and may require help.

Déjà Vu.

In *déjà vu*, a sensation closely related to depersonalization, a new place or situation instead seems eerily familiar, as if you had been there before. Déjà vu may take the form of strongly feeling that you can predict exactly what someone will say or do. One explanation of déjà vu is that you have indeed been there before. Being in the new situation has triggered off anxiety related to something disturbing about a past situation that resembles the present one. You've pushed your troublesome memory into the unconscious part of your mind; in the present-day situation, it partly resurfaces as déjà vu, as if your observer were saying: "This time I'm ready, I'm not going to be taken off guard like last time, this is all very familiar!" Brief episodes of déjà vu regularly happen during adolescence and are no cause for alarm. But when déjà vu occurs frequently, strongly, either by itself or together with other anxiety symptoms like depersonalization, it may be a warning sign that you are undergoing severe emotional stress.

Amnesia and Sleepwalking.

In *amnesia*, anxiety causes your conscious observer to shut down, as if a light switch had been turned off. With a mild amnesia, several minutes or hours pass that you can't account for, but during your absence you look and act pretty much like yourself. In severe cases, people have been found wandering about dazed and confused, unable to recall anything at all about themselves, not even their names. Amnesia may be caused by a sudden, strong, emotional shock, or by a reaction to uncharacteristic behavior you are deeply ashamed of.

A seventeen-year-old boy was a top student, and the treasurer of his class. Unbeknownst to anyone he loved to gamble, and he lost several hundred dollars playing poker "over his head." He suffered a day of amnesia immediately after he took all of the class dues in order to pay off his debts.

The most frequent cause of amnesia is a blow to the head. Memory loss here is due to physical rather than emotional factors. Many cases of amnesia get better without any treatment at all. Psychological treatment can increase the speed of memory return, or start it coming back when it doesn't seem to be returning on its own.

Amnesia is pretty rare during adolescence, but *sleepwalking,* or *somnambulism*, is much more common. Often it has already started in childhood. Experts think that during sleep some somnambulists may be acting out a painful, anxiety-making experience or thought which has been pushed out of consciousness while awake. During sleepwalking you may get out of bed, do things that seem meaningless, or talk nonsense. Your eyes may be wide open, but you are still asleep, and after awakening you have no memory of what you said or did. The meaning of supposedly nonsensical activity during sleep can be discovered in psychotherapy.

A fifteen-year-old girl was having somnambulistic episodes during which she would pack and unpack her bags as if she were going on a trip. With treatment she was able to regain the painful memory of seeing her father pack his bags after a bad fight with her mother, when she was three years old. He left and never returned. Through her somnambulism she was imitating him, trying somehow to come to terms with the painful moment of her loss.

By itself somnambulism doesn't usually lead people to seek therapy—help is sought when it is associated with other problems. For instance, the girl who packed her bags also was suffering from deep depression and school failure as well as sleepwalking.

The Anxiety Mix.

In textbook cases people suffer from one form of anxiety. But textbook cases are usually found in textbooks, not in the real world. If you are having anxiety symptoms, you probably won't complain of a phobia alone. Instead it's likely that you are being bothered by a mixture of anxiety symptoms, one of which is the most troublesome. Thus a dog phobia may be associated with anxiety attacks; a handwashing compulsion may be accompanied by tension headaches. In addition, as you shall see, anxiety symptoms often come mixed with other types of symptoms and problems.

Depression and Related Problems

Next to anxiety, *depression*, with its related symptoms, is probably the chief reason adolescents are referred to psychotherapists. Depression can range from the ordinary "blue" spell everyone has known at one time or another, to a crippling illness that threatens life. Depression is one of the first ailments to be described in ancient medical textbooks; it has occurred in every land and culture and time. In recent years researchers have made important breakthroughs in the causes and treatment of serious depression, but there is still much about the problem that puzzles the experts.

If an infant is deprived of its mother for several days, it first grows restless, cries long and loud, then sinks into a quiet, listless state, often refuses to be fed, and responds poorly to its surroundings. If the mother returns, the baby cheers up, starts eating well again, and responds normally. But if the mother doesn't return for a long time, or doesn't come back at all, the baby may remain permanently withdrawn and quiet, and in extreme cases even may fall ill and die.

These symptoms represent the earliest form of depression. They show how very sensitive human beings are, from infancy, to the threat of *loss*. Psychologists believe that loss, or the fear of loss, is the most important ingredient in many serious depressions. The first loss you fear as an infant is the loss of your parents' life-preserving physical care. As your mind develops, you start to worry more about the loss of love and approval, instead of the loss of simple physical care. If your father or mother gets angry at you, you may feel temporarily as lonely and sad as if he or she had actually gone away or stopped feeding you.

How good you feel about yourself as a child is closely bound up with how you sense your parents feel toward you. If you know they have good, warm feelings about you, it is easier for you to feel secure, happy about yourself. If you don't experience your parents as basically approving you, later on in your life you can become extremely sensitive about things you do or say that you imagine will make you lose the approval of others. As you grow up, anything that causes a loss of self-respect and self-esteem can lead you to feel blue or sad temporarily. But the harder it has been to keep up your self-respect as a child, the easier it will be as an adolescent or adult to lose good feelings about yourself and become more seriously depressed. Failing a test, getting passed over for a promotion, not being admitted to the college you have chosen, can turn into deeply hurtful rejections, proof that you aren't a worthy person.

Your feelings of self-esteem are also tied up with your physical well-being. To feel good about yourself, you must feel good about your body. Serious depression can be related to a loss of confidence in your body, sometimes due to deformity or long illnesses in childhood, sometimes with no real basis, but an incorrect view of your physique. Instead of seeing your body as good, whole, and strong, you mistakenly may see it as weak, damaged, and not as attractive as the next person's—a source of shame. Even without such problems you can grow very depressed when age, sickness, or injury deprive you of health. I've found that people who set a very high value on youthful good looks, like actors, models, or politicians, are often prone to get very depressed as they age. Depression after an amputation or loss of sight is common; here, a valuable body part or function is being mourned, just as you would mourn the loss of a loved one.

Many experts link serious depressions to an inability to deal with angry feelings. It's been found that a lot of people with depressive tendencies don't show anger easily. They seem to have been programmed to think that it is bad to get mad, and that if they get mad, no one will possibly like them. Instead of becoming angry, they feel guilty and turn their anger against themselves, punishing themselves for their "bad" feelings. A more normal example of this process is found in the grief you experience after a loved one dies. Psychologists think an important ingredient of this grief is anger at the dead person for leaving you. Of course you can't realistically blame someone for dying. Your anger seems so shameful and unacceptable that you turn it against yourself and become "normally" depressed.

Recent research has shown that hereditary and biochemical factors can play a part in causing especially serious depressions. At this point it's not clear whether a depression triggers off the release of certain substances within the body, or whether the release of these chemicals is due to some sort of glandular disturbance that then triggers a depression.

Sometimes a severe depression may be brought on by a real blow, like a death. Instead of eventually returning to good spirits, your grief continues on and even deepens. On the other hand a bad depression can occur for no "good," "outside" reason, without any obvious stress or hurt. Depression may develop suddenly, or gradually. It may then last for a few days, but in severe cases months or even years may pass before you return to a normal mood. Untreated, depression may go on indefinitely; however, most depressions are self-limited, meaning that they run their own course and disappear, like a cold or a bout of the flu. Some people with depression will suffer just one bout, while others have a number of bouts throughout their lives. Depressive illness is no respecter of persons or personalities; *any* type of personality can get seriously depressed. In fact, many people who have suffered depression are naturally cheerful, energetic, and enthusiastic both before and after their illness.

Let's take a closer look at the basic experiences of depression. Think of how you felt when a pet died, or a good friend moved away, or your team lost a game even though everyone played as well as possible. These events made you sad. Things that ordinarily might have made you excited or happy didn't reach you. You may have felt like crying, may have lacked pep. The world seemed drab, gray. After a short time things started looking up again, your mood brightened, and you returned to your old self. These are natural responses to loss or disappoinment which anyone or everyone, as I've explained, can feel. A more serious depression can be thought of as an exaggeration of sad feelings that don't clear up as easily.

First and foremost depression is a disorder of your *mood*. In turn your sad mood affects the way you *think* and, quite often, the way you *look* and *behave*. With a severe depression you feel very blue, lonely, and empty inside. Colors don't look as bright, taste and smell and other sensations often don't register as vividly. These feelings are usually worse in the morning and improve as the day goes on. Your facial appearance is likely to be as sad as your depressed mood—drawn, pale, unhappy. Your body seems to droop, your grooming may suffer. You move slowly, as if carrying a great weight. Your speech may be slow, your voice quiet. You may find you use fewer words, and that it takes a great effort to speak. You may cry easily. Depression brings with it ideas of pessimism, hopelessness, and helplessness. You find less pleasure in activities that previously interested you. You can become self-critical, blaming yourself for all sorts of failures and shortcomings, real or imaginary. In a bad depression you may have little faith you will ever get better, believe that little can be done by you or anyone else to help you. Feeling this hopeless, helpless, and unhappy with yourself, you may set up a vicious circle, withdrawing into a shell, shutting out people who want to help you, then feeling even more lonely, unloved, and worthless.

A severe depression often is accompanied by physical symptoms. You are fatigued no matter how much rest you get; you always seem tired and lack energy. You may find it hard to fall asleep and stay asleep. Typically you find yourself waking up in the small hours of the night, then lie in bed going over and over your worries until day finally breaks, when you arise exhausted. Instead of being unable to sleep, you may sleep too much. This is especially true of depressed teen-agers, who spend most of the day in bed. Your appetite may suffer, with resultant weight loss, or you may overeat and gain a lot of weight. Other depressive physical complaints include headaches; cloudy, fuzzy feelings in your head; backaches; and constipation.

Depression and anxiety are almost always intertwined. Anxious individuals feel depressed to some degree, and depressed people frequently suffer from some form of anxiety.

Bad depressions seriously disturb your basic ability to cope and function. A mother won't be able to take care of her children, a businessman will stop working, a teen-ager won't be able to attend school. But these very deep depressions aren't as common as milder ones, which don't interfere as obviously with everyday activity, yet still make it very hard for people to take joy in living. There are literally *thousands* of such individuals who suffer with less dramatic versions of the same feelings, attitudes, and behavior seen in serious cases of depression. In fact, depression may be one of our biggest public health problems.

As with anxiety, depression may be channeled into symptoms or activities that either substitute less painfully for it, or make it less painful. The physical problems related to depression may become the most important source of discomfort for a depressed person, instead of the awful sad mood. Depressed individuals may try to raise their spirits artificially with alcohol, drugs, gambling, or sex. Surprisingly a depressive may handle the "blues" by denial and reversal, appearing falsely cheerful and enthusiastic.

The greatest danger of depression comes when you feel so hopeless and worthless that life no longer seems worthwhile. It's difficult for someone who hasn't been there to imagine depressive suffering. One patient told me he felt as though he had "cancer of the soul." Suicide is often attempted to cure this terrible pain by removing the self from the world.

The pain of depression isn't the only reason people think about suicide. A suicide attempt is a very complicated act, often meant *not* to succeed. No suicide attempt ever takes place in a vacuum: There's always a message intended for someone, and that message is usually HELP! A suicide attempt may be a protest about how you are being treated. It may be a way of demanding that others change their attitudes or behavior toward you. It can be a cruel expression of hatred and revenge. Oddly it may illustrate a hope for life, not death. Death may be seen as the possible beginning of a new life, with a magical daydream of dying or being brought to the edge of death, then awakening without problems, as if the self has been reborn.

Most people have had a suicidal thought cross their minds at least once. *Anyone*, regardless of how strong he or she is emotionally, can be driven to suicide if there is strong enough stress. But certain people are more likely to try it than others: those who've tried before, who've lost an important relative or parent through suicide in the past, or who have recently suffered the loss of a loved one through death, divorce, or a relationship breaking up.

Adolescent Depression

Experts agree that teen-agers, especially young adolescents, tend more often than adults to channel depression into substitute symptoms, or to replace depression with behavior that makes it feel less painful but in the long run is as unhealthy. (One theory is that, as an adolescent, you are less willing than an adult to put up with the suffering of a pure depressive mood without doing something about it.) Much adolescent drug abuse is really meant to medicate a concealed depression. Reckless driving, and other kinds of antisocial or delinquent behavior may be aimed at wiping out depression by providing dangerous kicks. If you are depressed, you also may unconsciously seek to be hurt, or caught by the police, to "cure" deep feelings of guilt. If you have been feeling continuously, intensely bored with life, it's quite possible your boredom may disguise a depression. You also are more likely than a grown-up to hide sad feelings behind a giddy, artificially happy mask.

Frequent causes of depression in adolescence are parental death, separation, or divorce. As I've mentioned previously, the process of distancing yourself from your family leads to blue, lonely feelings typical of the teen-age years. But when a parent can't be present because of death or divorce, the ordinary blues may be transformed into severe depression. It doesn't matter to many youngsters that they continue to see a divorced parent on weekly visits. The loss of family stability is enough to upset the vital balance, bringing on depression and many other problems. In fact divorce-related difficulties bring at least a third of the youngsters I see into treatment.

You also may get depressed because of being rejected by a girl friend or boyfriend, leaving home for college, being turned down for membership in a team or social club, getting poor grades, or not being able to get into a college. Sometimes the most minor events trigger depression. I saw a girl who became extremely depressed after she failed her driving test. For her, not being able to drive meant that she was still a dependent little girl, instead of the "cool" person she desperately wanted to be.

Suicide is becoming a very serious problem for depressed teen-agers and young adults throughout the world. Of the twenty thousand Americans who succeed in killing themselves every year, at least half fall into the younger age groups. Suicide is now the second cause of death in adolescence. (The first is accidents.)

I've found that suicidal acts by teen-agers are often dismissed as "trying to get attention"; this is especially true when an attempt doesn't look serious, such as taking five aspirin or a teaspoonful of Clorox. Just because a method wasn't deadly doesn't mean a serious difficulty isn't there. If you have been thinking a great deal about killing yourself, or have made even the smallest attempt, secretly or openly, you *deserve* to be taken seriously. You should take your own problem seriously enough to have at least one consultation with a psychotherapist.

4 | *Psychosis*

The symptoms of anxiety and depression can make life very unhappy, but the majority of people with these problems still continue to work, go to school, and relate to others while no one guesses that anything bothers them. They hurt, but they continue to deal realistically with the world. Even when they do seem obviously unhappy, there is little that is disturbing about their appearance or their behavior.

I'm now going to describe certain conditions in which social relationships and the ability to function are seriously crippled, in which thinking, appearance, and behavior are likely to seem very disturbed to yourself and to others. The most important feature of these conditions, called *psychoses*, is that the experience of reality itself is extremely disturbed, very different from the way the average person sees and knows the world.

Psychotic individuals have lost touch with the people and the events around them. They have instead become involved with an inner world filled with strange and often frightening experiences, the most common of which are *hallucinations* and *delusions*.

When one hallucinates, one sees, hears, feels, tastes, or smells something that isn't there, but is manufactured by the imagination. Certain hallucinations aren't abnormal. You can hallucinate on the verge of waking up or falling asleep. Then you actually are slipping into or out of a dream. When fully awake, if you remember the hallucination at all, you will realize that it wasn't real. An *illusion* is an experience closely related to a hallucination, which you also can have without being troubled. In an illusion a real object is mistaken for something else, often under the influence of temporary emotional stress. Say you come back from a scary movie and open the door to your house or apartment. In the dark hallway stands a coatrack, and for just a few seconds, with the movie still at the back of your mind, the coatrack looks like a tall, menacing, hunchbacked stranger. You switch on the light—once more the coatrack is only a coatrack!

Unlike sleep-related hallucinations or illusions, psychotic hallucinations don't fade away. They are like walking dreams. One is convinced of their reality, althought after recovery from psychosis one may then know that they were unreal. Hallucinations of vision and hearing occur more frequently than hallucinations of the other senses. One may hallucinate ordinary objects or have extraordinary visions—Jesus and the saints, werewolves, trees with golden fruit. Basically anything wonderful or horrible that can be imagined can be called into being by the mind and experienced as if it were real. With *auditory* hallucinations one may hear the voices of familiar or strange people, or even one's own voice. The voices may feel as though they're coming from inside or they may be located at some point outside, even heard coming from the radio or TV. Voices criticize or reassure, threaten harm, or command that one should do harm to others or to oneself. They can speak in whispers or shouts.

A *delusion* is a false belief that has no basis in reality and is not held by other people from a similar social and cultural background. In a delusional frame of mind, one may be convinced that everything that's going on relates directly to one. People talking to each other on the street seem to be discussing the deluded person, not their private affairs. One may think one has caused important national or international events or that they in some way illustrate one's concerns. For instance, a man I treated believed that when the president mentioned unemployment during a TV speech, he was trying to pass the word secretly that the man's job was in danger!

With *delusions of persecution* one imagines that some individual or group is out to do one harm—a family member, a neighbor, the Mafia, or the FBI. The term *paranoid* describes a strong, suspicious feeling of being observed, talked about, watched, followed, or persecuted. At one time or another most of us have gotten a little paranoid with stress, yet have had the sense to know our suspicions are groundless. But in a delusion of persecution, one can't back away from paranoid ideas; sometimes, life is ruled by them.

In *delusions of grandeur* one imagines oneself very wealthy or powerful, or singled out for some mighty destiny. These delusions often have a religious flavor. A woman I treated was convinced God had chosen her to be the new Christ, come down again to rid the world of sin and suffering.

One theory about hallucinations and delusions is that they are *projections* of painful inner states of mind into the outside world. Thus, an eighteen-year-old girl whose emotional problems were so severe that she believed she was falling apart actually began to see the world fall apart. She hallucinated buildings crumbling and the ground splitting under her feet. The man I mentioned earlier who thought he was going to lose his job believed his boss was persecuting him. In reality he was very angry at the boss, but in his projection, it became the boss who was angry, and out to get him. This tendency to project our feelings upon others is in all of us, to some degree, but it can be tremendously magnified in a psychosis.

Psychoses may be caused by obvious physical factors such as severe illnesses with high fever, a blow to the head, or drugs like LSD, amphetamines, cocaine, and even marijuana and alcohol. These "physical" psychoses are usually brief, and one returns to normal after the cause is removed or wears off, as with most of the drug-related psychoses seen in adolescence.

The most common type of psychosis is known as *schizophrenia*. It is believed that at least two million Americans suffer from it, and unfortunately it is often an illness of youth, starting during adolescence or in one's twenties. No one knows for certain what causes schizophrenia. The best guess today is that it is produced by a mixture of factors, different for each victim, including hereditary, chemical, and purely emotional influences. Some experts think that the future schizophrenic is more dependent upon parents as a child, and more sensitive to separation experiences. The normal pressure of the teens to become more independent puts too much stress upon such an individual, leading to a schizophrenic blowup. LSD and related mind-altering drugs, including marijuana, can unmask a schizophrenic illness in a sensitive person. Instead of recovering from the "bad trip," psychotic symptoms continue past the point where the drug would have worn off.

Schizophrenia may come on very slowly. In the *chronic* form of the disease, the patient may appear quiet, odd, and withdrawn for months or years and may have many unusual ideas or inner experiences which are carefully kept from the world, until more serious symptoms and behavior make it obvious that help is needed. In sudden or *acute* schizophrenia, psychotic symptoms explode seemingly without warning, frequently in the setting of an important, stressful life change, especially a separation, like going away to college.

In most cases of schizophrenia, especially the sudden kind, one obviously is disturbed and the disturbance probably will upset others. One is likely to hallucinate openly, and the mind is flooded with delusional thoughts. Mood often doesn't relate realistically to one's surroundings, but to troubled thinking. One may be extremely angry or fearful if worried about imaginary persecutors, or very joyful if one believes God has summoned one to meet the saints in heaven. One may sit still as a statue if one thinks that lifting a finger can destroy a city, or may strike out at anyone who comes near if one is frightened of being murdered. Appearance is usually untidy and strange; one may use clothing or makeup peculiarly to illustrate psychotic ideas. With these severe problems, one may be too ill to function in school, on a job, and at home, and may have to enter a hospital for treatment.

Schizophrenia can occur in one spell or repeated attacks. Recovery is quick and complete in some cases, but slow and incomplete in others, especially if the proper treatment isn't followed or isn't available. Very sadly some people never recover from the first episode at all. They stay troubled or, after an acute attack, they simply slip slowly into chronic illness to lead rootless, disconnected lives. Still, despite its seriousness, having an attack of schizophrenia today doesn't have to condemn a person to such a dismal fate. At one time little could be done for the illness, and it was thought that long periods of hospitalization were necessary. But there's been a tremendous amount of research about the illness in the past thirty years, and with powerful new drugs and psychotherapy techniques, schizophrenia is more and more regarded as a treatable condition. It is now possible to take up a normal life after a schizophrenic attack, especially if it is the first or if one hasn't been ill for too long before an acute spell. It's possible for hospitalization to be brief, or even unnecessary in many instances. The key to success is early, effective treatment, often continued long after the storm has passed, to prevent schizophrenia from becoming chronic.

Schizophrenia should *never* be confused with a non-psychotic disorder known as *multiple personality* (an everyday expression for it is *split personality*). This is an extremely rare condition, although you would never know from the publicity given to books like *Sybil*. The individual's main personality submerges from time to time, and is replaced by other personalities which he or she is not consciously aware of. The causes of the multiple personality disorder are still uncertain. Some experts believe the secondary personalitites develop as a means of coping with extremely harsh treatment in childhood.

▌ *Psychotic Depression*

In very serious depressions one may sink into such a deep state of despair that one loses touch with reality and becomes psychotic. In psychotic depressions the tendency to be self-critical turns into delusions of responsibility for natural or man-made disasters; one may feel so evil that it seems necessary to commit suicide to remove such a powerful source of badness from the world. One may refuse food totally, losing so much weight that life is threatened. Meaningful work and human relationships stop. Depressions like these are more common in adults, especially older grown-ups, than in adolescents. They respond very well to medication and other up-to-date treatment methods. In *manic-depressive psychosis*, periods of deep depression alternate with times when one becomes *too* happy, overactive, and noisy, hardly sleeping, the mind filled with delusional plans for improving the world. This condition sometimes starts in adolescence, but is more common in adulthood.

Ignorant people often throw the term *manic-depressive* around to describe the changeable behavior and mood of adolescents, which really reflect shifts in thinking and feeling very typical and normal for this difficult time of your life.

5 Behavior Problems

If you've got a behavior problem, chances are you don't suffer from obvious psychological symptoms. Your chief difficulty, as far as others can see, lies in annoying, rebellious, or even destructive behavior that labels you difficult or bad. This doesn't mean kids with behavior problems don't hurt emotionally—many do, but have learned to hide their pain from the world and themselves behind a tough, uncaring surface. Only their "bad" acting up shows through.

With a behavior problem it is likely you won't easily seek help on your own; instead you will be forced into seeing a therapist *after* your behavior gets you into trouble. If you had a *very* serious behavior problem, I doubt you would be reading this book in the first place, because you would be sure there wasn't anything wrong with you and that your bad behavior had a good excuse. The best I can hope for is that you may use the following information to advise a friend who is getting into trouble and won't take adult advice, or possibly recognize the early warning signals of your own behavior difficulty.

After the many years I've been working with adolescents, I'm still amazed at how often adults overlook adolescent behavior problems—especially in the early stages—by chalking them up to pranks or natural high spirits. If you've been involved in repeated petty stealing and fighting in school, it is very likely that your behavior points to something more serious than simply kicking up your heels. Stealing a car for a ninety-mile-per-hour joyride shouldn't be dismissed lightly as a prank.

▮ *Juvenile Delinquency*

This is really more a legal than a medical term, covering a wide variety of difficult behavior that brings teen-agers into contact with the authorities in school, court, or social agencies. Typical delinquent activities of boys include playing hooky, drug and alcohol abuse, reckless driving, stealing, and acts of vandalism such as setting fires, or cruel, aggressive behavior toward animals or people. More typical problems of the delinquent girl include small-time thievery—especially shoplifting—and promiscuity, a kind of driven, unpleasurable sexual coupling with many partners, often leading to unwanted pregnancy.

Juvenile delinquency most commonly occurs in large cities among the poor. Bad social and economic conditions in slums contribute to unhappy family life; broken families of the ghetto breed delinquency (and many other emotional problems). But even if your home life is okay, if you are forced to live in a wealthy society where you have no wealth, where unemployment for people from your social or racial background is high and hope for education or jobs low, then it is easy for you to think you'll do better dropping out of a school that doesn't teach you much anyhow, to become a street-wise criminal rather than live like a loser.

Poverty doesn't explain away the rising tide of delinquency today. Delinquent activity is also found among teen-agers from middle-class and well-to-do homes. Experts are wondering whether life can't be made *too* easy for you if you live in a certain kind of wealthy neighborhood and family; if having so much given to you and done for you undermines self-confidence and drive, so that you can grow bored easily, eager to seek "kicks" through delinquency with like-minded friends.

I've shown that depression is easily converted during adolescence into angry, rebellious behavior. Since depression is connected with a painful early experience of losing loved ones, it's of great significance that many delinquent teen-agers, rich or poor, have suffered the loss of a parent during childhood through death, divorce, or abandonment.

Studies indicate that the parents of delinquents are often overpermissive, unable to lay down good rules and standards. Significantly they themselves may have a delinquent history, and consciously will pass on their antisocial beliefs. Or they may have reformed their previous bad ways to become very strict and upright, yet still send out hidden invitations to their kids to act up. The father of one of my patients was repeatedly arrested during his teens for car theft and drunken driving. He "shaped up" after getting married and became a successful businessman who prided himself on running his home with an iron hand. He was angry and puzzled about the behavior of his delinquent son. He would tell the boy: "You are just itching to take my car behind my back and ride around like a drunken bum!" Afterward he'd leave the car keys in plain sight. His son then did exactly what the father both dared and invited him to do. The son was really being *loyal* to his father by acting out the *same* impulses the father had struggled with during *his* teens. The father got plenty of secret, unconscious "kicks" this way while neither he nor his son realized what was going on.

Gangs

Forming groups with other kids is a natural part of your adolescence. And teen-age gangs have a lot in common with other adolescent groups, if one tries to see past the negative feelings the word *gang* stirs up. Of course the good things provided by a gang have to be weighed against the delinquent activity that is usually the price for membership. Some gangs are really only social clubs; their members manage to keep acting up just within the limits of the law. Others are gangs in the worst sense of the word, small criminal armies with a record of destructive behavior. If you are involved in a gang, it can be hard to tell if it is the social or the destructive type.

It's not surprising that gang activity, like individual delinquency, often arises in city ghettos. Living in poverty, you are particularly likely to feel unwanted by society. With or without good reason, you may think your family has failed you, too, and turn to other kids to form a substitute "good" family. You pledge loyalty to your gang and in return receive approval you don't seem to get elsewhere. The gang may fill your life, locking out relationships at home or in school. Gang membership brings a wonderful sense of belonging, emphasized by special names, clothing, and initiation rituals. But sadly this wonderful closeness may have to be bolstered by attacks upon the "enemy" outside—other gangs, adults, and their property. Just like a little country, gangs often have a territory—their "turf"—and elected officers. Gangs are chiefly organized by boys, but many of them have auxiliary gangs for girls, whose behavior can be just as violent.

It's been found that the average gang member isn't as messed up emotionally as the delinquent youngster who acts alone; it seems to take a certain amount of psychological strength to get along in a gang, an ability to have close relationships. But if you become totally submerged in gang life, you may still wind up taking part in behavior you might ordinarily avoid, to show your loyalty and win respect.

Running Away

The chief problem of about twenty-five percent of youngsters the law classifies as delinquent is *repeatedly* running away from home or institutions. Most kids who run away from home don't do it repeatedly. Often there is a very good reason for leaving—a drunken mother who beats a son, a father sexually abusive toward his daughter. Sometimes running away seems to be the only way you can bring attention to a hurtful family situation. You may run away for adventure or to show you can survive on your own. After a family quarrel, when you feel particularly misunderstood, the thought of "showing them" by packing up and getting out easily crosses your mind: You may actually have left home for a few hours in this situation, or slept overnight at a friend's house.

What distinguishes the delinquent runaway is that he or she seems to leave the scene over and over again, at the smallest sign of stress, to the point where running away really becomes a way of life—and often a great source of personal pride. One runaway boy boasted to me: "The place hasn't been built yet that can hold me!" Many chronic runaway youngsters come from the deprived social conditions and unstable family backgrounds typical of other forms of delinquency.

Recently, however, we've seen a wave of middle- and upper-class runaways. It started with the hippie movement of the late sixties and still continues. Unlike other delinquents, the runaway is usually a very timid loner, not particularly interested in violence or crime beyond petty theft.

Research indicates that runaway adolescents have been particularly unwanted and openly rejected by their families. They feel very worthless, very pessimistic about fitting in anywhere. Most runaways are boys, but reports from big cities increasingly tell of teen-age girls who run away from home to be picked up by vicious men, then lured into a nightmare world of drugs and prostitution from which they may never return.

More About Aggressive Behavior

Teen-agers are often referred to psychotherapists because of aggressive behavior, such as fighting in school, on the streets, or at home. You also may choose to battle the world with words and threats, rather than your fists. Aggression, physical or verbal, should be looked at as a symptom, not an illness in and of itself. You may be acting aggressively because you are depressed, because of delinquency, drug abuse (especially amphetamine stimulants, PCP, and cocaine), psychosis, or brain damage.

A problem with aggression may reach the point where you feel like hurting, even killing, others, and you may be even more ashamed and fearful about such murderous feelings than about suicidal ideas (they often occur together). As with suicidal behavior, kids who commit serious aggressive acts frequently give advance warnings, and terrible tragedies have occurred when others don't get the message. Most teen-age homicides occur in the home, and family members are the victims. At least once a year I hear of a case where a teen-ager has murdered his parents, even an entire family. The boy (it is usually a boy) is always described as a model youngster, who earned good grades, had many friends, and seemed to be completely well adjusted. In putting his story together, however, it is frequently discovered that the outward show of health disguised months of emotional torment, with severe depressions and outbursts of anger which were hidden from the world, or which the family chose to ignore, until his controls snapped and disaster struck.

I believe in taking an adolescent's aggressive behavior or daydreams as seriously as suicidal thoughts or acts. If you have been repeatedly troubled by homicidal fantasies, are afraid you might harm someone, or have already been involved in "secret" aggressive acts such as torturing a pet, or throwing stones from a roof when no one could see you, you need a consultation with a psychotherapist—and you shouldn't let anyone talk you out of it!

6 | *Physical and Sexual Problems During Adolescence*

Physical Problems

The normal growth spurt of adolescence can be quite upsetting until you get used to your "new" body. For some teen-agers physical changes are particularly upsetting, and cause emotional problems that require professional help.

Since you are so concerned with fitting in with others your age, it is likely that you will be very sensitive to anything that makes you feel different physically from your friends. There are tremendous differences in the degree of maturity among any group of teen-agers; if you are on either end of the scale physically, you may feel you stick out like a sore thumb. If you lag behind peers in growth, if you are shorter, if your voice hasn't changed, you may be embarrassed at looking and sounding like a "baby" just when you really want to appear grown up. In early adolescence boys get into a lot of locker-room comparisons regarding penis size and pubic hair. And girls anxiously compare their progress regarding breast size or menstruation. Lags in genital growth or the development of secondary sexual characteristics are often important causes for anxiety and shame.

On the other hand, if you look more grown-up than your age, you may be made fun of because of your height, or find yourself pushed into leadership roles you don't really want, or invited to take part in social and sexual activities you aren't emotionally prepared for. A shy girl with advanced breast development can develop a hunched-over posture just so her sexual maturity *won't* be noticed.

Time straightens most of these problems out. Sooner or later your growth slows down or speeds up until you do "fit in." But for some of you who take these differences particularly hard, psychotherapy may be necessary, especially when a problem with growth is combined with other emotional conflicts from your past or present life.

Physical conditions unique to adolescence often cause emotional distress; whether or not you need to consult a psychotherapist doesn't always depend on the severity of the condition, but on how well you handle it. The majority of you who suffer from bad acne are emotionally strong enough to deal with this ailment on your own. But even a mild acne condition may produce severe depression and anxiety if you feel very insecure about yourself to begin with.

The condition known as *gynecomastia*—enlargement of the breasts—is frequently a great source of embarrassment to a teen-age boy. There are two kinds of gynecomastia. The more common type affects both breasts, and is caused by enlargement of fatty tissue around the breasts. It is seen in kids who've been chubby during childhood. When these youngsters stretch out during adolescence, their breast enlargement usually disappears. The other type of gynecomastia generally involves only one breast, with enlargement mostly around the nipple, in the breast tissue itself. This is seen in boys who aren't fat, and may *not* disappear with more growth. Gynecomastia doesn't mean there's anything seriously wrong with you, but try telling yourself that after you get cruelly kidded in a locker room and secretly wonder if you've been turning into a girl! If the second type doesn't go away, it can be treated by simple plastic surgery, but many surgeons will wait until you are further into your adolescence so the operation doesn't have to be repeated.

Adolescents with weight problems are often referred to psychotherapists. It's frequently assumed there must be an emotional reason for an overweight condition, but this isn't necessarily true. You may have a familial or glandular tendency to put on weight. If you are overweight as an adolescent, chances are you were chubby as a child. If you are heavy and emotionally healthy, there is no point in seeing a psychotherapist to help you lose weight. Studies show you can handle your problem on your own, with proper attention to diet and nutrition. But if your overeating is directly related to emotional stress and frustration, if eating has become a channel for dealing with painful feelings, psychotherapy can be both necessary and helpful.

Our society is extremely weight conscious. Being made fun of by peers and your fear of getting "left out" socially may lead you to get upset if you gain just a few pounds more than you think you should weigh. This is especially true of adolescent girls. During normal adolescent development there are frequently periods of chubbiness before your weight redistributes. A girl who doesn't understand, or can't cope with this normal process, may get into unhealthy crash dieting. I've treated about as many kids whose problem was unhealthily *worrying* about weight as I have treated overweight individuals.

The fear of becoming too heavy is exaggerated in a very serious emotional illness called *anorexia nervosa*. This condition most frequently strikes young teen-age girls who have developed such a distorted view of their bodies that they think a normal appearance is revolting. They drop weight to such alarmingly low levels—seventy to eighty pounds—that their health is seriously threatened. They can't stand the sight of food, and they hide food they are supposed to eat. They are often very active at first, considering their amazingly low weight, but in the later stages of the illness they become very weak, often have to be hospitalized, and may not survive. Anorexia nervosa has been getting a lot of attention recently on TV and in the press. So please remember that the condition isn't that common, and shouldn't be confused with other kinds of weight loss. Even if you are emotionally stable, you can still drop a few pounds during times of stress. And most youngsters who are depressed enough to lose weight still don't show either the overconcern with their weight or the extreme weight loss shown by someone with anorexia nervosa.

The condition known as *bulimia* also occurs most commonly in teen-age and young adult women. A bulimic person goes on frequent big eating binges, then feels so physically uncomfortable or distressed at the thought of gaining weight that she makes herself vomit by putting her fingers down her throat. Doing this repeatedly can lead to serious changes in body chemistry from lost stomach fluid, or even cause damage to the esophagus—the tube that connects the mouth to the stomach. The bulimic is often as overconcerned with weight as a youngster with anorexia nervosa: sometimes, the two problems occur together. Worry about weight usually masks other severe insecurities and self-doubts. The longer bulimia goes untreated, the harder it is to "break the habit." Prompt diagnosis and treatment is extremely important.

The longer any illness goes on, the greater the impact upon your emotional life. Chronic physical illness during adolescence presents great emotional challenges; it makes you even more preoccupied with your body, and often limits normal activity, increasing your dependence upon others at the very time you want so much to be your own master. Because of the psychological stresses caused by physical illness, you may develop additional emotional problems, may have trouble in handling prescribed treatment or getting along with your doctor. So you may need psychological first aid in addition to your medical care.

Illnesses or injuries that demand long rest periods away from school and social life are especially likely to cause depressed feelings, which can continue after the physical problem has passed. For instance depression is often seen after *infectious mononucleosis*, a viral infection commonly striking adolescents which produces sore throat, high fever, and extreme fatigue. The depression may last for months, although the mononucleosis is gone.

Chronic diseases that force you to change your diet or interrupt your regular routine to rest or take medicine, can make you feel scared and resentful. You may act as if your illness doesn't exist, and forget or refuse treatments, thus upsetting your family and your physician. I've frequently seen this situation develop with teen-agers who suffer from *diabetes*, an ailment in which blood sugar is elevated because of the lack of the hormone insulin. (Insulin helps to convert the sugar found in food into the energy the body needs to perform its tasks.) The treatment of adolescent diabetes is likely to require self-injected insulin, restriction of foods containing high amounts of sugar and carbohydrates (including most of the junk food you're fond of), and adequate rest and attention to hygiene. The majority of diabetics (and many others who suffer with chronic diseases) can live normal, productive lives if they take proper care of themselves. But if you are a typical adolescent diabetic, you won't tolerate these changes in your life-style easily. By neglecting proper care, you may even get sick enough to wind up in a hospital. It's here that the psychotherapist can be helpful in showing you how to make the best possible adjustment to the reality of your physical problem.

Physical illnesses are always influenced by your feelings. A depressed individual often will take longer to heal a fractured leg or recover from pneumonia. There are conditions in which emotional factors seem to play a particularly important role; these are known as *psychosomatic* illnesses. In these ailments a physical response to emotional stress can produce uncomfortable symptoms and long-lasting, or even permanent, changes in various organs of the body. The most common psychosomatic conditions include asthma—a narrowing of the air passages of the lungs, causing attacks of wheezing and difficulty in breathing; stomach ulcer—inflammation of the stomach lining, causing belly pain, nausea, and vomiting; ulcerative colitis—inflammation of the large intestine, causing diarrhea, cramps, and bloody bowel movements; migraine headache—a headache accompanied by changes in vision and nausea, so severe that you often have to stay in bed for a day or two.

Psychosomatic illnesses often begin during childhood or adolescence. Symptoms last a long time, sometimes an entire lifetime, with many flare-ups and periods of improvement. While these conditions may be crippling, the majority of patients can continue to live reasonably normal lives, especially with proper medical care. At one time experts thought the main cause for psychosomatic illnesses was emotional, but research has shown they may be brought on due to strong allergic or hereditary influences as well. You usually won't need psychotherapy just because you have a psychosomatic illness. You can be cared for by a skilled physician who knows what medicine to give and can provide emotional support for you, too. But if the psychological factors in your case are very important, the medical doctor will ask you to consult with a psychotherapist. In no way is psychotherapy supposed to replace your medical care, but I've treated many adolescents who had fewer asthmatic attacks and migraines once they sorted out their feelings.

The causes of *bedwetting* and *stuttering* are still not known. Current research rates physical causes as more important than psychological factors. These conditions both tend to begin in early childhood, occur more often in boys than girls, and generally improve without treatment during the teens. In a small number of cases, problems continue into adolescence and adulthood.

Bedwetting and stuttering often cause anxiety and shame, leading to emotional problems such as depression and behavioral difficulties, especially when the symptoms don't get better at puberty. Psychotherapy may help by discovering the stresses buried in your past that have gone into forming the symptoms, or by assisting you to adjust better to the symptoms for as long as you have them. Psychotherapy is usually combined with other treatments—speech therapy for stuttering, medication and bladder-training techniques for bedwetting.

Reading difficulties may develop in childhood or adolescence for purely psychological reasons. Anxiety often interferes with the concentration needed to learn to read. But we now know that most reading difficulties have a physical basis, traceable to difficulty the brain has in receiving images sent by the eye. The eye may see a letter correctly, *c*, but in sending a picture of the letter to the brain, it somehow gets scrambled and reversed, so that it looks like *ɔ*.

This kind of reading problem is called *dyslexia*. It has nothing to do with intelligence. If you have it, chances are your IQ will be at least normal, and maybe brighter than average. Dyslexia occurs seven times more frequently in boys than in girls. There are special reading-therapy techniques to reeducate the brain in seeing letters and words correctly. For the best results this therapy should start during childhood. Unfortunately many youngsters with dyslexia get overlooked, and because they can't read properly, they are mistakenly thought to be emotionally troubled or unintelligent. The longer you go without reading therapy, the greater your chances are of becoming emotionally upset in addition to your dyslexia, as you fall further behind in school and feel more and more inadequate, depressed, and frustrated. By the time you reach your teens, emotional problems may actually be worse than the original reading difficulty. An adolescent psychotherapist treats reading problems due to purely emotional factors, and also the emotional problems that stem from undiagnosed dyslexia or other related learning disabilities, such as problems in simple mathematics. The therapist is trained to be alert to the possibility that dyslexia may be at the root of your troubles. Special testing quickly reveals dyslexia, and if it does, you may be sent for reading therapy in addition to receiving psychotherapy (see Chapter 13 for more about reading therapy).

Sexual Hang-ups

It's been said that sex gives us some of our best and worst moments. Certainly some of your most uncomfortable and wonderful sexual experiences will happen during your teens. While sex isn't *everything*, it is a very important part of your life, involving deep psychological meanings besides the simple satisfaction of physical need. The sense of being sexually desirable is closely tied up with how good or bad you feel about yourself generally. Sexual feelings are connected to the entire range of your emotions, from joy to anger.

People with emotional problems in other life areas may develop additional sexual difficulty. For instance, if you're feeling depressed because of financial worries, you may find your sex drive is slowing down. Sexual anxiety may also cause symptoms that spill over into other life areas; thus, a handwashing compulsion that's based on a fear of masturbating may take up so much of your time that you can't study effectively or enjoy being with your friends. Whatever your reason for seeing a psychotherapist, it's likely that you have *some* important question about your sexuality. Quite possibly a concern about sex may be your *main* problem.

Sex can become a source of trouble during your teens because it is then that you become consciously aware of shameful, fearful, sexual fantasies, daydreams, or night dreams of having relations with someone of the same sex, of having sex with a close relative or friend, of having sex in unusual or hurtful ways, of watching secretly while others make love. Such sexual fantasies are deeply rooted in childhood experience, as mentioned in the discussion of anxiety symptoms. Children develop complicated ideas about sex, based on truths and half-truths, overheard conversations, odd noises coming from their parents' bedroom, or watching animals "doing it" in the street. Out of a tangled web of confusing and exciting information, each child weaves an answer to the riddle of sex. Even being told "the facts of life" doesn't make your early sexual fantasies fade away. Childhood images and fears about sex often return during adolescence, with the onset of a mature sex drive. Ordinarily they create some discomfort, then sink beneath the surface as you start having a well-rounded sex life. But sometimes early sexual wishes, fantasies, and fears cause problems, spinning off all sorts of symptoms like phobias and compulsions, actively interfering with satisfaction during sexual activity.

Problems with sexual performance bring many adults, and some older teen-agers, into psychotherapy, where they are treated very successfully. In the male these problems include the repeated inability to have or keep an erection, ejaculating or "coming" too quickly, inability to come at all, holding an erection indefinitely without pleasure, or experiencing little if any pleasure after orgasm. The medical term for these difficulties is *impotence*. In the female *frigidity*, *dysparunia*, and *vaginismus* are the most common sexual difficulties. Frigidity is an inability to get excited and reach a climax during sex relations. (Many women can be aroused without having a climax; lack of orgasm here is due *not* to frigidity, but to ignorance on the part of the woman or her sex partner about how to achieve climax.) Dysparunia is the medical name for pain during sex relations, often caused by vaginismus, a contraction of the walls of the vagina so severe that the man's penis can't enter easily.

Note that I have used the word *repeated* about problems in sexual performance; *no one* should be called impotent or frigid on the basis of a few unpleasant sexual experiences, especially at the beginning of his or her sex life. Studies show that most women aren't aroused the first time they have sex, and that most men have had an episode of impotence at one time or another, frequently during puberty, without anything serious being wrong. People of both sexes regularly go through brief periods of sexual "turnoff," feeling uninterested sexually, without having big emotional problems.

Sexual hang-ups may not be revealed in performance difficulty. Instead a problem with sex may show up in the form of having sex in adolescence too early with too many unattractive, unappetizing partners and little real pleasure, as is the case with promiscuous delinquent teen-age girls. There isn't any exactly right time to start having sexual relations. When and if you begin having sexual intercourse in your teens will depend on many social, family, and religious influences. But research does seem to indicate that a lot of random, casual sexual activity before you are emotionally mature enough to deal with it may either be a sign of psychological difficulty, or in itself can cause difficulty later on in forming deep, loving relationships.

Sexual hang-ups may originate not simply in childhood fantasies or wishes, but in actual disturbing sexual experiences during your early years and adolescence. You can become troubled because of sexual activity with near or distant relatives your own age, or from having relations forced upon you by grown-up relatives or strangers. The term for sex relations with a close relative is *incest*. It's not rare for the psychotherapist to treat a teen-age girl who has been forced into incestuous relations with her father, or an uncle. As a result she may mistakenly think she's the guilty party. Out of her sense of her badness, she may act like a prostitute, become promiscuous, or a horror of sex may lead her to reject relations altogether and become frigid. Adolescents of either sex who have been raped or molested sexually may similarly become disgusted and turned off by normal sexual activity and require professional help.

There's a debate in our society today about *homosexuality*, a sexual desire for individuals of your own sex. Some experts say homosexuality is a disease that should be treated with psychotherapy to change the homosexual into someone with normal sexual interests. Other experts, as well as an increasingly large number of "liberated" homosexuals, claim that homosexuality is no more of a sickness than *heterosexuality* (having sex with someone of the opposite sex).

While the debate continues, the adolescent psycho-therapist still has to deal practically with teen-agers who are referred because of homosexuality. If you are having a problem in this area, or someone thinks you are, the first thing the therapist will do is determine whether in fact you are homosexual or bisexual (meaning that you can enjoy sex with people of either sex). Do you enjoy the thought or the reality of homosexual relations, even though you may feel guilty? Has your pleasure been long-lasting, with frequent homosexual experiences? Single homosexual events happen frequently in adolescence, without necessarily meaning that you are homosexual or in any kind of psychological distress. There are adolescents—usually boys—who are gripped by a fear of being homosexual because they worry about their ability to have success-ful relations with the opposite sex. They are not actually aroused by men, but they doubt a woman would find them attractive, or that they'll be able to satisfy her. Because they fail to measure up to some supermasculine ideal they've set, they conclude they must be homosexual. This problem may require treatment, but it's *not* true homosexuality.

If you have been having deep, persistent homosexual feelings, whether you've acted on them or not, the therapist will help you decide what you really want to do about them. Many homosexual youngsters don't see a therapist because they want to, but because their sexual activity has been discovered by their parents who are frightened or angry, and who want them to "act normal." Often these kids have known about their sexual direction since childhood. They don't want to change and do not want psycho-therapy, at least not right now. In recent years I've seen many ado-lescents with this outlook.

If this is the case with you, there is no point in entering psychotherapy against your will. Your parents may have to be seen by the therapist in order to help them adjust to your homosexuality. Tragically, the parents of many homosexuals exhaust themselves in searching for a magic "cure," angering their child to the point where he or she rejects them, or else they become so angry *they* drive their child away.

If you do want psychological help about homosexuality, what is the reason? Do you need guidance concerning problems of living that have arisen because of homosexuality, that aren't related to homosexuality, or do you want to change your whole sex life? Setting the problem of their sexual preference aside, homosexual people suffer from the same difficulties and symptoms as "straight" people. They may doubt their attractiveness and worry about success on the job or in school. Many homosexuals only want help from a psychotherapist with "ordinary" problems, or in handling the negative reaction of others to their sex choice. But if you aren't satisfied with being homosexual, if you have a genuine wish to change your sex life, the therapist will make every effort to help you toward this goal, since studies have shown it is a young homosexual, strongly wishing to become heterosexual, who stands the best chance of "switching" with treatment. If you aren't able to switch, psychotherapy will help you accept homosexuality without shame or self-hatred, so that you can live the best life possible within the setting of your homosexuality.

At least once a year I'm called by parents who are terribly upset to discover their child, usually a daughter, has been having sexual relations. Although most of the girls I've seen in this situation aren't psychologcally troubled, the parents assume something must be very wrong. The truth is that many youngsters today have started sexual activity at an age which in their parents' day would have been thought unacceptable.

Even if your sexual activity isn't a sign of emotional difficulty, you and your family may still find brief psychological guidance useful in helping your parents adjust to your decision. The psychotherapist can help you get permission for contraception, if you are a girl, and haven't used it already. (In most states, a girl who is legally underage needs permission from her parents to get contraceptive pills or a diaphragm from a doctor.)

Adolescent pregnancy is a serious matter for girl and boy alike. Consultation with a pyschotherapist can help you make a wise decision about issues of marriage, abortion, and child placement. You may need further assistance after you have made your decision. Often, in this situation, a psychotherapist will consult with the parents of the boy and girl, to calm down what is almost sure to be their stormy reaction.

7 | *Drugs and Drug Abuse*

The problem of adolescent drug abuse became common in the late 1960s and early 1970s. You don't hear so much about drugs like LSD today, but it is still very much on the scene, along with a wide variety of pills, marijuana, and alcohol.

Drug abuse is the self-administration of a substance, man-made or found in nature, for no good medical reason. Instead, the drug is taken to produce pleasurable physical and emotional reactions, in strong enough doses or long enough to cause psychological and/or physical damage, often accompanied by unusual or difficult behavior. Some abused drugs have recognized medical value; others have no use at all.

Abusing drugs may produce a state of *psychological dependence,* an emotional craving for a drug.

The degree of dependence is related to the amount taken, the length of time the drug is taken, and the personality of the user. Some produce *physical dependence*, as well as psychological dependence, a condition in which the tissues of the body have gotten used to the drug, so that when it is withdrawn the user experiences uncomfortable, even violent physical reactions. *Addiction*, a term that isn't used much by doctors today, refers to an extremely strong physical dependence. Experts now rate psychological dependence over physical dependence as more important in keeping you heavily involved with drugs. The condition called *tolerance* develops when increasing amounts of a drug are needed to give the same physical and/or emotional effect.

There are many different drugs that are abused today, with widely different physical and emotional effects, patterns of dependence and tolerance, and legal penalties for possession or dealing. Abused drugs are surprisingly available everywhere, in big cities or small towns, in slums or wealthy neighborhoods. There's a great deal of peer pressure to experiment with drugs, so that you can feel "with it," one of the gang. As once was the case with smoking, coming to terms with how you are going to relate to drugs is part of growing up throughout America and much of the rest of the world. Sometimes the facts about drugs get lost in the battle between the generations over this complex subject. Many important medical and legal drug issues are being hotly debated by experts. I won't discuss them, and will only tell you about the drug problems you might have that could require a therapist's help. If you're interested in more hard facts, you can check the books listed in the Appendix.

I think of drug users as falling into three categories: *tasters* who try a drug once or a few times, then don't want further involvement; *irregular users* who take drugs occasionally for kicks, over the weekend, at parties, or sometimes in stressful situations like examinations; *heads*, for whom the use of drugs has become the biggest concern of life. Heads are so strung out that they can't function without drugs. Most adolescent drug users belong to the first two categories. If you are a taster or an irregular user, chances are you don't think of yourself as having emotional problems, and won't see a therapist unless your parents find out and force you, or you get arrested, and a lawyer or court official requests psychological consultation. Usually, in this case, a therapist won't find anything to treat; the problem is then turned back to where it came for parents, legal officials, if they are involved, and you to work out. Parents may have to be shown by the psychotherapist that they aren't dealing with an emotional illness, but a conflict in values between the generations, such as exists with a teen-age girl and her parents over her sexual activity. The therapist isn't giving a seal of approval to your drug tasting here, but is only trying to make parents more aware of the circumstances that make many normal teenagers experiment with drugs.

I don't want to give you the impression that being an occasional drug experimenter automatically means you can't develop drug hang-ups. Studies have shown that unavailability of drugs keeps many young people away from serious drug abuse; when drugs do become more available—say, after moving away from home or attending a different school—these youngsters can develop significant problems.

Rarely, an experimenter will have a bad psychological reaction to a drug—a panic reaction with marijuana, or a "bad trip," a sort of minipsychosis, with LSD. These experiences are terrifying, often bad enough to warn you off drugs forever. Luckily drug panics and bad trips are brief, especially if your personality is stable to begin with. After helping you over the "bummer," usually no further treatment is required.

The head is the type of person who is most likely to need psychological help. Unfortunately most heads don't get referred until they are in serious trouble with the law, or extremely ill, emotionally and physically. If you're a head, it probably won't be easy to figure out whether emotional hang-ups like depression first got you into drugs, or if your heavy drug use started mostly because of peer pressure. The therapist will determine the different social and personality factors that have contributed to your problem, examine your pattern of drug abuse, then work out a treatment plan, including safe, supervised withdrawal if necessary..

There are heads who come to recognize how badly hung up with drugs they are and then make good use of office psychotherapy. But unfortunately many are too drug dependent, too physically ill, too psychotic or depressed, to handle outpatient treatment responsibly. So at least to start, they require hospitalization of placement in special live-in drug programs (see Chapter 13).

8 | *Knowing When You Need Help*

If you have a temperature of 104 degrees, feel too weak to get out of bed, and your throat is so sore you can't swallow, it's obvious you are quite sick and need a doctor. You won't argue too much about this. But what if your temperature is only 100 degrees, your throat hurts only a little, and although you're tired, you can still get to the kitchen and make yourself some soup? Chances are you've only got a minor cold, and there's no need to waste a doctor's time. You'll rest up, take aspirin, and stay away from school until you feel better. If you get worse, you can always give the doctor a call.

Like most physical symptoms, the majority of psychological symptoms are mild, and often *do* go away without any professional help. You can't live in this world without becoming sad or anxious from time to time, just as you can't avoid catching a cold or bruising your knee in a fall. These minor hurts of the body or the mind usually heal in time. Mild symptoms—phobias, compulsions, hypochondriacal sensations—often appear briefly during adolescence without any clear reason and disappear just as mysteriously. Generally when you are upset, you will restore your own vital balance by working things out on your own, or with a little help from your natural network of relatives and friends. But how can you tell when your own resources are failing you, or when your network has given all it can to help, but simply isn't doing the job?

There isn't a set formula for deciding if you are upset enough to need psychotherapy. The decision is always very personal. Some people tolerate suffering better than others. Some people believe more in solving their own problems than turning to outsiders. Some people are just less inclined to examine their reasons for feeling or behaving as they do. This doesn't mean one type of person is better or stronger or wiser than another; it's just that we each have different ways of coping with life stress. Each of us also has a unique *breaking point*, a point where our troubles have gotten very bad, where the world is treating us very badly, where people ordinarily there for us can't be there, or can't understand what we are going through. My guess is that some of you are reading this book to see if you—or someone you know—has reached a breaking point and needs professional guidance.

You're probably at that point if psychological symptoms are seriously interfering with your ability to have good relationships with family or friends, to do productive work in school or elsewhere, or to enjoy the recreational and creative activities that were important to you before your symptoms began. If symptoms or problems are making it hard for you to get along in only one of these life areas, say your school work, I think you should seriously consider seeing a psychotherapist, although you may be able to wait for your situation to improve. But if your functioning is severely crippled in *several* areas, I think you should go for help *immediately*.

If symptoms that have been mild and bearable until now have been getting steadily worse over the past few weeks or months, if they are joined by new symptoms, so that more and more of your ability to cope is being affected, you shouldn't delay seeing a therapist any longer, because things will only get worse if you wait. Let's say you've been having unexplained physical problems for a while (headache, tiredness, dizziness), and now you find you are spending much more time at home, resting up, thinking about your health instead of being with your friends. Let's say you're getting afraid of school, too, because you worry about catching cold there, and you're washing your hands repeatedly for fear of infection. What's happening here is that hypochondriacal feelings have been joined by a school phobia and a handwashing compulsion, all of which are combining to interfere increasingly with a normal social life. You certainly don't need any further warning signals by this time to tell you you're in serious trouble.

It's especially hard when you are adolescent to know if you are depressed enough to go into therapy, sometimes to know whether you are depressed at all. How can you tell whether your blues are average for your age or not? If sad feelings don't seem to lift, if you are "bummed out," gloomy most of the time, if you've had other depressive symptoms, like trouble falling asleep or early waking, poor appetite, and weight loss, at the very least you should try one session with a psychotherapist to see whether you need treatment. If any of the substitute depressive behavior I've outlined previously reminds you of you—drug abuse, reckless risk taking, delinquent activity—sit down quietly, look at your life, and you may realize you've been going through what's called a *masked* depression. As mentioned earlier, I advise *immediate* consultation if you've been thinking repeatedly of hurting yourself or someone else, or if you have made a halfhearted suicide attempt, or have been secretly doing hurtful things which make you feel ashamed, but which you can't stop—torturing a pet, tormenting a younger brother or sister.

Perhaps your unhappiness seems chiefly due to outside

pressures, rather than deep inner conflicts or symptoms. Your parents' personal or marital difficulties may be spilling over into their relationships with you, causing great suffering. An emotionally troubled sibling may be making your life miserable. Is it worthwhile to see a therapist if your problems are mainly a result of other peoples' problems? Of course! Psychotherapy can help you learn to handle these outside stresses better, teach you not to react in ways that only make a bad family situation worse. If you are growing increasingly desperate and depressed about coping with difficulties created by parents or other family members, if problems at home are seriously interfering with your ability to get along in important life areas, then you should seriously consider having a consultation with a therapist.

People don't come into therapy just because they are in great emotional pain. Not everyone seeking help is unable to function, suicidal, symptomatic, floundering in a family crisis. You can go to a therapist for aid in solving less urgent difficulties: what kind of work to do, whether to go to college or not, whether to stay with a childhood sweetheart or start dating others. These problems might be worked out elsewhere, discussed with friends or parents. But psychotherapy can offer a unique opportunity to examine puzzling challenges in a calm place with a specialist who isn't personally involved with you, who can be more objective about your situation than someone who knows you perhaps a little too well.

What should you do if people are telling you you need help, but you think you don't, or you aren't sure? Ask yourself if these people are truly in your corner. Do your parents want psychotherapy for you to turn you into the kind of person they think you ought to be? On the other hand, just because your parents may not see things your way, or may have been wrong over other issues in your life, doesn't mean that they're wrong about your needing help! Certainly, I'd pay attention when a good friend or an adult you like and trust outside your home says you should consider psychotherapy. Think especially hard about why you are fighting treatment if several people recommend help for pretty much the same reasons. One person might be wrong, but if you hear the same message from different people, with different relationships to you, who are reasonably unprejudiced, the chances are you should listen to them.

Answer this question honestly: While you are saying no to psychotherapy, is there a small voice whispering, "They're telling me the truth, I'm just too scared to admit it"? That voice comes from the healthiest part of you, and it is very wrong to disregard it. Deciding to visit a therapist doesn't bind you to more than a few sessions at most. If you really feel free about not having to stay in therapy when you don't want to, it may be easier for you to stay in therapy as long as you have to! And a good therapist isn't going to keep you in treatment one session longer than you truly wish! In fact, if you shouldn't be in treatment at all, the therapist will say so, right up front. That may not make others happy, but the therapist is there to do the right thing for you, not to win a popularity contest.

It's possible that you may have to deal with people who want to persuade you *not* to see a therapist, once you've made up your mind to do so. They may make light of your problem, tell you you're not as messed up as you think, criticize you for babying yourself, or for not being strong enough to work things out on your own. Perhaps they have private reasons for not wanting you to go. There are people fearful of therapy because they're scared to find out about their own serious problems. They may try to make you just as fearful, because if they can win you over to an antitherapy position, they can then reassure themselves their hang-ups aren't bad enough to require help, either. In Chapter 10, I'll tell you more about all the unreasonable reasons you, your parents, or other grown-ups may use to help you avoid psychotherapy.

Well-meaning people may be convinced, for the best possible reasons, that you are really doing fine and don't need help. Perhaps you do seem okay. But you may be looking so good because you've been doing such a great job of concealing your problems from the world, putting out a mighty effort that has probably added to the troubles you already have. Anyway, outward signs of success and achievement don't amount to a hill of beans when you are hurting badly inside. When you come right down to it, you are the only one who knows the entire story about your problems. You shouldn't let others, well-meaning or not, stop you from doing something about it.

9 | Psychotherapy—
What Is It,
Who Does It?

What Is Psychotherapy?

There are as many definitions of psychotherapy as there are experts defining it. My definition is practical. *Psychotherapy* is the healing of troubled thoughts, feelings, and behavior that have led to a troubled life. There are many different, reasonable, and effective forms of psychotherapy. The method still used most commonly with adolescents is *individual outpatient psychotherapy*, in which you meet regularly with a therapist at an office or clinic to discuss your problems, while continuing to live at home and to go about your regular activities. Individual psychotherapy may be combined with other psychotherapies such as group, family, or drug treatment, or specialized forms of help such as reading therapy, or vocational or educational guidance, which I'll tell you about later in this book.

Individual psychotherapy involves a number of healing experiences which come into play at one time or another during the course of treatment. Some of these experiences will occur more often or be more important than others, depending upon your personality, problem, and needs.

Getting It Off Your Chest.

It's likely that you are coming to the therapist with troubles you've never shared with anyone. When painful feelings stay locked up inside you, you're like a boiler that's been heated up, with no place for the steam to escape. Emotional pressure builds, small problems look much bigger, and really big problems grow overwhelming. The first service a psychotherapist provides is being a good listener to the story you have been aching to tell, but have been unable or unwilling to tell until now. In therapy you may open up immediately, in the first session. The therapist just asks why you came, and your story rushes out like water pouring through a broken dam. But many people, especially teen-agers, don't reveal their problems easily until they can risk trusting the therapist. To help you on your way, the therapist will let you know you won't be punished, judged, or made fun of—reactions you may already have gotten from others when you tried to talk with them. From the first the therapist will accept where you are "coming from."

The therapist knows when to listen, when to keep quiet, when to ask a question, when to guide the session so that it is as easy as possible for you to speak about hurtful issues. The therapist also knows when to stop you from letting off more steam than is good for you. The relief of getting a problem out in the open can quickly be replaced by distress at having spoken too openly, so that you feel exposed, ashamed, and defenseless. The therapist knows when too much openness is bad for you.

If you are like most new patients, you'll feel much better

just for having revealed a little about your difficulties. Your burden won't be as heavy, now that it is being shared by two.

Reassurance and Support.

A tape recording can listen, but it will only give you back exactly what you put into it. Like a good friend, a psychotherapist does more than just listen sympathetically; he or she will respond supportively to your story, recognize how much you've been hurting, let you know that others have had similar problems, and make you feel you're not unique in your suffering. The therapist will tell you if he or she thinks you've been given a raw deal, and will support your healthy, constructive ideas about your life, whereas others may have criticized them. You'll find reassurance that things will get better, be shown strong parts of your personality you may have overlooked, and discover that you've already done a great deal to help yourself. The psychotherapist lends you strength, comforts you when you are down, feels happy with you when things are going well, offers hope when you're hopeless, and gives you the promise of peace when you can't find peace within yourself.

However, a psychotherapist isn't a "sob sister," won't weep over you as if you were a poor, trapped victim who can't do anything about your situation. The therapist will support you *realistically*. He or she won't applaud you for qualities you don't possess, and won't go along with unrealistic ideas just because they are yours, although you'll never be put down for having them. A-braham Lincoln once posed for a photograph, and the photographer told him he could ink out Lincoln's warts. Lincoln refused, saying: "Let them see me as I am, warts and all." The therapist accepts you "warts and all," your right judgments and muddled opinions, your good side and your not-so-good side. You've had no choice but to be who you are right until the moment you enter therapy; thereafter all sorts of choices may be open to you if you can realize them. If you can make this calm attitude of self-acceptance your own, you are in a better position to help yourself become a happier person.

Understanding Your Situation Better.

Most people with emotional problems have a feeling of great confusion and disorder about their lives. When you are troubled, the past, present, and future can seem all scrambled up, without any rhyme or reason. You probably aren't used to thinking about your life too logically. Perhaps you have been too close to what's happened to make sense out of things; you may have forgotten past stressful events, may be protecting yourself by overlooking connections because it's too painful to admit them. Just fitting your life story together logically is very helpful at this time. By taking a careful history the psychotherapist can show you that you weren't dropped out of the sky into your present difficulties. The therapist and you will assemble many seemingly unrelated events into an understandable pattern. You will come to see the chain of cause and effect that brought you to where you are today.

Here's an example of what this process is like: A few years ago I saw a boy whose parents were divorced. He lived with his mother. Recently the father had started canceling out of his weekend visits with the boy at the very last minute. On Monday the boy would come to school very depressed and would get into bad fights. He was *totally* unaware of the very obvious (to me) connection between the canceled visits and the Monday fights. Because he loved his father, he felt guilty about the bad feelings the father's cancellations were producing. Instead he carried over his anger about the weekend into the classroom. Once I made this link clear to him, he was able to stop taking out the angry feelings meant for his father on others and speak to him directly.

A psychotherapist may show you connections that bridge many years, to help you discover that forgotten childhood events still influence you today. The therapist may investigate an event that took place just a few hours ago—an argument on the ballfield or at home—in order to demonstrate the causes and effects that made you have an unpleasant reaction you don't understand.

Sometimes the therapist will have to make an educated

guess about the motives of another person, or about an event you can only partly remember. If that guess is correct (and a good therapist never makes wild guesses), this new information will make you understand the person better, or help you remember the event more clearly, opening the way for further connections. In making these guesses you and the therapist are like two detectives, fitting clues together to solve your problem. Like good detectives you will always wonder if more clues are needed, or if the guess is incorrect and there are other explanations to be considered.

Sometimes the therapist is as interested in discovering what you thought happened as in the *reality* of what happened. Your mistaken ideas about a life experience may be an important source of problems. For instance, a girl became anxious and sick to her stomach whenever a boy tried to kiss her. She stopped dating because she thought "all boys were animals." It was obvious that most of her dates were reasonably well-behaved, decent fellows who weren't out to attack her, despite her fearful image of men. One of the chief reasons for her sexual anxiety and her unwholesome view of men turned out to be a forgotten childhood memory of finding menstrual blood on her parents' bedsheets one morning, making her believe her father had hurt her mother during some terrible deed he had forced upon her. Even though she consciously knew the facts of life, she had developed an unconscious fear of being harmed by an angry man during sex. This fear surfaced during her adolescence in anxiety attacks when she became involved in the mildest sexual situations, like kissing.

When you understand the chain of causes and effects that has led you into your current difficulty, you feel more connected to yourself. You see that upsetting emotions you've been trying to protect yourself from are there for a good reason, even if the reason no longer exists today. When the girl could understand how her sexual attitudes had been influenced by her childhood experience, her anxiety symptoms dropped away and she was able for the first time to enjoy kissing a boy.

The therapist may help you achieve a very complete

understanding of the background of your problems. This kind of understanding really takes a long time and usually isn't needed by the average teen-ager who comes for therapy. Making some general connections between the past and present, helping you recognize the causes and effects of your behavior today in situations directly related to your difficulty, will be enough to make most of you feel reconnected to who you are. The therapist knows when to stop exploring your life, and to let you get on with the business of living it.

Education–Psychological and Practical.

It's been said that a really good teacher makes himself or herself unnecessary, by passing on knowledge so that the student can now make the best use of it without needing a teacher anymore. The psychotherapist is a teacher, and the subject is personal psychology and human relations. You will be given powerful psychological tools by the therapist to keep on learning and growing after your treatment is over. And by learning more about yourself, you will also learn about what makes others "tick."

Each session you will find out a little more about how the mind works, about psychological development from childhood through old age, about the forces in family life and society that help mold you, about the important messages you send to yourself every night in your dreams. The "textbook" of your psychological education is your life and your relationships, including your relationship with your therapist. You will discover, for instance, how you take feelings you originally had toward important people in your life, and apply them to the therapist without realizing it. This process, called *transference*, is found in every relationship you have, but when it gets out of hand it seriously interferes with your ability to appreciate the true nature of others and to trust, love, or learn from them. The therapist is objective enough to make you aware of how you project qualities that really belong to someone else upon him or her. With this knowledge you can deal more healthily with your relationships outside the therapist's office and see people for who they really are, not whom you think they resemble.

In addition to educating you about psychological issues, the therapist will, if necessary, give you practical information about a wide range of topics. This is an especially useful helping experience for growing adolescents, because you may be too ignorant, or too blocked by your problems, to have gotten the important realistic knowledge you need to further your progress into adulthood. Sometimes your parents or teachers have been unwilling to educate you, or perhaps you have been unable or unwilling to accept adult instruction.

A therapist may educate you on practical matters directly, or give you the names of books to read, pamphlets to send away for, courses to take, or films to see. I've given "gut" information on everything from sexual anatomy and how to go about making a date over the telephone, to organizing better study habits. I'm constantly amazed at what adults assume a kid already knows when in fact he or she may be tremendously ignorant about the basics of getting along in life regarding social skills, managing money, or personal hygiene. Many teens are too ashamed to ask for guidance.

I once saw a tall, athletic fifteen-year-old boy who everyone believed was quite a "ladykiller" because of his good looks and sophisticated behavior. Actually he felt painfully shy around girls, avoided dating, and was completely misinformed about sex. He came to me because he had been getting increasingly depressed about inventing wild sexual exploits for his locker-room pals, when he had hardly ever held a girl's hand. We worked on the psychological reasons for his fear of getting close to girls; I also gave him straight information about sex and socializing that, as I look back, probably helped him to have better social relationships as much as my investigating his emotional conflicts.

By being educated your natural reach is extended. But your therapist will be very, very careful about just how much educating to do. Because you are likely to be very sensitive about areas of ignorance, the therapist won't talk down to you. And before the therapist dishes out information, he or she will make sure you really want it. Sometimes it's better to let someone else do the educating, or let you find out on your own, once you've understood what you need to know more about. If it seems unlikely that anyone is going to educate you, or you are a long way from being able to get information you really need to make progress, the therapist will feel comfortable in helping you along.

Sometimes education means telling you well-known facts—the reasons for menstruation, what contraception or venereal disease is, how alcohol affects the body, the age the law says you can drive a car by yourself. Just as often the therapist will discuss social situations where cold facts or absolutely right answers can't be given, only ways to behave the are generally considered reasonable which you are then free to follow or not. Here's an example:

A boy who had just started dating wondered why he was always being turned down. He was a lonely, shy fellow. It was a very big step for him to call a girl up at all, but the negative responses he kept getting were only making him feel more like a "creep." I found out he was trying for a Saturday-night date on Friday afternoon or Saturday morning. It never occurred to him that he was calling at a time when a girl was likely to already have a date. I also pointed out that girls, like boys, could be insecure about their image, that even if they didn't have a date, they might turn someone down who called so late in the week because they didn't want to give the idea that they were available at the drop of a hat. I told him times were changing, that there were girls with more liberated attitudes who weren't so worried about their image, and might accept a late call. All things being equal, however, he still stood a better chance by calling earlier, unless it really bugged him to act like everybody else. Because he couldn't see past the ceremony of a Saturday-night date, I also told him he could ask a girl out for other nights of the week, or other times of the day, like a Sunday brunch. Much to his surprise, when he put this new knowledge to work he got results quickly.

Guidance.

Many people mistakenly believe a psychotherapist won't tell you what to do, won't give you specific advice about how to handle a problem. Instead the therapist is supposed to help you find out about yourself, so you can make wise choices on your own. How you deal with the world outside the office is supposed to be your business, and your responsibility.

With most adult patients, this hands-off policy does work best. Adults typically have greater independence and knowledge of the world, and require little specific advice. But a hands-off attitude won't work with many teen-agers. It's natural during your adolescence to want and to get a certain amount of proper guidance from grown-ups, including a psychotherapist.

Education and guidance tend to go hand in hand during therapy. A request for hard facts about sex, or information about social behavior, doesn't come out of nowhere. Instead you usually come in with a particular situation where guidance, practical advice, and education will all be helpful. In my previous example I was teaching a boy new to dating that Saturday morning was not the best time to ask a girl out for Saturday night, and guiding him toward other possibilities, too.

Depending upon your situation, guidance may be direct and forceful, or gentle and general. The therapist may recommend a particular plan of action, or map out several alternatives for you. The therapist may avoid direct guidance, show you only what your possibilities are, and let your make up your own mind.

Guidance consists of telling you what to do, and sometimes, what *not* to do. *Forceful* guidance more often involves what *not* to do: The therapist shows you you're getting into an extremely dangerous situation, or that you are involved in behavior that is highly destructive to yourself or others, and tells you up front to get out of the situation or stop the behavior. I do think you have a right to make mistakes and learn from them. In many situations a therapist will hold back from giving advice so that you can have the very valuable experience of learning to take responsibility for your actions. But I also think it is wrong for the therapist to sit by and do nothing when you might get hurt, or get into serious trouble, because of your own or someone else's problems.

I treated a sixteen-year-old girl who fell head over heels in love with a boy who had a criminal record a mile long. She thought he was a misunderstood genius. There wasn't anything she wouldn't do for him. Then one day he asked her to help him rob a drugstore. She was supposed to distract the storekeeper's attention while he did the actual robbery. She was very upset, but decided to go along with him. She felt that this way she could gain his confidence. Besides, he was the one doing the crime, and no one would suspect she was involved, according to his plan. She asked me what I thought. I told her she was playing games with her life and her conscience. She had a very strong sense of right and wrong, and I could see she was troubled, no matter what her excuses. I pointed out that if the boy really cared for her he'd straighten himself out, instead of dragging her down. I told her not to take part in his scheme. If this was the way he repaid her affection, she'd be better off out of the relationship. She became very angry, and said I couldn't understand what a wonderful person he was, how bad his childhood was, I was like everyone else who couldn't believe her, et cetera. She threatened to leave therapy, but I held my ground, stating I'd rather lose a patient by doing the right thing than hold on to someone by doing a wrong thing. Midway through her arguments she broke into tears and cried: "What am I fighting with you for? You're only telling me what I know already!" She refused to help the boy and eventually broke off seeing him. Several months later he and another girl were arrested for holding up a supermarket.

In less obvious situations than this one, the therapist is much more careful about guidance, always weighing the benefits against the ills of advice. In general the therapist does want you to leave treatment being able to make freer choices for yourself. By indicating a plan of action or a way of behaving, the therapist runs the risk of undercutting your self-reliance and independence. The therapist will let you know that guidance is there for you if you want it, but that you won't be bothered with unwanted advice, except in a true emergency.

A therapist's guidance usually centers around specific family, school, or social situations. He or she won't tell you what to do about major life decisions, such as what college to go to, what job to take, what profession to follow. In these matters you either know better already or can find out better by yourself. The therapist will help you work out problems standing in the way of a major decision, possibly help you clarify what your alternatives are, but encourage you to make the final decision yourself.

Many times in offering guidance the therapist is really offering you an *opinion*. An opinion is not a law, but an educated guess, based on the therapist's training, knowledge of the world, and judgment, as well as his or her personality and personal values. Since a therapist is only human, his or her opinion could be influenced by a special prejudice or way of looking at the world. That opinion might be altogether wrong, or perhaps right for someone else. The therapist has no business labeling a personal belief as a fact of nature and trying to cram it down your throat, because you will surely choke on it.

It *is* important for you to know the therapist's viewpoint on a variety of subjects—drugs, sex, politics, or religion—even if you deeply disagree, especially when other grown-ups you know have been vague or fuzzy about their beliefs. It is a vital part of adolescent development to register different viewpoints, take from them what makes sense, and reject what doesn't. A psychotherapist won't get upset if you reject his or her words of wisdom, or if you only buy part of the package. After all, if everyone accepted everything they were taught, how would society continue to change and grow? A therapist will explore with you the problems you must face if you decide to go against the grain, but won't stop you from marching to a different drummer.

Entering Your World.

Much of the therapist's work consists in helping you make changes in your inner emotional world. With adults a therapist probably won't become involved at all with anyone in the patient's outside world. With people your age this often isn't possible. You are involved heavily with your family. You may have been referred at the request of a school, a court, or some other agency who may want follow-up reports on your progress. At the very least your therapist probably will have some brief contact at first with parents, school, or an outside agency to get a fuller picture of your problem.

There are circumstances where more than this is required, where the therapist may be asked by you or an outsider to help change something in your world. Giving this kind of assistance is very risky. It may mean that people other than family members will find out you are in therapy. The therapist never knows whether this will be used for or against you. If the therapist does help you out of a rough spot, you might get the idea he or she is there for continuous handholding, to rescue you from every stressful situation. Or you might resent the therapist bitterly, feel that you have been robbed of the freedom to act in your own behalf.

But what if you really lack the power to change something that needs to be changed, have tried your utmost without success, and having failed, have fallen deeper into despair? The therapist will then balance the benefits of entering your world against the harm it might cause. In general, a therapist will step into your life only in moments of great crisis or serious need, when you are unable to act for yourself, or have exhausted all your possibilities for action.

Thus if a seventeen-year-old girl says she wants me to force her father to raise her allowance by my telling him she is very nervous because it is too low, I'll refuse. It's not a major problem; it's something she should be working out on her own rather than using therapy as a club over her father's head. If a seventeen-year-old girl tells me her father won't let her wear lipstick, listens in on her phone calls with boys, and calls her a tramp because she wants to go out on dates, and if I know she's not exaggerating, then I'll speak to her father to get him to examine his strict, unhealthy attitudes and change them.

When the therapist has to enter into situations outside your family, contacts are kept brief and to the point, and the therapist will get out as quickly as possible. Here's an example:

A sixteen-year-old boy developed a phobia about going to gym class. He was too ashamed to tell the school about his problem, kept cutting the class, and got into trouble with the school authorities. He entered psychotherapy and wanted to keep treatment confidential. However, his phobia remained so troublesome that he couldn't go near the gym. After a few sessions I suggested he let me speak with the school and get him a temporary suspension. At first he was reluctant, but finally agreed when I told him that not going to class without some reasonable explanation was sure to make problems for him beyond the phobia he already had.

Many schools have a guidance counselor. I spoke briefly to his school's counselor, told her about my patient's problem without getting into his personal history in detail, told her he would probably get over his symptom within a few months, but he couldn't handle the gym class now without being flooded with anxiety. She readily agreed to recommend a temporary medical suspension to the principal's office, which was okayed. She knew how important it was to keep therapy confidential; the only people who were aware of the psychological reason for the suspension were the counselor, an assistant principal, and the school nurse. My patient chose to tell his friends he had a back problem that kept him out of class, so no one bothered him except for some good-natured joking about how lucky he was to get out of gym. Several weeks later he was feeling better. I had him go to the counselor and tell her he was ready to start class again. She called me to make sure, and that was the end of the problem.

Not every situation is solved so easily and may need more frequent contact between the therapist and the outside person. The principle is still the same: The therapist will do what is necessary for you, and will get uninvolved as soon as possible.

For most adolescents, contact outside the family, if it occurs at all, will be with school personnel—teachers, guidance counselors, headmasters, assistant principals. The therapist may give advice in planning a school course load so that you won't be stressed beyond your ability to handle your work. The therapist may recommend that you have special educational help, such as tutoring. The therapist's timely advice may mean the difference between your being allowed to stay in school or asked to leave.

If you have gotten into legal trouble, the adolescent therapist will probably become involved with probation officers, lawyers, and court officials. Judges often allow an adolescent to stay out of jail or a juvenile home as long as the youngster gets psychological guidance. If it is the right thing to do, the therapist will recommend treatment over imprisonment. If the recommendation is approved by the court, the judge often will require the therapist to keep regular contact with a probation officer during treatment. If imprisonment is unavoidable, the therapist may be asked to help the court decide what kind of place a youngster should be sent to. Instead of a standard correctional institution, the therapist might recommend a more "open" juvenile institution where better psychological treatment is available.

If your problems are such that you can't remain at home, the therapist may work with social agencies to find a good place for you to stay. If you are in some kind of vocational training, the therapist may give advice to your work program about the best approach to use in teaching you a skill, or finding you employment. If you suffer from a psychosomatic illness or from other chronic physical problems which you aren't handling well, the therapist may work very closely with your physician, keeping the doctor posted on the emotional side of your illness, working out the best approach to your medical program.

The Therapist as Role Model and the Corrective Emotional Experience.

I've described what a therapist does, but a vital part of psychological healing in individual therapy depends upon who the therapist *is*. During adolescence you identify with many of the ideals and goals of others. This doesn't mean you become a carbon copy of someone else's personality. Instead the important beliefs of others are joined to yours, and something new and uniquely your own is then born. "Old wine is poured into new bottles," the saying goes.

The personality of the psychotherapist can become a source of healthy identification, especially if you stay in therapy for some time. To use the psychological term, the therapist acts as a *role model*, someone to pattern yourself after in a constructive fashion. You may thus find yourself imitating the therapist's mannerisms or way of talking or dressing. A friend of mine was leading a therapy group of delinquent boys. The group had been having trouble getting off the ground. After sharing some common experiences, one member said at the end of the session: "Hey, Doc, maybe there is something to all this group baloney!" My friend is a pipe smoker. At the next session, most of the members showed up smoking pipes, even though they were cigarette addicts. As it turned out one of the pipes had been boosted from the elevator operator! The boys were totally unaware that they were pleased with the therapist's leadership and were imitating him.

But surface imitation isn't the important factor of role modeling. There are deeper, much more helpful identifications with the therapist's calm, tolerant, flexible approach to life. Possibly you haven't had the right kind of people to model yourself after, or haven't been able to make good identifications because your problems have led you to push others away. In the quiet of the therapist's office, effective identifications can begin, and from these you begin to build bridges to the significant adults in your life with whom you need to identify.

Role modeling doesn't happen quickly or mechanically.

The therapist doesn't consciously decide, "Now, I'm going to act this way so that Jack will learn to behave as calmly as I." You don't consciously say, "I'm going to try Dr. G's style on for size." Instead role modeling and identification take place gradually, mostly outside the awareness of you and your therapist.

Many people in therapy find they are treated with more respect and consideration there than on the outside. Some experts believe the *corrective emotional experience* is the reason people get better in psychotherapy. Hurtful outside treatment is corrected by the therapist's caring attitude. I personally don't think your problems will be solved simply by the therapist trying to make up for the love or attention you never got, or think you never got. If this is what you are looking for in treatment, you must get disappointed. A teacher of mine said that in therapy "love is not enough." A truly corrective emotional experience in treatment will certainly include sympathy and kindness, but the other ingredients I've described will take you further down the path toward emotional maturity.

∎ *Psychotherapy: Who Performs It?*

Forms of psychotherapy, although not labeled as such, were practiced by physicians and priests in ancient times. Sometimes the job of doctor and priest was combined, since it was believed that health problems were caused by angry gods or evil spirits. Witch doctors in primitive cultures today, besides giving charms and spells, offer guidance, support, and reassurance to their "patients" just like psychotherapists working in a big city. Studies show that for many emotional problems, their help is at least as effective.

In the Western world, the healing of the mind gradually became a medical problem rather than a spiritual or religious matter. For the past few hundred years most psychological treatment was chiefly performed by medical doctors. In the past thirty to forty years this situation has changed enormously. Today physicians called *psychiatrists* still practice psychotherapy, but they've been joined by therapists who've received training in fields other than medicine. This has caused debate among professionals as to who is qualified to do therapy, and confusion for the public about the differences between medical and nonmedical psychotherapists.

I'll try to clear up the confusion by describing the background, training, and qualifications of the various mental health professionals you are most likely to meet when you look for help. As for the question of who should perform therapy, I believe that well-trained, well-supervised nonmedical therapists are capable of treating many of the problems psychiatrists deal with.

Until the 1940s psychological treatment in hospitals and clinics was influenced by a *team* concept, which strictly set out the role of each mental health professional. The *doctor-psychiatrist* was the head of the team; he or she actually treated the patient. The chief nonmedical assistants on the team were the *psychologist* and the *psychiatric social worker*. The psychologist was supposed to give and interpret psychological tests, which helped the psychiatrist understand what was troubling the patient. Psychologists also were trained to design research projects in mental health. At that time it was believed the psychiatrist should have little to do with family members, in order to keep the treatment as confidential and as free from outside influence as possible. Yet it was necessary to have some contact with the family to get information the patient might not be able to supply, and to keep family members posted on the patient's progress. The psychiatric social worker's job was to act as a link between psychiatrist and family, also helping the patient with realistic problems such as finding a place to live, getting welfare assistance if necessary, et cetera.

Since the 1940s psychotherapy team tasks have been followed less strictly as the disciplines of psychiatry, psychology, and social work learned more from each other. Psychologists and psychiatric social workers no longer just did their traditional jobs, but also started practicing individual psychotherapy themselves.

Gradually, special programs were set up for their training. These developments occurred because nonmedical professionals wanted to become directly involved with patient care, and also because of the increasing acceptance of psychological treatment, leading to a greater public demand for therapy, and a need for more therapists. Today medical and nonmedical therapists work together, doing psychotherapy in clinics and hospitals throughout America. And, like psychiatrists, many nonmedical psychotherapists also treat patients in private practice.

Here are the requirements for becoming a psychiatrist (a medical psychotherapist) and a psychologist or psychiatric social worker (the two most common nonmedical psychotherapists): To train to be a *psychiatrist*, you attend college, then four years of medical school, where you learn how the body functions in sickness and health. As part of learning to care for ill people, you take basic courses in psychology and do simple psychotherapy. After receiving an M.D., or Doctor of Medicine, you take a year of hospital internship, where you apply what you have learned during medical school to the daily treatment of sick patients. Then you take a three- to four-year residency in psychiatry at a hospital or clinic. You receive advanced training in the cause, prevention, and treatment of emotional disorders. You are carefully instructed in individual psychotherapy, the use of drugs, and other physical treatment methods. After graduating residency, you are qualified to enter private practice or to work in a hospital or clinic.

To become a *clinical psychologist* you must finish college, then take a four- to-six-year training program in psychology that is usually given in a university graduate school. You take courses in many of the same subjects a psychiatrist studies, including personality development, normal and abnormal behavior, and psychotherapy. You also receive specialized instruction in subjects such as psychological testing, designing research projects in mental health, and correction of speech, learning, and reading difficulties.

You have at least one year of internship in a psychiatric hospital or clinic or agency, where you learn to diagnose and treat people with emotional problems under careful supervision. In performing psychotherapy you won't be allowed to give drugs, but as part of your training you will take general course work on drugs and other medical subjects. After you complete an original piece of research or clinical work, called a *thesis,* you are awarded a Doctorate in Clinical Psychology, or Ph.D. *Clinical* means that you have a great deal of practical experience in treating people, instead of doing research in the laboratory or working in some other area of psychology. You can now treat patients privately or in a hospital or clinic.

Psychiatric social work is only one branch of the field of social work, just as clinical psychology is a branch of the general field of psychology. Social work originally was developed to help poor people get in touch with services to provide shelter, clothing, food, and work. The psychiatric social worker's services have shifted away from these practical realities to psychological needs. To become a *psychiatric social worker* you go to college, then take two years at a university-connected social-work school, which gives you the degree of M.S.W., or Master of Social Work. In the M.S.W. program you are taught about subjects such as the kinds of institutions and agencies that provide social services. You also take courses in simple counseling and psychology, but your study usually is not as deep as that of the psychiatrist or psychologist. You have supervised "field work" in institutions such as hospitals, family agencies, Y's, and community centers, helping individuals and groups with a wide range of social and emotional needs. Because of your brief training, as a newly graduated psychiatric social worker you are probably better qualified to do a simpler form of psychotherapy, giving guidance, support, and reassurance in situations that are not too complicated.

I do want to stress that the skill of qualified therapists, both medical and nonmedical, begins to draw closer together with more experience after training is finished. A therapist's ability is especially likely to increase if he or she takes advanced courses in psy-

chological treatment after finishing basic training, or if he
or she works at a place where supervision by older professionals is given. Many therapists do not immediately enter private practice, but see patients under supervision at a clinic, agency, or hospital. Special institutes for postgraduate training in psychotherapy are
set up for medical and nonmedical therapists. These programs have
very high standards of admission, and take anywhere from two to
seven years to complete. Psychotherapists who have finished this
type of training are extremely capable, whether their original degree
was in psychiatry, psychology, or social work. There are also
therapists who prefer not to take on any more schooling after
graduation from basic training. They go into private practice right
away. They view experience with patients as their best teacher, and
in addition they may take selected courses to improve their skills.
Often they will pay an older professional to supervise them in private cases, thus arranging their own excellent training programs.

Most psychotherapy is still done by psychiatrists, psychologists, or psychiatric social workers. Nonpsychiatric doctors
with an interest in psychotherapy may do simple counseling in their
offices. The training of clergymen, school guidance counselors, and
psychiatric nurses now usually includes some course work in psychology and psychotherapy, so that these professionals can under-
take simple counseling tasks that come up during their regular
work. They also are taught when it is proper to refer a patient who
has a difficult problem to a therapist with greater training. Some
clergymen, counselors, and nurses have been allowed to receive
advanced training at qualified psychotherapy institutes. They generally will choose to practice psychotherapy as their chief work, instead of the profession for which they originally trained.

Today increasing use is being made of people with *no*
previous training who provide simple counseling and guidance
through community clinics, drug treatment centers, hot lines, and
other crisis programs. These people receive training and supervision
from qualified mental-health professionals. To justify therapy by
non-professionals it is said that you might find it easier to trust

someone closer to your own background, even with limited training, than a fully trained therapist from a completely different background. Thus an ex-drug addict, born and raised in the city ghetto, might be in a unique position to help a streetwise youngster in a drug-treatment program. Supposedly a troubled college student might find it easier to relate to a student his own age in a peer counseling program than to the college psychiatrist.

I think this kind of counseling does have its place, often in persuading someone to go into treatment with a professional. But it also has *very* serious limitations. It *cannot* be a substitute for psychotherapy of a severe, troublesome, emotional difficulty like a phobia. It's possible that in our enthusiasm to see that everyone who wants help gets it, we may have gone a bit overboard. Today experts are trying to figure out just what types of problems a nonprofessional can handle. Personally I would be very cautious about being helped by a total nonprofessional, even under supervision, if I were an adolescent. I would certainly be very quick to ask for professional guidance if I felt my problems weren't improving.

Where Therapy Is Practiced.

In private psychotherapy, treatment takes place in the psychotherapist's office, located in an ordinary apartment building, a medical office building, or the therapist's home. A therapist may practice privately alone, or share offices with other therapists, physicians, or other professionals. Despite what you may have seen on the *Bob Newhart Show*, most private therapists do *not* have secretaries, and take care of appointments, bills, and other matters by themselves.

If you can't afford private psychotherapy, you can be treated at a clinic run by a hospital, a psychotherapy training institute, a community agency, union, religious or charitable organization. There may be a waiting period between your screening and the actual time you start therapy, although clinics try to arrange their schedules so that very distressed people can enter therapy quickly, even immediately.

A clinic therapist may be a private therapist who works part-time, or a therapist in training. The idea of treatment with a student therapist may put you off, but remember that usually the student will be supervised by an experienced senior therapist. I've trained many excellent students over the years. Whatever they lack in experience, they more than make up for in interest and enthusiasm, qualities that may have faded in an older therapist who's "seen it all."

At a clinic you may make arrangements for appointments and payments directly with your therapist. However, most clinics do have secretaries who handle the business side of your treatment.

The practice of psychotherapy, private or clinic, still tends to be concentrated heavily in large cities. Small towns don't have nearly as many therapists available, so that if you live in a small town and need help, you may have to travel to the nearest big town or city to get it.

▌ *Adolescent Psychotherapy and the Adolescent Therapist*

A teacher of mine called adolescent psychotherapy the poor relation of adult treatment. Modern psychotherapy techniques originated around the turn of the century, and were applied mainly to adults at first. Experts always thought that many adult emotional problems could be traced back to childhood, yet many years were to pass before child psychology became a recognized branch of general psychology, and special training programs in child therapy were founded. Adolescents *still* weren't receiving the attention they deserved during the first half of this century. A little *was* known about teen-age emotional development, but adolescents still were dealt with like adults in therapy, and few teen-agers entered treatment.

During the past thirty years we have become much more sophisticated about the special problems, talents, and needs of emotionally troubled adolescents. The specialty of adolescent psychotherapy is young, and there aren't as many training programs for learning how to treat adolescents as there are for adults and children. Nevertheless a typical training schedule for mental-health professionals is likely to contain at least one course in normal adolescent psychological and physical development. The trainee usually will be required to perform therapy with at least one adolescent under the supervision of an adolescent specialist. A large number of programs now offer several years of advanced study in child and adolescent psychotherapy to the graduate mental-health professional.

Since the field is pretty new you will find very good older therapists who treat teen-agers even though they don't have special training—it just didn't exist when they went to school. What they do have is a natural "feel," a "knack" for working with adolescents, combined with long experience. There are unfortunately many therapists who are better trained to treat adults, but who still see teen-agers as well. A therapist may be qualified legally, have every proper credential and degree, without owning the knack, without being sensitive to the special issues of treating adolescents. I'd like to tell you a little about the particular qualities, the *X* factors that a talented adolescent therapist has, so you can recognize them when they are there and when they are not.

An adolescent psychotherapist must have the personal qualities of any good therapist—he or she must be patient, kind, a good listener, neither critical nor judgmental, and should have a basic liking for people and a lively curiosity about what makes them tick. A good memory helps, too. The more "together" a therapist is, the better he or she can help others get their lives together. Dealing with patients' problems touches on one's deepest emotions and conflicts, so the therapist should know what makes himself or herself tick, psychologically. Many therapists actually undergo therapy to do a better job, or simply to solve their own problems.

People often see a psychotherapist as someone who sits behind a desk with a great stone face, rarely speaking while patients pour out their hearts. This is an exaggeration, but a therapist does tend to be pretty quiet with most adult patients, a less active approach that usually doesn't work with adolescents. You want to speak to a real person, not a wax dummy. If a therapist is too quiet, you'll probably think he or she is either weird or bored, and drop out of treatment quickly.

It's very important for an adolescent therapist to be absolutely honest about his or her life-style, beliefs about therapy and other issues, and especially about mistakes or misunderstandings that occur during treatment. You don't admire adults who don't take a firm stand about what they believe, and probably get irritated when grown-ups act as if they were always right and their word is law, without ever questioning their beliefs or admitting errors. You don't need a therapist who repeats these unhelpful tendencies.

I've known therapists who thought they could make better contact with teen-agers by "talking their language," and who ended up talking and dressing like a grown-up adolescent. There's nothing you have a keener eye for than phoniness. As one boy told me, "You can put a monkey in a tuxedo, but he's still a monkey." If it isn't natural for a therapist to dress and talk "hip," you'll quickly get on to the game and get fed up or lose respect. An adolescent therapist *does* have to have a good knowledge of things you are interested in, from rock groups to football teams, since you often will express important feelings in the course of talking about topics that are important to you. Your therapist should know about some of these topics, not to impress you, but just to understand better what you are talking about. If I don't know the meaning of a slang term, or have never heard of a new rock group, *I* ask. That's the way I learn, and besides it generally gives my patient a good feeling to teach this expert something he doesn't know. Don't ever hesitate to educate *your* therapist in an area of your life about which he or she seems ignorant.

If you are like most adolescents, you probably are moody and unpredictable at times, saying one thing when you mean quite another, changing your feelings or attitudes quickly. Some therapists don't work well with teen-agers because this changeability drives them "batty." But a good therapist won't get rattled or irritated at your quick shifts of mood or opinion. He or she will stay firm and calm while you do the jumping around.

Many teen-agers in therapy come from very permissive backgrounds, where no one has ever placed limits on hurtful or unsocial behavior. Your parents may not have realized that saying "no" to you is a way of showing they care. Styles in raising children change, but kids grow up healthiest when respect for their needs to express themselves is combined with discipline that is firm, fair, and never cruel. Kids from overpermissive homes may act defiantly toward the therapist, but often they are inwardly crying out for the controls they never got. A psychotherapist may be the *first* person in your life who ever said there were things you simply *couldn't* do. For instance I've told youngsters flat out that in my office they weren't allowed to treat me disrespectfully, curse at me, or break things. Your therapist may extend limit-setting outside the office, indicating to you that it isn't okay for you to get drunk, stoned, or to sleep around. As mentioned previously, your therapist may have to be quite forceful in disapproving of self-destructive acts of behavior that is harmful to others. In rare instances the therapist may even tell you you can't continue therapy if destructive behavior continues. Of course a skilled therapist knows just how far limit-setting should be carried. It's not helpful to set a limit you have absolutely no intention of following, especially early in treatment when you and the therapist don't know each other well. It doesn't show much common sense for the therapist to demand that you magically stop the very behavior you came to get help with in the first place. If your therapist does have to set strong limits, he or she will treat you considerately, without making you feel rejected and bad.

Instead of setting limits there are plenty of times when a

good adolescent therapist will give you the room to experiment that others outside haven't allowed. Just as there are parents who are too permissive, there are parents who are so strict their children hardly have space to grow. Although your therapist may run the risk of displeasing your parents or other important adults in your life, he or she will be ready to stand up for your rights to have different values, or a different life-style, as long as it is healthy. The parents and teachers of a brilliant student I saw last year were so wrapped up in his soaring grades and marvelous future that they ignored the fact that his life only consisted of lonely studying. He had developed compulsions about doing homework, and had become deeply depressed. He finally begged for treatment. As he began to improve and make friends, his grades slipped, and his parents became angry with him and with me. They thought he was getting worse, not better. I brought them into the office and explained forcefully that high grades and getting into a top college weren't the most important signs of an adolescent's success. What really mattered was that their son now had a decent social life, instead of living like a studying machine. I told them he had been headed for a breakdown, and they should thank their lucky stars for his improvement. They got the message and stopped pestering him about his schoolwork.

A good adolescent therapist possesses a high degree of objectivity, the ability to look at your situation coolly and calmly and search out the real truth in the frequently different stories you and those who know you tell. Adolescents frequently paint a picture of themselves as innocent victims of adults they believe are stupid, unfair, and cruel. Out of sympathy a naive therapist can be trapped into buying the whole story, neglecting to see realistically how you may be provoking your parents into getting angry. The opposite problem is buying an adult description of you as a rude, crude monster who needs to be "straightened out," turned into the kind of wonderful human being your parents want, which means denying who you really are. The skillful therapist can't swallow your parents' view whole, for that could mean a loss of appreciation of your viewpoint, which actually may be far more on target.

Finally, a good therapist won't need to have his or her job praised openly. This is a heavy burden. After all, being human, a therapist wants some recognition for good work done. But if you are like most teen-agers, you'll stay in therapy until you've gotten what you need, then when you are on the right track you'll leave without showering the therapist with flowers. Big displays of gratitude are hard to afford when you're trying to become independent from adults. A good therapist gets enough satisfaction from knowing inwardly how you've been helped. Don't think you owe him or her a testimonial.

10 | *Reasons for Avoiding Therapy*

Negative feelings about psychotherapy are always present to some degree, both for someone thinking about entering treatment, and for a person already in treatment. Adolescents are especially likely to express resistance to therapy openly. Most grown-ups come to a therapist under their own steam, but the average teenager is usually *pressured* into having a consultation. While your resistance may be frustrating to outsiders and even puzzling to yourself, there are very powerful, sometimes very good reasons for your avoiding or delaying therapy.

Our society is supposed to be more enlightened now about emotional difficulties and more accepting of people in psychotherapy than in the past. No doubt things are better than fifty years ago, when it was generally believed that only very disturbed people in a sanitarium or hospital needed treatment. But even with all the therapists there are today, and all the publicity about mental health, you'd be surprised how many people still think that seeking psychotherapy means there must be something terribly wrong with you. With such mistaken ideas there has to be fear, and it is very human to turn fear into cruel laughter at someone else's expense. Teen-agers don't take well to the hint that something is bothering them emotionally, and often are equally unable to show kindness and understanding toward someone else in trouble. Like most adolescents, you probably fear being labeled a "kook," "nut," or "weirdo" by your peers. Sadly, your fear may have prevented you from appreciating how common your problems are, or how many of your friends live with similar difficulties. The truth is that most patients in therapy are no different in dress, manner, speech, or behavior than anyone else. The big difference is they've had the wisdom and courage to see a therapist about problems others choose to hide.*

Linked to the misbelief that you have to be "off the wall" to see a therapist is the equally common misbelief that a therapist is a nut. TV comics fill their acts with bad jokes about crazy "shrinks." Supposedly a therapist must be crazy to start with since he or she wants to sit with troubled people all day, or else just sitting with nuts will make the therapist nutty. It's only a short step from these fairy tales to the idea that therapists do crazy things to patients, making poor, unsuspecting people worse off than they were in the first

*I'm not saying all your worries about being labeled a "mental case" are completely unreasonable. Teasing by peers is a real possibility if you reveal you are in treatment. So perhaps you'd be better off not discussing therapy with friends at all, or only with a friend you really trust. I wish I could tell you that revealing you are in treatment to a school or an employer has always been greeted by a fair judgment, but this doesn't always happen, and probably won't until school officials and employers are better educated about mental health. So you're better off keeping your therapy to yourself when you are trying to get into college or are applying for a job.

place with hypnotic spells, strange machinery, psychedelic drugs. But as I've shown you, psychotherapy is based on sound scientific theory about personality, mixed with a liberal helping of plain, old-fashioned common sense. And it is practiced by highly qualified, dedicated professionals.

Your avoidance of therapy may stem from the typical adolescent struggle to become independent and have a "space" of your own, without grown-up interference. At a time when you are so involved in proving to grown-ups you don't need their help, it's naturally much harder for you to admit that your ability to take charge of your life is getting shaky, and that you require outside assistance.

Your parents, and other adults in your world, also may be highly resistant to treatment, sometimes even when they recommended therapy in the first place. Parents see their children as a reflection of their child-raising ability. If you develop problems, they may automatically assume they are to blame, thinking they've hurt you by something they've done, or by failing to provide the love or guidance that supposedly would have made you healthy. They may mistakenly believe that your troubles will reflect badly upon them in the therapist's view, or that family secrets (and what family doesn't have them?) will be exposed in therapy. So your parents may deny your problems to protect themselves from the therapist's imagined shaming and blaming.

Your parents may overlook your troubles because someone in their own lives suffered emotional difficulties, and had to be hospitalized. They worry about a similar fate befalling you. Frequently parental denial of your conflicts will go hand in hand with denial of their personal or marital difficulties. Parents sometimes fear the therapist will turn you against them, thinking you will get better in therapy by learning how to hate and accuse them better. Nothing could be further from the truth.

Finally, your chances for help may be sabotaged because of grown-ups mistakenly chalking up serious emotional problems to adolescence itself. Adults often go on about how crazy teen-agers are, but in the same breath they allow as how kids always outgrow their wild behavior in time. While adolescence is marked by a certain amount of ups and downs, the average teen-ager just isn't as wild and unpredictable as adults think. Deep spells of depression or obvious delinquent behavior are all too often dismissed as typical for an adolescent, when they would never be ignored in an adult.

It's thought that for every teen-ager who does consult a therapist, there may be as many as *ten* others who will never go for badly needed help. Now that I've explained something about how therapy works, the kind of people who practice it, and the reasons for avoiding it, I hope you will use this knowledge so that you don't become one of the unknown psychological casualties of adolescence. If it's your parents who've been stopping you from seeking help because of their resistance, I'll tell you what you can do about this in the next chapter.

11 | *Your First Consultation*

Entering Therapy: Early Moves

If it is your idea to see a therapist, think carefully about how you want to break the news to your parents, or the adults responsible for your welfare. Choose a quiet time and place. Although your problem upsets you, try not to alarm them about it. If they're like most grown-ups, when they hear about your decision, they will probably get worried even if your difficulties aren't serious. Even if your problem is such that there is a realistic reason for them to be worried, if they get *too* upset, they may not be able to think clearly about the best way to get you help.

Explain your problem as *simply* and as *generally* as possible, without exaggerating or overdramatizing. I wouldn't go into detail about symptoms neither you nor they understand very well, about very private matters of personal relationships. I think it is terrific if you can be open with your parents, but there are also issues which are really your private business. For instance, parents don't usually discuss the intimate facts of their love-making with you, and you don't have to spell out the details of your sexual life.

Try to be as reassuring as you can under the circumstances, especially if you feel you are pretty stable except for one or two issues that need straightening out. If your parents panic, don't let their panic panic you. Try not to get drawn into long debates about your problems, unless you genuinely feel that the act of asking for help has made it possible for your parents and you to speak more openly. And don't let improved communication with them take the place of therapy, if you know deep inside you still want help. If you really don't want to talk with anyone but a therapist, just tell your parents you feel this way because of the personal nature of your problem, not because you don't respect or care for them. Tell them that in time, with a therapist's help, perhaps you may be ready to discuss your difficulties with them, or maybe your therapist can speak with them after the consultation.

Above all don't blame your parents for your problems. Probably they're going to do plenty of self-blaming, or at least self-examination, when you tell them you want help. Accusing them may be completely unfair. And even if they are responsible for many or all of your hang-ups, blaming them may put them on the defensive, so that they will become even more resistant than they were in the first place.

Most adults will support your wish to have therapy. Rarely they won't. They will turn you down flatly, or delay, telling you to think things over, wait awhile to see if you get better. Watching and waiting may be okay up to a certain point, but I wouldn't do it if you are hurting badly, or if you know your parents deal with many problems by repeatedly delaying.

If you are getting nowhere fast, you may have to reveal facts about your condition that otherwise you would have kept private—how seriously suicidal you've been, or how deeply involved with drugs you've been. You may have to stop the discussion, and speak to them again in a day or two until they get the message. If nothing works, try going to a relative, a family friend, a physician, or a clergyman, to see if they can convince your parents. Don't just go to anyone. If possible seek someone your folks know and trust, whose opinions they respect. Don't go to someone who has a bad relationship with your parents, or an ax to grind with them, where the knowledge that you're upset could be used for gossip or to put your parents down. If there is no one who can persuade your parents to get you help, you may feel you have no choice but to see a therapist against your parents' wishes, or even without their knowledge.

Very rarely an adolescent makes an appointment with me and reveals in the office that the visit is a secret from his or her parents. He or she won't accept further help unless I agree to have *no* contact with family members, not even a phone call. If this plan appeals to you, you should know that it is against the law in most states for a therapist to treat you under the so-called age of consent for any length of time, without a parent's or guardian's permission. This age is generally eighteen and below for a girl, sixteen and below for a boy.

When *I'm* faced with this problem, I first try to find out the reasons for secrecy. Perhaps the adolescent is getting harshly treated at home, being abused physically and or sexually, like a girl who's being forced to have sex with her father, or a boy who's beaten severely and frequently by alcoholic parents. In this situation the teen-ager doesn't want parents to find out about his or her getting any sort of help, because he or she is afraid of being punished. The teen-ager may also be worried that the parents will get punished legally if the secret is leaked outside the office.

If you are being abused by your parents, you *must* let *someone* in authority know, whether it is a therapist, a policeman, a family physician, or a clergyman. I tell an abused teen-ager that I can do almost nothing about painful feelings related to abuse as long as the harmful parental behavior goes on unchecked. In such a case I make an educated guess about how reasonable parents are likely to be about outside help. If I think parents may accept assistance, I tell the teen-ager to say that help has been sought, without going deeply into the reasons, and I myself will call the parents to set up a meeting. If I'm certain that telling parents will only lead to further angry abuse at home, I offer to help the patient report abusive behavior to the proper authorities, even to find a place to stay temporarily if there is real, immediate physical danger, until the parents can be placed under proper supervision, or it is decided the adolescent should be permanently removed from home. This is a very complicated situation, and a therapist may be risking legal action by parents in return for giving you such help. But I believe the risk has *got* to be taken for the sake of the young person's physical and emotional health. Laws in many states that require a therapist or physician to report abusing parents to authorities make this situation easier to handle.

It's more likely that your reasons for wanting the therapist to have nothing to do with your parents aren't nearly as dramatic. Possibly you're worried your parents will "mix in" to therapy if they've interfered in other areas of your life. You *may* have a perfectly good reason for your concern, but there *are* better ways of handling the situation.

I tell young people opposed to the idea of my seeing their parents how careful I am about confidentiality (see below). I also explain the realistic legal need for parental permission. I say I'll need only a brief contact, one office session, or just a phone conversation, to get treatment off the ground. I've found that an adolescent's objections usually fade when it's understood how strongly I feel about keeping treatment safe from outside interference. But if you still have doubts after reading this, I'd suggest that you ask to be present when your parents are interviewed.

The adolescent therapist is occasionally called by a relative who wants a youngster to have therapy, offers to pay, and asks that treatment be kept secret from parents. The relative really may have the teen-ager's welfare upmost in mind, but far more often I've found that relatives have reasons for mixing in that aren't well intentioned: long-standing, bitter feelings about the parents that have nothing to do with the adolescent's problems, or a jealous desire to interfere in the child-parent relationship. So I tell relatives that I will only see an adolescent with his or her parents' full knowledge and cooperation.

When a relative offers to pay for your therapy, think carefully. Is this arrangement really going to be helpful to you, even if your parents do know about it? Is the offer made free and clear, or are there hidden strings attached? Will you now be expected by the relative to be loyal to him or her in family arguments? When parents really can't afford treatment, and a really well-meaning relative wants to pay, I'll go along with this offer, but only if everyone knows who is doing the paying, and no one will feel angry, guilty, or obligated—truly, no strings.

Actually, most adolescents don't go to a therapist on their own, in secret or not, but because a grown-up has *told* them to. Quite possibly you're reading this book because someone is asking or demanding that you have a consultation. I've discussed how to deal with this situation in the chapter "Knowing When You Need Help." It's been my experience that the majority of teen-agers seen because of an outside recommendation for therapy *do* turn out to need help, although not always for the reasons the outsider had in mind. A good therapist also knows how to handle the less common cases where help isn't required.

If I were you, I'd agree to a consultation without making a big fuss, but with the *clear* understanding that you will be given the opportunity to make up your mind afterward, without pressure, even if this means postponing or refusing treatment. If for any reason you don't believe your parents or guardian can find you an objective therapist on their own, insist on going to a third party, whom everyone in your situation trusts, to find you a therapist.

Finding a Therapist

▮ There are national organizations of qualified psycho-therapists with local branches in major cities. They keep lists of therapists in the surrounding area, their specialities, sometimes the fees they charge. These organizations include the American Psychiatric Association for psychiatrists, the American Psychological Association for clinical psychologists, and the American Association of Psychiatric Social Workers for members of that profession. If you can't find branch offices listed in your phone directory, write to the national offices to find out where they are located (see Appendix). In addition, private psychotherapists and psychiatric clinics are often listed with your county medical society, your local United Fund or Community Chest, various mental health groups, and the central office of your religion.

Most people seeking help would rather be referred to a psychotherapist through someone they know and trust. If you need this personal touch, a general practitioner or clergyman you've known for many years is usually a very dependable referral source. As mentioned, family doctors and clergymen get a lot of training today in psychology. Many treat simple emotional difficulties. It's been said that for every person a psychotherapist sees, there are probably a hundred successfully counseled by a general practitioner, priest, minister, or rabbi. These professionals are often the first to see someone in deep emotional trouble. Their guidance often does wonders in resolving a problem altogether, or reducing the anxiety about going on to see a therapist. It's the mark of a fine doctor or clergyman that he or she will really take time to talk with you. You won't automatically be sent to a "shrink."

Making an Appointment.

I like the idea of teen-agers making the first appointment on their own, but in reality parents or other grown-ups usually make the first contact with a therapist. Your parents may want to speak to the therapist before you do to make sure they get a chance to tell "their side." Like so many situations that come up in treatment, there's never one right method for your therapist to follow.

For effective treatment to take place, you must believe your therapist can be *trusted,* you must know that your relationship will be kept *confidential.* The therapist therefore will always be very careful during any contact with outsiders. In return the therapist asks that you always take certain basic *responsibilities* for the realistic details of psychotherapy. After all, a big aim of treatment is to help you become more independent.

In line with these principles of *trust, confidentiality,* and *responsibility,* your therapist will usually speak briefly on the phone with your folks, get an idea of what your problem is, then speak to you right away. If you are not available, the therapist will ask that you call later to set up your own appointment. (There are several exceptions to this approach, which I'll discuss presently.) You can be sure that in this first telephone conversation, and in any contact thereafter, your therapist will treat your parents with respect, but will do his or her utmost to protect your privacy.

When you telephone for an appointment, the therapist will speak briefly with you, then try to schedule a session that won't conflict with your school, or any other important activity. I don't think it's a good idea to see the therapist knowing that you are missing something important, since this can make you feel anxious, resentful, and less willing to talk. I doubt you will want to discuss your problem at length over the phone. Most people prefer to wait until they see the therapist in person. The therapist as a rule also doesn't want to get into long telephone discussions on first contact, for it's impossible to offer advice about a situation the therapist can't know much about without seeing you face to face for a good talk.

If your problem sounds like it's been going on awhile, and you aren't in great pain, the therapist will set up an appointment within a few days to a few weeks. If you are in the midst of a crisis such as a bad drug trip, the therapist will see you within a day or the same day, or will refer you to someone else who can. Of course what the therapist thinks is a crisis may be different from your parents' or your own opinion. Parents often get very upset about a problem that may indeed require help, but not immediately. Sometimes the therapist can be helpful just by telling parents to calm down and accept your own less upset view of a situation. When the therapist then sets up a later appointment, you will get the feeling that he or she doesn't overreact as others have.

Here are the exceptions to your setting up an appointment before your parents are seen:

(1) If you are about age eleven to fourteen, you may prefer that your parents be seen first. At this age you are often realistically more dependent upon your parents, closer to childhood than adulthood. You're usually more used to seeing a doctor with your folks, to the doctor speaking to your parents first. You may feel a little scared about going to a therapist alone, at least the first time. You may have trouble getting to the office because of transportation difficulties. However, if you do decide to see the therapist regularly after your consultation, you'll be expected to come in on your own, as part of your responsibility to therapy. If you are driven to the office, it's best to be dropped off and picked up without anyone speaking to your therapist.

(2) Regardless of your age, even after reading this book, you may still be so worried about seeing a therapist that you want to send your parents ahead of you to see what the therapist is like, or insist on being seen together with your parents, using them as a shield. I wish for your sake you didn't have to be so "uptight," but if this is the way you feel, your therapist is likely to go along with your wish to test the water. Probably after you've heard your parents' report, or met the therapist with your family present, you'll feel better about being seen alone.

(3) Your particular symptoms or problems may not permit you to come alone at first. If you are phobic about traveling on a subway or a bus alone, you may not want to come to the office

by yourself because you are so panicky. If you are very depressed, having psychotic experiences, you may be too troubled to get to a therapist under your own steam, or to tell the therapist what he or she needs to know to be helpful to you. Under these circumstances a therapist may decide to see your parents first by themselves, then bring you in to be seen, until you are well enough to come in by yourself.

You may not feel like seeing a therapist at this time, no matter what your parents say, no matter what advice I've given. This is your right, whether your reasons for refusing therapy are correct or wrong. But your decision may leave your parents feeling very worried, so they may call a therapist for some help in dealing with your situation anyway. Every adolescent therapist gets these calls. The therapist may tell your parents that there is little they can do even if you need help to force you into something you don't really want. Instead the therapist may suggest that they "hang in," take pressure off you to see a therapist, and wait for you to recognize a need for treatment.

Occasionally a therapist may offer to meet with your parents to discuss your situation further, because it's felt your parents can use guidance to deal better with the problems you seem to be having. This help can make them feel better and take pressure off you. It also may make you rethink your refusing help, especially if you see the changes your parents make because of their sessions. If a therapist does decide to consult with your parents, he or she will tell them not to keep their visits a secret, but to let you know they are getting help the best way they can, given your wish not to be treated.

If a therapist does get involved in counseling your parents, and you then decide that you want treatment, he or she has to figure out: (1) whether to see you and stop your parents' sessions, (2) whether to continue sessions with your parents while you are in treatment, or (3) whether to keep working with your parents and send you to someone else. The best course depends on how long your parents have been seen, whether your treatment will take pressure off your parents so they don't need help anymore, whether seeing your parents would make it hard for you to trust the therapist, and finally whether the therapist's investment in seeing your folks' point of view is so strong that it would then become difficult for him or her to treat you fairly.

▌ *Your First Consultation*

Don't be surprised if you begin to get nervous as the time for your consultation approaches. Many people have strange notions of what's going to happen in a therapist's office—they'll be hynotized, be given truth serum, be forced to confess dark and shameful secrets. It's one thing to know in your mind that these things won't happen. But "head" knowledge isn't always enough to stop your heart pounding. Breaking the ice with any stranger never is easy; if you don't watch out, you can build the therapist up into a very fearful stranger indeed, a mixture of Frankenstein and the Wizard of Oz.

Your first meeting won't be such an ordeal if you remember that your therapist isn't a mad scientist, a sorcerer, or a computer with a brain for a heart. He or she is another human being just like you, with very human feelings, hopes, dreams, and even problems. You aren't going to have your mind dissected or be forced to talk about anything you don't want to. You are under *no* pressure whatsoever to tell your entire life story right after you walk through the door.

Many of you probably think a therapist's office is like a busy doctor's office, with a nurse, an examination room, and an eye chart. Perhaps you expect the therapist to wear a white coat. The reality is quite different. There will probably be a quiet waiting room, with enough seats for a few people. The therapist's inner office will usually be furnished informally, so that it will look more like a living room, or a comfortable den. Most therapists have a desk, but they usually prefer not to sit behind it when seeing patients. Your therapist will probably sit in a chair a few feet away from you, close enough so that both of you can easily see and hear each other, yet not so close that you'll be breathing down each other's necks. You'll find that the light of the office is kept soft; bright lights often make people uncomfortable. However the office is furnished or lit, it will provide a peaceful, relaxed setting.

Unless you are attending a clinic, there probably won't be a secretary, or indeed anyone greeting you when you arrive. The therapist probably will be in session with another patient, so you'll let yourself into the waiting room. If the therapist shares an office, there may be another patient waiting, but chances are you'll find yourself alone. A fan or a radio may be going—that's to prevent any conversation that might spill over from the inner office being heard outside.

If you come early, you may want to use this free time to collect your thoughts, possibly think a little more about what you want to get from your meeting. If you've already been mulling your problems over, you might just be better off taking a few deep breaths, relaxing, or reading a magazine. You probably won't have to wait very long because psychotherapists tend to keep to their schedules.

If other patients *are* present (more likely to be the case in a clinic), you may feel uptight about sitting with them. Simply remember that they are there for the same reasons you are, to get help with their problems. You may feel like one big sore thumb sticking out, but your head *isn't* made of glass. No one can look inside and know about your secret troubles.

In the following pages I'm going to describe my own approach to a new adolescent patient and family, so that you can get a better idea of what your first consultation will be like. Remember that no approach is automatically the right one, nor are there any set rules to be followed by you or the therapist after you've been invited into the office. In most respects my approach probably resembles the one your therapist will use. Of course your therapist may have similar ideas about what psychotherapy is supposed to accomplish but a *different* way of working than mine.

I begin a first session by jotting down vital statistics— the patient's name, age, address, names of parents and important family members, telephone number. I don't take any more notes after this, because I prefer to write notes after a session is over or at the end of the day. Many therapists do take notes while you are talking. You may find this distracting at first, but you will get used to it after a while. If note-taking continues to bother you, courteously ask the therapist to stop.

While I need a great deal of information about my patient, my most important job in a first session is to help someone feel comfortable in a situation most people find at least a little threatening. If a patient feels comfortable right away, I get right down to discussing the problem, and to taking a complete life history. If someone feels very uncomfortable, I save "deep" questions for later on in the session, or for another session, concentrating instead on helping him or her feel less nervous. Sometimes this can be done quickly. If you are very uptight, it may take several sessions before you can talk easily. So you may be surprised to find that instead of getting into "heavy" issues, you will be discussing the World Series, the latest rock-and-roll hit, or even playing chess. I have even taken both of us for a walk in the park nearby if I thought it would make the patient feel more relaxed.

I always ask an adolescent what he or she knows about me and the work I do. I never assume that anyone has completely realistic information about therapy. Sometimes before I can even begin to investigate a problem, I will have to clear up mistaken notions about treatment that might get in the way.

I ask the patient to tell me as simply as possible why he or she has come to see me. If I have had any contact with parents or outsiders, I'll tell the patient what they have said and, in connection with any further outside contacts, I promise that I will keep whatever I'm told strictly confidential. If it is necessary to meet with parents or other people, I say I won't reveal anything the patient doesn't want me to. The only exception to this rule is if I think the youngster is in serious danger of self-harm or harming others. If a danger exists, I say I will break confidentiality in order to protect a patient from injury or death, or the legal consequences and crushing guilt that he or she would suffer if anyone got hurt.*

In collecting information I don't fire questions from a prepared list. This approach makes adolescents feel they're getting the third degree, or that the therapist is more interested in gathering facts than in the person behind the facts. If you begin to have a "third-degree" feeling during the first interview, I advise you to let the therapist know immediately.

I encourage adolescents to tell their story in whatever order seems most natural, skipping from one topic to another, from family life to school matters, from the past to the present. As the story unfolds I always listen carefully, avoiding issues that too obviously are upsetting, trying to put pieces of the picture together, clarifying issues that seem unclear or memories that are fuzzy, if I can.

Regarding a youngster's symptom or problem, I'll ask the following questions: When did the trouble start? How long has it been going on? Did it start gradually, or all at once? Are there other problems or symptoms besides the main one? What else was happening when the trouble started? Were there sudden stresses, illnesses, losses? What life areas have been seriously affected by the trouble, and what areas have been unaffected?

Since today's emotional problems may be a signal that

---

*In nearly twenty years of treating adolescents, I've only had to break confidentiality for these reasons several times. Later, patients have always told me how glad they were that I could act in their best interest at a time they couldn't.

something has been wrong for a long time, I try to get a complete picture of what a youngster's life has been like from infancy right up to today. Facts about family life are always important, but especially so with adolescents. Since you probably live at home, and are still closely involved with your family, what they do and feel affects you very deeply.

I ask for the name, age, and a brief thumbnail sketch of each family member, and ask how each gets along with my patient. I'm not only interested in parents, brothers, and sisters, but in anyone living under the same roof—grandparents, aunts, uncles. People like maids, gardeners, or boarders may be very important figures in your family life. I may ask about significant people who live outside the family—relatives, neighbors, teachers, friends. Who are the youngster's favorite people, and least favorite people? What are their outstanding good and bad qualities? Who in the family considers my patient his or her favorite, or least favorite? Have any relatives had emotional problems, been treated by a therapist, or hospitalized for psychological disorders?

Adolescent problems are especially likely to be related to problems parents have with each other, so I want to know how their marriage looks through my patient's eyes. What about each parent's family, social, economic, and religious background? How did mother and father get along with *their* folks? How did they meet? What was their courtship like? If my patient was adopted, what, if anything, does he or she know about the natural parents?

If parents are unhappy, what does my patient think is the cause for their disagreements? Is my patient blamed for their problems? What are their fights like? Have the parents ever separated or talked about divorce? If they are divorced, what are the arrangements for seeing the parent my patient doesn't live with? If divorced parents have remarried or are living with someone, what is the new partner like? How does the patient get along with half-brothers or half-sisters?

There are tremendous differences from one society to

another in how feelings are expressed and problems are handled. I'm concerned about these differences, in how typical or untypical my patient's family is for its cultural background. Economic factors strongly influence family life. So I want to know about the parents' work. How happy are father and mother—if she is a wage earner—with their work? What are the work hours? Is the family comfortable financially or poor? What kind of neighborhood does the family live in? Does my patient live in a house or an apartment? Does my patient have a private room, or share a room with someone else? I ask for a description or a drawing of the living space, especially my patient's room. People always say a great deal about themselves in how they furnish and use their environment.

Each family develops a special style for living together, communicating, making decisions. I get a rough idea of family style by asking how the family gets its tasks done—cooking, taking care of chores, going on vacations. Who makes decisions, and how are they made? Some families are run like democracies—children have a big vote in making family policy. Others are run like kingdoms—one or both parents hand down decisions that the children have to follow without questions. Most family "governments" fall somewhere in between these types.

Since adolescent beliefs so often collide with the values of others, I want to know what the family's basic ideas are about religion, morality, and politics, and whether the patient shared these beliefs before adolescence. What is the parents' vision of how life is meant to be lived? How does my patient's vision differ from this?

Turning to the past I ask about early memories of parents, family, and neighborhood. Even if you have a good memory, it isn't likely you can trace your own history back much before your third or fourth year. So I ask what my patient has been told by others about early life experiences he or she can't possibly remember, including birth and infancy. What was his or her reaction to going to school for the first time? How has my patient gotten along with classmates and teachers throughout schooling? Have grades and conduct been good or bad? How did the patient handle stresses like a move to a new neighborhood, the arrival of a baby brother or sister, personal injury or illness, or changes in the family due to sickness, divorce, children growing up, and leaving? If my patient was adopted, when and how was this revealed, and what was the reaction? Who have been important influences, good or bad, among friends, relatives, teachers, religious figures? What have been favorite athletic, creative, and leisure activities?

Sex is often hard for adolescents to discuss. I don't believe in making a big deal about it in early sessions unless it is easy for my patient to discuss or if it is obviously very important because of the nature of the problem. I introduce the subject by saying simply that sex is a natural part of life; since my patient is alive and kicking, I know he or she must have sexual thoughts, feelings, and probably some experience. I state that these are things young people often want to keep to themselves, but that in doing so, a teen-ager possibly can develop ideas and fantasies that can be very troubling, unless they are brought out into the light and cleared up with realistic information.

If I can, I ask for childhood theories about sex and birth. When and how did my patient learn about "the facts of life"? To what degree has he or she undergone physical changes of adolescence, and how well have these been handled? Has the adolescent girl had her first menstrual period? How was she prepared for it? Has the adolescent boy had wet dreams?

Masturbation is a particularly difficult topic to get into with an adult, but it is often vital for you to discuss it with the therapist, since fear and shame connected with it cause so many problems. I help my patients talk about it by taking the strong position that masturbation is one of the many, ordinary expressions of a deeply inborn need for sexual satisfaction, an activity which continues throughout adolescence and adulthood. At what age did my patient begin to masturbate? What "stories"—images, daydreams—occur with masturbation? Does my patient think masturbation will harm him or her in any way? How often does my patient ordinarily masturbate, and has there been an increase or decrease in masturbation? There isn't a normal or acceptable figure for masturbation. Some people masturbate daily, or several times a day; others several times a week or less, showing how widely we differ in the strength of the sex drive. But a sharp increase in masturbation may indicate that you are handling a rise in anxiety or tension through this physical tranquilizer, while a decrease may mean that you are becoming very guilt-ridden, or depressed, with a general lack of energy showing up in your sexual life.

If an adolescent patient has had sex relations, I want to know when sexual activity started, if sex has occurred with many others or just one partner, if it has been enjoyable or not, if there have been any difficulties in sexual performance, if there has been any homosexual or bisexual activity, if contraception has been used, and what my patient knows about contraception.

I always inquire about my patient's view of the future. What does he or she want in coming years regarding education, work, marriage, leisure? Would he or she bring up children any differently than he or she was raised? Is he or she optimistic or pessimistic about solving emotional problems? Does he or she feel good or bad about the future of the country, and the rest of the world? Many experts believe more teen-agers have emotional problems today because serious social problems like the threat of nuclear war or environmental disaster make them feel more scared and helpless than someone growing up a hundred years ago.

Just because you don't have a degree in psychology doesn't stop you from forming your own ideas about your problem. I always ask what my patient believes is at the root of the trouble. The answer tells me a lot about my patient's common sense and ability to think psychologically. I'm struck by how often adolescents come up with explanations that are amazingly to the point, summing up some complicated psychological issues very simply: "When I get angry I hold it all in, then I feel like a time bomb that's going to

go off, and the least little thing will make me blow!" "No one under-
stands me, but sometimes I don't think I even understand myself,
and I get so frustrated I take out my troubles on everybody around
me."

Toward the end of my first meeting or meetings, I ask a
series of questions that will tell me more about my patient's level of
education, judgment, and ability to concentrate and think clearly.
Who were the last five presidents? What is the capital of France? I
ask for an interpretation of a proverb like "Don't cry over spilled
milk" and how the patient would handle an imaginary situation like
a fire in a crowded theater. Other questions help me understand
more about the patient's inner life, fantasies, daydreams, such as: "If
you were born again as an animal, fish, or bird, which would you
choose, and why?" "If you had to spend a year on a desert island
with just one person, who would you pick, and why?" "If you could
have three wishes, what would they be?"

These are all standard questions; try not to react to them
as if they were a school examination. You won't be graded on your
answers. The therapist isn't interested in whether you are right or
wrong, but in your personality and your problem.

In order to get to know you and your problem, your
therapist will usually need to spend one to three sessions with you
alone. A session will last about an hour, sometimes three-quarters of
an hour, sometimes an hour and a half, but rarely longer.* By the
end of your first session(s), the therapist may have a pretty good
idea about what's bothering you, and already have figured out what
to recommend about further treatment. On the other hand the
therapist may feel that more information is needed from outsiders or

---

*If you feel you are being cut off just at the point you are really getting
into your story, you should tell the therapist to arrange a longer
interview for you the next time. If you feel you are getting tired by a
long interview, you should tell the therapist that you wish to stop, and
ask him or her to schedule you for a shorter session the next time.

from additional tests before definite suggestions can be made. The therapist obviously will have formed some general impressions about your problem. You certainly have a right to ask for an opinion at this point, even if the therapist can't say too much. If the causes of your problem seem very clear, and if you are willing to listen, many therapists will tell you up front what's causing your difficulty, even after just one session.

In my experience teen-agers do indeed want to know what's wrong with them, but they often hold back asking because they are scared of being told they are seriously mentally ill. Don't let your fear prevent you from getting information that will make you feel better. If I can, I always tell new patients *what* I believe is troubling them, sometimes even using the psychological name for the condition. I explain, if I am able to, *why* I think they are troubled, too. I may give a general explanation about why people develop their particular difficulty, and if I have a good idea about deeper causes of a problem or symptom, I examine them. Here's an example:

A seventeen-year-old boy was referred to me because he had wrecked his car while drunk and gotten his license suspended. He was failing in school, his sleep and appetite were poor, and he seemed uninterested in anything except getting into trouble. His problems began two years earlier, after his father had died of brain cancer. The father had been cheerful and outgoing his entire life, but in the last months of his illness, as the cancer spread, he became increasingly ill tempered. He would yell at my patient, calling him a shiftless, no-good bum who would never amount to anything, despite the boy's good school record.

At the end of our consultation, I told the boy I thought he was suffering from an unrecognized depression that had begun after his father's death—at the time he could only say he felt numb—and still continued to the present time. I said depression was often related to an important loss, leaving one feeling sad, empty, and helpless. It would be normal to grow depressed after an important family member died. But in this case normal feelings of grief were complicated by his father's cruelty during his final months. I explained that we often feel angry at people who died, because we loved them and they left us alone. Sometimes our anger makes us feel guilty. But he felt even *more* guilty because he had been very angry at his father *before* his death. He had wished that his father would die, so he wouldn't be hurt anymore by the father's constant rages. After his father's death he denied his grief, only feeling numb instead. But then his depression began to surface through his eating and sleeping difficulties, in concentration problems which lead to school failure, in loss of interest of enjoyable activities, and in self-destructive, accident-prone behavior. He felt so terribly unhappy, so guilty, that he didn't know whether to strike out at the world or at himself.

My explanation can be thought of as a sort of psychological aerial photograph: photography from high up gives you a big picture of territory, outlines of land, buildings, houses. You can't see what's actually going on inside a house. For that you need more detailed pictures, taken closer up. I told my patient that while I could give him a big picture at the end of one session, it wouldn't magically improve his problem. To feel better he would have to spend more time filling in details about his relationship with his father before he got sick, or how he had handled strong angry feelings toward other people. Nevertheless, just having the big picture gave him relief, for now he realized the *nature* of his problem (a depression); recognized a little about its *causes* (buried anger and guilt toward his father); and knew something about its *treatment* (further therapy sessions to clear up the issues mentioned above).

Your psychotherapist will try to gear an explanation about your problem to the kind of person you are and your needs at the moment. The above case was pretty clear-cut. The boy was eager for help, anxious to understand more, so I could give him a fairly detailed picture. But you may not want to hear a complicated explanation, or may be too upset to understand one. If your therapist's explanation is too confusing, too complicated, too incomplete, too simple, say so. Perhaps he or she can do better.

On the other hand, try not to be angry if the therapist honestly can't say too much about your troubles at this point. There are many adolescents whose situations I can't understand as quickly as the boy's above. Sometimes I may only be able to say what a patient is suffering from, without knowing why. Or I may know the nature and cause of a youngster's troubles, without being sure of the right treatment approach. There's nothing wrong with the therapist telling you that he or she needs further information, contact with your parents, special tests, a school report, before your question about your problem can be answered fully. After all there are many times after a physical examination when a medical doctor won't know all the reasons for a patient's physical symptoms, and will ask for further tests.

12 | *Meeting with Parents*

If you are in your early adolescence, between age twelve to sixteen, you are probably still very involved with your family; your problem is involved with them, or involves them in some way. Your therapist may want to meet with your parents (or guardian) and possibly other family members before or after the consultation, to learn how they view your situation. If you are an older teen-ager or young adult, not too involved with your family, not seriously troubled or in trouble, it is more likely that the therapist will choose not to meet with your family at all. Arrangements about practical matters like fee, insurance coverage, et cetera, will be made over the phone or through you.

Your psychotherapist wants to accomplish more than getting information about you from your parents. Parents have as many doubts and fears about therapy as teen-agers, sometimes more. While meeting with your folks the psychotherapist will give them realistic information about treatment, explore their attitudes about therapy (and correct them if necessary), calm their fear or guilt about your problem, and let them learn about his or her personality and methods. The therapist thus builds an atmosphere of trust with your family, insuring good working conditions for your treatment, now and in the future.

When I meet with parents, I say that since I'm going to ask many questions, they should feel just as free to ask me questions in return. I immediately stress the importance of confidentiality. Usually the subject comes up when parents ask me what their child has told me. I state I can only give them a general idea, because going into details will ruin the adolescent's confidence in me. I explain how valuable this trust is, and ask parents to put up with the frustration of not knowing exactly what I have been told, or will be told, because the rewards are so great.

On the other hand I reassure parents that things they've revealed to me in confidence won't be leaked. If letting the cat out of the bag about a past event will only cause everyone pain, and there is no really helpful reason for revealing it, I prefer to keep it buried. But if keeping a secret has played a very important part in the present problem, I ask that it be brought out into the open. I may suggest that they tell the secret to their youngster in my presence, or I may ask their permission to reveal it in a private session. But often the best plan is for parents to share the secret with their child at home, without bringing in a third party.

The problems that arise with unnecessary secrets are illustrated in the case of a fifteen-year-old girl whose mother had developed diabetes. The mother had to be hospitalized for several weeks, but was quite well when she was released. She did have to take injections of insulin to keep her blood sugar under control. Mother and daughter were very close, and the parents were afraid the daughter would get too upset if she found out about the diabetes. So they decided to tell her that the mother had been in the hospital for a minor checkup. The fact that the mother was taking insulin was concealed.

In the next few months the daughter overheard talk about her mother's diabetes, without finding out exactly what it was. She also discovered insulin needles several times. As a result she developed wild ideas that her mother either had a fatal illness or had become a drug addict. She grew anxious, couldn't sleep, lost weight, and finally was brought to see me on the recommendation of her pediatrician who also hadn't been told about the mother's condition.

When the parents finally confessed their secret, I pointed out that in their overeagerness not to hurt their child, they had created a problem that really *was* upsetting her. I learned the mother was extremely worried about her health. Despite the doctor's reassurance, she was afraid she was going to die within a few years. I told her that *her* worries had made her overestimate the seriousness of her problem, and underestimate her daughter's ability to deal with it. Like most such secrets this one cried out to be told. The parents had hinted about it, the teen-ager already knew a shadowy version of it. After their meeting with me the parents went home and told their daughter the truth: Her mother did have a physical problem, but she could still live a normal life. The girl was tremendously relieved, and her symptoms quickly improved. I saw her for a few sessions, during which she discussed her anger at being treated like a baby. After this she required no further therapy.

Other secrets which the psychotherapist may have to get out into the open include the adolescent's having been adopted, born out of wedlock, or born out of a love affair mother or father had with someone else; a past history of parental separation and reuniting, before or after the youngster's birth; a parent or family member having been hospitalized for severe mental illness, or imprisoned. If you worry about any of these possibilities, or feel that vital information is being held back, let your therapist help you find the truth.

Sometimes an entire family may share a secret, and *everyone* will decide to keep it from the therapist, including the patient. A sensitive therapist knows that people can deal only with disturbing issues when they are ready to, not one second before. With more time and trust family secrets usually come out. So you mustn't feel ashamed if you still feel unready to share a secret with the therapist at first, nor should you be worried that the therapist will get angry at you for having kept back a secret when you finally do reveal it.

In taking a history about the adolescent patient from parents, I cover much of the same territory outlined in the previous chapter, but this time from the grown-ups' viewpoint. It's then quite common to find that parents and patient will have given two entirely different versions of the same event. Which is right? What is the truth?

A therapist frequently discovers that you and your family members each have a piece of the truth about an event, but each believes it to be the *whole* truth. Each party may be too close to the action, too personally involved, to get the big picture of what happened. Differences in stories told about the past are also due to tricks of memory. We naturally tend to forget things that are upsetting, or to shuffle painful memories around to make them less painful. The therapist listens carefully to everyone, then steps back from the "action," to put his or her own objective, complete picture of the event together.

Many events vital in shaping your life cannot possibly be remembered, because you were too young, or weren't even born yet. Your therapist will review these events with your parents, including details of their early lives, their family history, courtship— years before you came along. I'm always interested in what kind of pregnancy the mother of an adolescent had, in the smoothness or difficulty of birth, in the adolescent's development in early infancy and childhood. Any of these life experiences may contain the seeds of future emotional hang-ups.

I ask parents what the adolescent's reaction was to past

stressful events—losses, illnesses, births of sisters and brothers, moves. I may already know about these occurrences from talking with the teen-ager; now I'll see how the parents' and patient's memories of them match up. If the adolescent hasn't been seen yet, the parents' history alerts me to trouble spots to get into when I interview the patient. I pay special attention to emotional signs and symptoms in childhood the parents may have forgotten—phobias or compulsions; troublesome, aggressive behavior; personality features such as shyness, sensitivity to criticism, moodiness, stubbornness—all possible forerunners of the present trouble.

Your therapist will end your parents' consultation by summarizing his or her findings and making recommendations to your parents alone, with you present, or both (see the next chapter for a further discussion of "The Treatment Plan"). Speaking with your parents alone allows the therapist to describe your situation in language that might not be easy for you to follow, or to give your parents some guidance about issues in their lives together that affect you. On the other hand, sharing findings with you and your family often creates a feeling of closeness that's been absent for a long time. Everyone feels "we are all in this together, we each played a part in this problem, how let's all do something about it together." Such a feeling leads very naturally into drawing up a treatment plan.

In my summary to parents, I'm simple and honest. I discuss general reasons why teen-agers develop the type of problem their youngster has, and describe the causes I've been able to discover so far for their child's particular difficulty. If there is still a lot that is unclear, I say I'll need more time with the teen-ager to form a definite opinion, possibly more tests as well. If a symptom can be treated easily, I'll say so. If a problem looks serious, I won't play it down or sugar-coat it. I believe parents need to know if treatment is going to be long, and what it is going to be like. I've found the overwhelming majority of parents do appreciate a therapist's being up front. Usually their fears will be calmed by knowing that even a serious problem isn't mysterious, and that something can be done about it.

Like most parents, your parents probably will ask your therapist: "Where did we do wrong?" Shame about unhelpful behavior—either real or imaginary—may make your parents hold back important facts that could help the therapist understand your problem better. It might even make them shrink from having you get the therapy you need. So your therapist will say strongly that he or she has no interest in blaming them. I tell parents that, with most emotional problems of adolescence, no one has consciously acted in a hateful, harmful fashion. Usually no one is to blame, but everyone concerned is *responsible* in some way regarding the adolescent's trouble, including the patient.

I tell parents that blame creates guilt, which can make it even harder to handle a teen-ager's troubles effectively. Even assuming your parents haven't always been helpful, I don't know anyone who has been 100 percent correct in raising their children, including me. Your parents weeping over their past harmful behavior won't help you one bit. What *will* help is for them to identify and understand their unhelpful behavior, so that it is not repeated.

13 The Treatment Plan and the Therapy Contract

The Treatment Plan

Once he or she has a good basic idea about what has been troubling you, your psychotherapist will work out a treatment plan with you and your family. *A treatment plan* is an approach uniquely tailored to your particular problem and personality. *Working out* the treatment plan *does not* mean the therapist will deliver a neat package of recommendations to be followed automatically. Quite often a great deal of discussion will take place before a treatment plan agreeable to everyone is arrived at.

A treatment plan deals with the following questions: Is psychotherapy needed at all? What type and amount of psychotherapy is required? Should family members be involved? Are additional tests or examinations needed? Is any other treatment besides psychotherapy required? Who should be the therapist? What will the cost be? Should there be another opinion before therapy is begun? Let's examine these issues.

❚ *Is Psychotherapy Needed?*

The problem that brings the teen-ager into the office may simply express a conflict between the generations, without anyone on either side of the gap needing psychological care, such as when parent and child violently disagree about the child's style of dress, grooming, or makeup. This situation doesn't require therapy; occasionally a few sessions may be spent with parents alone, or with the family, to try to resolve the conflict, or at least to help them live better under the same roof with their differences.

Adolescents may be very upset when they make an appointment, only to calm down by the time they actually come in. At that point they either don't want further sessions at all, or aren't sure about continuing. Here's an example:

A sixteen-year-old girl experienced a deep depression after she broke up with her first real boyfriend. She had never known such sadness, couldn't think of anything else but the breakup, and broke into tears at the drop of a hat. She was afraid she might be "flipping out," and asked her parents if she might see a therapist. Her appointment was set for several days later. By that time her mood had brightened. I couldn't find any danger signs in her life history; she seemed to be feeling better and had very mixed feelings about seeing me again. We decided she was dealing well with a painful experience, a natural part of growing up, that had temporarily thrown her off balance. I couldn't see any reason for more meetings now, so I told her to get in touch if her mood plunged again.

When you and your therapist aren't entirely sure you need further therapy, and your life definitely feels as though it's in better shape now, there's nothing wrong with taking a wait-and-see attitude. You can arrange another session within a few weeks if you wish. An emotional checkup in which you touch base occasionally with a therapist in itself is a form of therapy.

Ten percent of the adolescents who consult with me either don't require therapy, or fall into a wait-and-see category. The rest definitely need more help.

Type and Frequency of Treatment

Adolescents vary a great deal regarding the kind of therapy needed, how often they are seen, and how long the entire course of therapy takes. If you are basically stable and your problems are obviously due to an outside stress that isn't too serious, your troubles may improve quickly with the therapist's support. If you aren't having painful symptoms, but are simply puzzled about an important life choice that is hard to make, such as whether to go to an out-of-town college or stay at home, you may need only a short period of treatment.

Short-term Psychotherapy.

Short-term therapy lasts from one to twenty sessions, several weeks to months. The therapist will usually see you once a week, unless you are very upset, or pressed for time. Some therapists make a contract for a set number of sessions. The limit on interviews often acts as a push to get you moving. In short-term work the psychotherapist will be quite active, won't encourage you to dig deeply into yourself and talk about your past, and will focus instead on present-day issues and their realistic solutions.

Long-term Psychotherapy.

Long-term therapy may be recommended to you (1) when an emotional crisis is only the surface indicator of much more serious problems that affect many parts of your life; (2) when, without any immediate crisis, it's found that you have actually been suffering for a long time with a symptom or a problem that you either weren't aware of, or hadn't wanted to do anything about until now; or (3) when you are basically all right emotionally, but are still having great difficulty dealing with a tough family situation that you can't leave yet, and that will go on for some time unchanged.

Long-term therapy is often required in conditions like serious phobias and compulsions, schizophrenia, chronic depression, anorexia nervosa, and repeated delinquent activity. The sudden onset of a psychosis or a suicide attempt may in fact represent a tip-of-the-iceberg signal that you have been troubled for some time. In this case it will probably take you a long time in therapy to feel better. Difficult family situations calling for a long-term approach include living with a psychotic, alcoholic, or severely depressed family member, living with parents who continuously battle each other without any question of separation, living with a divorced parent who is still very upset at being alone and still fights repeatedly with his or her ex-partner, while you keep getting caught in the middle.

Long-term therapy may involve a deep examination of the way past events and relationships have shaped your present difficulties. It also furnishes the same kind of practical guidance about your life today found in short-term psychotherapy.

The number of regular weekly visits in long-term psychotherapy ranges from one to five per week. Experts have argued about the best number for adolescents. Personally I'd rather see teen-agers *less* frequently, because they lead very busy lives, and want so much to become independent, to work things out on their own. Unless they are seriously troubled, or going through a big crisis, most of my young patients only see me once or twice a week.

Your psychotherapist's recommendation to come in *more* than once a week *doesn't* have to mean that you are more troubled than someone who only comes in once. Perhaps your therapist feels more comfortable seeing patients more frequently. Many do. Perhaps you are the kind of person who will find it easier to open up, to develop a better working relationship, when you are coming in more often. You will then find you remember more about what happened during the last session when it took place several days ago, rather than a whole week ago. Yout therapy will go smoother and faster.

The type of psychotherapy that requires the most frequent contact with the therapist is called *psychoanalysis*. You probably have seen cartoons of a patient lying on a couch, with the therapist setting in a chair behind the patient. Many people believe *all* therapy is done this way, but the couch is used *mainly* in psychoanalysis. Not being able to see the therapist, you are freer to relax, get in touch with your daydreams and fantasies. Psychoanalysis offers you the deepest possible examination of your personality and your past. It takes many years and is very expensive, unless done in a clinic. The high frequency of visits, from three to five a week, is definitely *not* related to the seriousness of your troubles. In fact you have to be pretty strong emotionally to undergo this extremely deep therapy.

Psychoanalysis isn't used very often with teen-agers today. I myself don't do it much with younger teen-agers. I believe it can be very helpful if you are in your later teens, are interested in getting a very complete understanding of yourself, and if it is already part of your makeup to think carefully about what makes people tick. If self-examination isn't "your thing," if you are more interested in doing rather than thinking, I doubt you will find psychoanalysis worthwhile.

It is hard to predict how long you will have to stay in long-term therapy. Your therapist can give you a rough idea, but the guess may turn out to be shorter or longer than the time you will actually spend. Psychoanalysis is generally the *longest* long-term treatment, taking up to seven years or more. Most of my patients who need long-term therapy stay with me a year or so. Personally I like the idea of adolescents spreading their wings and flying on their own; if they have trouble staying up, they can always come back for a few more lessons. But, like other therapists, I treat some teen-agers for many, many years, sometimes into their young adulthood. I know that sounds like an awfully long time, but the problem may just be serious enough to require it.

There are other forms of psychotherapy that may be recommended for you, instead of or besides regular individual psychotherapy. These include group therapy, family therapy, hypnosis, biofeedback, et cetera. Your therapist may also want you to take medication, under his or her guidance, or under the supervision of a psychiatrist, if the therapist is not medically trained. I'll discuss medication, and other types of therapy, in Chapters 18 and 19. If your therapist thinks your problems and/or your family's problems are too serious for you to remain at home, he or she may recommend hospitalization or placement in a nonhospital setting such as residential treatment center, group home, or boarding school. Out-of-home placements are described in Chapter 20.

▮ *Involvement of Family Members in Your Therapy*

In most cases the only outsiders involved in adolescent psychotherapy are parents and family members. If they asked for the consultation, outside agencies like schools or courts usually are content to know that you have been placed in treatment. But more frequent contact with family members may be necessary for the therapist to keep them posted about your progress, advise how to make things better for you, and find out more about the pressures affecting you at home.

The amount of contact your therapist will have with family members will depend on (1) the influence family problems play in creating your difficulties; (2) the extent to which your problems upset the family; (3) the degree of your family's resistance to therapy; (4) the degree of *your* resistance to the family's getting involved with your therapy; and (5) whether your therapist believes in the value of continuing family contact.

Some therapists still feel that *any* contact at all with the family can be extremely hurtful to treatment; on the other end of the scale, there are therapists who believe it is ridiculous to work with a teen-ager without the family actively being treated. Most psychotherapists fall somewhere in between these two extreme positions, although there has been a shift over the past twenty years toward the therapist having more involvement with the family than less.

If family therapy is recommended as the main treatment for your problem, your therapist will obviously be having a great deal of contact with your family (see page 133). If your main treatment is individual psychotherapy, family involvement will be much more limited, and will fall into one of three patterns:

(1) After the first consultation, your therapist agrees to have no further involvement with any family member at all, except in real emergencies, or when there is some vital piece of information the therapist must know. If the therapist is contacted under these circumstances, he or she will decide (often with your help) whether to meet with parents in the office, discuss the situation more over the phone, or plan no further contact with them for the time being.

This limited approach will usually be advised if you are an older teen-ager whose problems aren't that severe, or don't directly involve the family, or if you are a younger teen-ager who is functioning well, and who doesn't upset the family continuously.

(2) After the first consultations, the therapist will see your parents or family every three to six months to keep them posted on your progress. You may or may not choose to be present at these sessions. This approach is usually recommended if you are a younger adolescent, where there is a resonable but not urgent need for the therapist to see your family to find out how you are doing or to answer general questions they may have about your progress.

(3) After the first consultations, your parents or family will be seen *regularly* by another therapist who keeps in touch with

your therapist over the phone. Your therapist will have no direct contact with the family, except in an emergency. Your therapist may make suggestions to the other therapist about how family problems should be handled, or give no advice, simply filling in the other therapist about your treatment, and getting information about what's been happening in the family. If you can't even deal with this limited contact between the therapists, your therapist won't communicate anything about your treatment except in an emergency, and the other therapist will have to work in the dark. (I hope you *don't* choose this method. I use it very rarely, if it's the only way I can get a youngster to agree to treatment.)

The other therapist may be a psychiatrist, psychologist, or psychiatric social worker. Your therapist naturally relies on his or her "partner" not to reveal details about your treatment. The other therapist may talk to your folks occasionally over the phone, see them as often as once weekly, or only when serious problems arise.

This approach is most often recommended if you are a younger adolescent, your problems seriously affect your family's life, your family's difficulties play a big part in keeping you upset, your family needs a great deal of guidance, and you, for whatever reasons, are dead set against any involvement of the therapist with them. Bringing yet another therapist into the picture can be complicated, but it is very helpful for teen-agers who need to feel that regardless of a terribly messy family situation they can still keep the therapist for themselves alone.

▮ *Additional Tests and Examinations*

Your psychotherapist may want further tests before therapy begins or while it is going on. Usually the therapist will have enough information after meeting with you and your family to begin treatment, but he or she may still want further examinations to understand your problem better, or to make sure something else hasn't been overlooked. If you aren't that upset, and it is unclear whether psychotherapy is needed, the therapist will delay treatment until any special tests are completed. But if you are in very great trouble, the therapist will start seeing you at once, and change your treatment if further studies show anything new.

Your therapist may refer you to a clinical psychologist for *psychological testing*. From the results the psychologist can quickly construct a detailed picture of your personality, filling out the clues your therapist has picked up. Testing can help your therapist make important decisions about the areas of your life that need particular exploration, the use of medication, placement away from home, et cetera. Occasionally testing may show that an unsuspected physical condition affecting the brain is present.

When you go for testing, the psychologist will not ask you much about yourself. The idea is to let the tests speak for themselves. Some tests involve phsyical performance: You will put colored blocks together according to a design you're shown and the time it takes to do this will be measured. Your vocabulary will be tested, and you will solve mathematical problems. Other tests give free play to your imagination. You will be shown a series of pictures and asked to make up a story about each, or given a series of ink blots and asked what each reminds you of. As with the simple tests the therapist has already given you, the purpose of psychological testing is *not* to grade you. Don't get hung up on whether you are giving good, smart, or crazy answers to questions. You aren't there to impress the psychologist with your mental health. The more honest you are in answering the questions, the truer the picture of you, and the better your therapist will be able to help you.

Psychological tests take about three to five hours to complete. The psychologist will have a report ready for your therapist in about two weeks.

Most psychotherapists ask you to have a complete *physical examination* done by your family doctor if you haven't had one within the past year, or by a physician of the therapist's choice, whichever you choose. This is particularly necessary if you've been having physical symptoms, such as headaches or dizziness. Some physical illnesses can cause emotional symptoms, and your therapist wants to make sure that you don't have such a difficulty.

A *neurological examination* is a very detailed study of the way your brain and the rest of the nervous system work. Vision, hearing, taste, smell, balance, coordination, touch, and muscle strength are some of the items thoroughly tested. This may be done by your own physician, or a specialist called a *neurologist*. The neurological examination is recommended when there may be a possibility that your problem is related to some physical disturbance of the nervous system, such as a brain tumor, the after-effect of an old head injury, or epilepsy.*

Additional neurological tests include X rays of the skull, and the *electroencephalogram* or EEG. The EEG measures the electrical activity of brain waves, and picks up areas of abnormal activity, as in epilepsy. To do an EEG, pads are applied to different spots on your scalp which are attached to wires leading back to a recording machine. The pads are held in place by jelly or a net. This sounds and looks scary, but is totally painless. Remember the EEG measures the electricity your brain puts out—it doesn't put electricity *into* your head!

In an *audiogram* you put earphones on and tell when you can hear recorded tones of different loudness and pitch. The audiogram measures how good your hearing is, and can pick up cases of undetected deafness which have caused emotional difficulty.

---

*Epilepsy, also known as *fits* or *seizures*, is a neurological disorder that often begins in childhood or adolescence, and is related to abnormal electrical activity within the brain. In a typical epileptic seizure, the victim loses consciousness, falls down, and shakes uncontrollably. In rarer forms of the disease, the fit may consist of strange experiences, such as visual or auditory hallucinations, or outbursts of aggressive behavior. Today epilepsy usually can be brought under control by medication.

You may be referred to an *opthalmologist*, a specialist in vision, to see if your problem is in any way related to an undiagnosed difficulty in seeing. A speech problem such as a stammer or stutter may be explored by a *speech therapist*. Your reading ability may be tested by a *reading therapist*. Reading problems may be caused by emotional or physical factors, or both, and can lead to as many hang-ups as hearing problems, if undetected.

You may find these tests scary, uncomfortable, or just plain boring, but try to put up with them. Having them can mean more effective treatment. Ask questions about any test you are asked to take—before, during, or afterward. And above all, make sure *you* get the results in simple language you can understand. Experts often assume that teen-agers either aren't interested in test findings or won't be able to deal with them. Nothing could be further from the truth, in my experience.

Do not get frustrated if a specialist who has tested you says that your therapist will tell you the results. He or she may not want to speak out of turn or may want to rely upon your therapist who knows you better to go over the findings.

▌ *Additional Treatment Besides Psychotherapy*

About 10 to 20 percent of the adolescents who consult with me require some sort of special help besides psychotherapy, or instead of it. You may need *medical treatment* of a condition that has directly caused an emotional problem, or is associated with emotional stress. *Surgical treatment* may be necessary to correct a facial deformity, take away an unsightly scar, or restore an enlarged breast to normal size—all conditions that frequently cause psychological difficulties.

Psychotherapy may still be needed even after successful medical or surgical treatment. Although plastic surgery may do wonders for your appearance, your old self-image may continue to bother you because you have lived with it for so long. Or having felt unattractive, the sudden awareness of your new attractiveness may make you feel extremely uncomfortable, and may require that you receive help. I do think you should be *very* careful about getting plastic surgery or cosmetic dental work unless you have very obvious cosmetic troubles. I've seen many adolescents who pinned their unhappiness on their looks. Then they became even more unhappy when a bobbed nose or capped teeth didn't magically remove psychological problems that weren't related to their appearance.

Severe speech disorders often do *not* improve with psychotherapy alone. The *speech therapist* uses various educational techniques to break poor speech habits, teach smoother, clearer, easily flowing speech. Deaf adolescents also gain from instruction in lipreading.

The *reading therapist* educates reading-disabled teenagers in how to look properly at a printed page and in developing a smoother, more rapid reading rate. Both speech and reading therapy sesssions usually are held once or twice weekly, individually or in small classes.

In addition to their emotional difficulties, many youngsters who do poorly in school have never learned *how* to learn. Their work and study habits are terrible. The *educational therapist* helps you organize your study time more effectively, prepare assignments, and take examinations. The educational therapist may give individual or group tutoring in difficult subjects. He or she also can work with your psychotherapist and school to plan out the program of courses best suited to your needs.

If your study habits are very poor, you may require weekly educational therapy sessions for a while, but many youngsters benefit from just a few sessions.

If your present school can't meet your needs, your psychotherapist may recommend that you change schools, then refer you to a particular school, or advise you to see an educational therapist or your school guidance counselor to discuss placement. There are other experts who specialize in *school placement*. They usually have been teachers at one time, and have a broad knowledge of the different types of public, private, and boarding schools in your area and elsewhere. A school placement specialist may also be consulted at the end of your high schooling, to discover which college is best suited for you.

Vocational counseling usually is recommended to older teen-agers and young adults who are having trouble figuring out what kind of work to do. Using a combination of special tests and personal interviews, the vocational counselor points out work areas you are likely to find interesting and also may tell you specific jobs to aim at. The counselor can leave it up to you to find work, once you know your interests, or may assist you in getting a job, teaching you how to fill out forms and how to handle a job interview.

Vocational counseling, educational, speech, and reading therapy are done generally by psychologists with special training in these fields. They may give these services privately, or through schools, low-cost clinics, and community and religious agencies.

▍ *Who Should Be Your Psychotherapist?*

The psychotherapist you first consult with may *not* end up treating you. He or she may not have time to do more than a consultation, or his or her fee may be more than your parents can afford if prolonged treatment is needed. In this case the consulting therapist will refer you to another therapist who can give you the right kind of help, at the right cost. Clinics and agencies usually employ a screening therapist or team of therapists to figure out what sort of psychotherapy you need and how soon. Frequently the therapist who screens you will *not* be the one who treats you.

There may be special reasons why you should be treated by a different therapist. The consultant may believe you will do better with someone of a different sex, different age, different personality, or way of working.

You may have heard about the marriage broker used in some societies to help families arrange a good match between young people. Like a marriage broker, a skillful consultant will try to arrange the right kind of match between your personality and that of your new therapist, so that you have the best chance of having a successful therapy experience.

I do think it is *extremely* important that you be told in advance when a psychotherapist is *not* going to be able to handle your case after your consultation. If a private therapist or an agency knows this, you should know it, too, and be given an opportunity before you see the therapist to choose someone else who *can* treat you after the consultation. Too often I've seen teen-agers who felt cheated or rejected when they spill their entire story and then are told they have to speak with yet another therapist. They may feel so hurt they will reject any further help. Don't let this happen to you.

∎ Getting Another Opinion

It's human nature for people to want to accept a therapist's opinions without too many questions. They are hurting so much that they can't afford to let themselves think twice about a therapist's recommendations. After all, isn't the therapist supposed to be an expert?

In America today the public is becoming increasingly consumer-conscious. We believe we should have a right to know more about the quality of goods and services we buy, and we search carefully to find the best possible product at the best possible price. Yet the same person who will look carefully before buying a house or car will often plunge right into major psychological treatment without a second thought.

It is *vital* that we become consumer conscious in health

matters, too. More patients have been getting a second opinion when important surgical and medical treatment is recommended. You and your parents have the same right to a second opinion concerning psychotherapy. You shouldn't be afraid to challenge your consultant's opinions, or worry about hurting his or her feelings by seeking advice elsewhere. You may wish to consult with someone else because you aren't satisfied with what you've been told, or because you don't like the consultant, even though you agree with his or her advice, or just because you want to double-check.

If you wish, your consultant can give you the name of a second therapist. If you want to feel as sure as possible that the second therapist's opinion won't be influenced by the first, then choose him or her yourself, or let your parents arrange a consultation.

Remember, a good therapist won't get upset if you decide to get a second opinion. If your consultant does get upset, angry, or seems to be taking your going elsewhere very personally, you probably shouldn't be there in the first place.

▌ *The Therapy Contract*

As you and your family work out a treatment plan with the therapist, you also will be working on the obligations you have to each other concerning your therapy. I think of these obligations as a *therapy contract*, an unwritten agreement that gives the best chance for successful treatment. You, your therapist, and your parents (and occasionally other family members or outsiders) each have obligations in the terms of this contract. The contract always has a certain amount of give and take. It will be personalized, open to change, but also will contain certain ground rules that never change.

The therapist agrees to use all his or her skill and understanding to help you solve your problem, promises to deal honorably with you, and to behave with respect and consideration toward your family.

For their part, your parents should agree to respect your right to confidentiality in therapy. They should not nag you to find out what is happening in your sessions, and should keep strictly to the arrangements they have made about how and when they are allowed to contact your therapist.

Money is an important term in many contracts, including the therapy contract. A private therapist sets his or her own fee for a session. If you are treated at a clinic or an agency, the fee probably won't be set by the therapist, but by an administrator. Most private therapists and clinics work on a sliding scale. Each patient pays according to what each can afford. As you might expect, private help is much more expensive than clinic treatment; a private therapist's lowest fee is probably higher than the top fee you would be charged at most clinics.

Depending on what part of the country you live in, and on your therapist's training and experience, private therapy sessions generally cost between $25 to $85. The average national fee charged by a psychiatrist is about $60. The average fee of a nonmedical psychotherapist tends to be lower. Fees tend to be higher in big cities. Therapy at an agency or clinic may cost nothing, only a few dollars, or may run as high as $30 or more per session.

Family health-insurance plans often cover a certain amount of private psychotherapy for teen-agers. Many parents aren't aware that they have this coverage in their health plan, so tell your parents to check.

Although it is good for you to know what you are being charged, I don't think it is helpful to involve you directly in taking bills home and bringing checks back. Most therapists prefer to bill parents by mail and receive a check the same way.

Your parents should also avoid laying guilt trips on you about how hard it is to pay your therapist. The necessities of life should not be sacrificed for treatment. Your parents shouldn't ruin themselves paying for therapy they can't afford, because such a sacrifice will put such pressure on you that your therapy eventually becomes impossible. Ideally your work with the therapist should take place without your worrying that you aren't getting well fast enough. Rather than ruin treatment, it would be better for you to see a private therapist who charges less, or go to a good clinic.

Unfortunately some parents who can afford treatment still find it necessary to keep reminding a youngster about the cost of treatment. Perhaps this is another example of how parents continually make a child feel guilty. Perhaps the parents really are well meaning, but are getting frustrated with what they feel is a lack of progress in therapy. Any way you look at it, guilt trips about the cost of treatment are always destructive. If your parents are laying financial guilt trips on you, tell them to stop. If they don't, let the therapist know what's happening, so he or she can straighten the situation out.

Concerning your part of the therapy contract, you'll be expected to treat your therapist courteously. This doesn't mean you have to salute the therapist when you enter the office, just that you give him or her the same consideration and respect you would wish to receive. If you have strong negative opinions or objections about the therapist, you'll be expected to speak openly about them. But you don't have to be abusive or get physical to make your point. The therapist doesn't expect you to act like a goody-goody, but there is a bottom line of offensive language and behavior which will be drawn. If you step over that line, the therapist will try to help you understand why you are treating him or her badly, but only up to a certain point. If your abusive behavior continues, the therapist will certainly ask you to leave the session, and even to leave therapy if you don't show any desire to clean up your act.

Regarding confidentiality, you should be responsible enough to keep what goes on between you and the therapist private. You shouldn't let anyone pressure you into talking about what goes on in treatment, and should avoid the temptation to get your friends' or family's opinion about something that occurs during a session. It may occasionally be all right to speak about your therapy in a general way, but more often talking about therapy only leads to unnecessary arguments at home, and unhelpful comments from outsiders. The one exception to this rule is when you keep getting the feeling that your therapy is not working out, that you are not getting better, or that there is something peculiar about the way the therapist is acting. If your therapist refuses to discuss your feelings about these issues with you, then you must share your doubts with your parents, or whoever is responsible for your treatment.

Regarding fees, most teen-agers simply can't afford to pay a therapist for their sessions, but sometimes it may be good for you to handle a portion of the fee. If I think it will make treatment more meaningful, I ask a youngster to pay me as little as a quarter. One teen-ager who had been spoiled by his wealthy parents got very angry when I asked him to give me a dollar out of his huge allowance for each session. He thought he had treatment coming to him, like everything else in his life. The dollar fee turned out to be quite significant. It was the first time anyone had demanded that he take some responsibility for himself, without his parents rushing in to rescue him. Paying the dollar made him feel that he had an important say in his treatment, instead of thinking of himself once more as a baby. Eventually he took responsibility for other parts of his life as well, and felt very proud of himself because of his new-found maturity—all for a buck.

Another important term in your contract is to get to your sessions on time. Therapists work on a tight schedule. Either they see several patients back-to-back and then take time off to relax, or they leave themselves a few minutes at the end of each session to take notes or unwind. If you come late, the therapist can't extend your time past the time your session would be over, without keeping another patient waiting, or interfering with time set aside for rest.

Your therapist will probably extend you a few minutes if there is a very good reason for your lateness, or if you are truly upset at the end of a session by something you've been working on. But most of the reasons for being late don't really justify special treatment, and it is very rare to get so anxious in a session that you will require extra time. Of course if it is the therapist who is running late, it is only fair to give you your full time, or if this can't be done for any reason, for you to have the time made up by adding it to another session later on.

It will also make you feel more mature and responsible to come on your own to therapy. Your therapist will insist on this, unless the office isn't easily reached, you are too young to drive, or if you are too troubled to travel alone by public transportation. Under these circumstances, your therapist will expect you to start traveling on your own when you get older or healthier. If your parents do have to bring you for your sessions, your therapist will not speak to them privately, as a rule. I've seen treatment ruined because the therapist innocently spent a few moments chatting with a parent after each session. The adolescent thought that whatever was discussed in the session was going right into the parent's ear, and dropped treatment very quickly. If your therapist does this, tell him or her to stop.

Of course there are always questions and issues that won't be covered in a therapy contract, no matter how carefully every matter is considered at the time. But a good therapy contract is like the cornerstone of a well-planned building. The architect may change a detail of the plan here and there, add a hallway, redesign a room, but the cornerstone always will hold the weight of the building securely. A well-thought-through treatment plan and therapy contract will make allowances for change, growth, and unexpected new possibilities, while continuing to support the healing relationship between you and your therapist.

Now that you've learned about the mechanics of getting treatment started, let's discuss the actual week-to-week experience of your psychotherapy.

14 | The Unfolding Story of Psychotherapy and Your Psychotherapy Session

Psychotherapy

The experience of psychotherapy is like reading a good story. At the beginning you don't know anything about the characters, where they have come from, or what the author has in mind for them. As the story unfolds the plot falls into place. You learn more about the background of the characters and their typical ways of acting and thinking. You become more interested in them and want to know more about their past, present, and future. Soon you really start to care what happens to them. Sometimes you can figure out how the story will end, but the ending may come as a complete surprise. Along the way you'll often be surprised by the unexpected feelings or behavior the characters display when unexpected events happen to them.

At the beginning of psychotherapy your therapist knows something of your story, but despite all the questions that have been asked, there is still an enormous amount that neither you nor the therapist can know. Initially the therapist has had little actual experience being with you. As psychotherapy unfolds the therapist learns more about your history, but just as important, he or she learns at first hand how you typically act, think, and feel right in the session. The therapist develops a better idea about where you have been, where you are, and where you are trying to go. A therapist wouldn't be doing this work if he or she weren't interested in people, but the more time spent with you, the more he or she really comes to care, deep down, about you. By the end of therapy the therapist may have a good idea of what direction your life will take—or may be totally surprised when you take an unexpected turn on the road toward adulthood. There is no lack of surprises during therapy.

Unlike the reader of a story, the therapist doesn't just take in your tale. He or she is constantly at work, helping you point your story in a more hopeful, happier direction. While this is happening you are learning more about yourself, and you also learn more and more about the therapist's story, too. Probably you won't ever know as much about the therapist's life as he or she knows about yours. But chances are you will discover a lot about the kind of person your therapist basically is.

Psychotherapy has a life and story of its own, as two total strangers meet and slowly build a healing relationship. This story is always different. No healing partnership is exactly the same as another. The therapy story at different times may be dull, exciting, stormy, funny, or sad. At its best it is a very moving story, and one that will change you for the better, as well as affect the therapist a great deal. I don't think we therapists always appreciate how our personalities become richer for having been with our patients.

Rarely the story of psychotherapy can have an unhappy

ending, at least temporarily, because a teen-ager isn't ready to accept help, or the therapist can't find the right way to give it. But this turn of events doesn't have to be tragic. Perhaps the adolescent and the therapist will be able to meet again in the future, at a time when the adolescent is ready for help, or the youngster will leave one therapist and find another who can "tune in" better to his or her story, with happier results.

If you think of psychotherapy like a story or novel, you can imagine each psychotherapy session as a chapter in which a little more of the story gets told and a little more about the cast of characters is revealed. This unfolding *isn't* always as exciting as a good book. In movies and TV programs about therapy, every session seems filled with high drama: Patients break down in tears as they spill out long-buried secrets, threaten to jump out of the therapist's window, or show up for an appointment with a totally new personality. Movies and TV shows run an hour or two, and the audience expects to be entertained. But psychotherapy often takes many sessions, and is basically a slow, undramatic process. You may be disappointed when you find that most sessions aren't filled with high tension, but then you probably won't find therapy as painful as it has been pictured either.

When reading a story you usually get a sense of where the plot is headed because you are outside the action. But as the chief member of the cast of characters in your therapy, you may not be able to tell at the time how one session fits into the overall plot, because you are too close to the action, too personally involved to get the big picture. Often it's only weeks or months or even years later, that the meaning of a session or a particular stage of therapy becomes clear to you. Then you can say: "That was when I was trying to find out if I could trust Dr. Greenberg and if he would put up with me. So I was really trying to bust his chops!" or "That was when I was feeling so helpless and so angry at my family that all I could do was complain about how awfully they were treating me, instead of doing something about it."

Therapy has dry stretches where nothing very much seems to be happening. Yet when you look back you find that this dead time wasn't so dead after all. Something was beginning to happen that you just weren't aware of. Perhaps you were trying to adjust to new ideas you were developing about yourself or your world. Maybe you were working up the courage to explore an area you had never worked on before in therapy. Remember that quote from the Bible about there being a season and a time for every life process? In therapy you often will spend time simply getting ready for change.

Think of each psychotherapy session as a piece of a jig-saw puzzle which is your life. When you start working on a puzzle you are able only to fit a few pieces together here and there. Then you see an edge, a frame, a pattern falling into place. Next big pieces of the picture fall into place, sometimes in a flash. But for this flash to occur, you had to go through the slow, frustrating process of fiddling with smaller sections of the puzzle. It was only then that the larger sections, and finally the entire picture, could become clear. Similarly in psychotherapy (especially long-term psychotherapy), you may go through many sessions where a bit or piece of your life is examined before the really big pieces of your picture fall into place, and you can see your entire life situation clearly.

▌ *Your Psychotherapy Session*

An average psychotherapy session usually lasts about forty-five or fifty minutes. But your therapist may make your sessions short at first if you are too jittery or upset to last out a regular interview. Longer sessions may be recommended if you are someone who finds it hard to get started talking, or if you live a long distance away and can't visit the office very often.

What should you talk about? *Don't* think of your session as a period in school; the therapist *isn't* running a classroom, and there isn't a set assignment. Occasionally the therapist may ask you to think some more at home about an issue, but whether you do so or not is up to you. You certainly won't be marked on your therapy "homework."

Unless you have something definite on your mind, it's not a wise idea to try to find a particular topic. In fact the harder you strain to prepare for a session the less helpful it probably will be. Surprisingly some of your best sessions occur when you start with nothing to talk about; the session just seems to flow naturally, out of seemingly unimportant topics.

Your therapist may have an idea of what's recently been on your mind, but *won't* call on you to give a recitation on any special issue. You won't be required to pick up where you left off, either. Perhaps something new has happened in your life, and your situation has changed since the last session. The therapist will gear the beginning of each session to where you are coming from right now, today.

Some therapists feel comfortable starting out by letting you sit down and waiting for you to talk. Others start the ball rolling with a statement like: "How have you been since the last time we talked?" or "What's happened since our last session?" An adult often won't need more than this to get started. But if you are like most teen-agers, it won't be nearly as easy for you to talk, and you will need more help to get started and to keep going. The typical picture of adult psychotherapy is the patient doing the talking, while the therapist occasionally interrupts to ask a question or make a statement. But the typical picture of adolescent therapy is an active conversation, with you and your therapist talking back and forth to each other.

If you feel stuck for a beginning of your session, a good idea is to be as honest as you can and simply say whatever comes into your mind. If nothing comes into your head, tell your therapist. And don't be concerned if what you are thinking seems silly, beside the point, or shameful. Let the therapist worry about whether what you are saying makes sense or not. Just say it.

Sometimes thoughts that seem silly when you air them this way have a way of connecting with other thoughts that are quite important. A girl whom I was treating because she couldn't make friends was sitting in her session with her mind blank, when suddenly the thought of a dog she had seen on the street that day popped into her head. The thought seemed ridiculous, and she started to push it aside. I asked her to say anything that popped into her head about the dog. She said that recently she had thought about getting a pet. A dog was a good pet, it was always loving and grateful for the care you gave it. You could trust a dog, you could risk giving it your affection, but if you trusted people, they just ran numbers on you. Just the other day, she had told some girls at school she had begun to hang around with about a boy she had a crush on. They said they would keep her feelings a secret, but the same afternoon they spread her secret around the whole class. She felt like dying. It reminded her of the time when her older sister had ratted on her to her parents that she had been reading a book about sex she found in their bedroom.

You can see how unsilly this "silly" thought about the dog was. In her session the thought became a bridge that led us to discuss strong feelings of mistrust she had about others, a problem very much related to her lack of friends, which was the reason she came into therapy in the first place.

Once you've gotten started, you'll find that no two sessions are ever exactly the same. The subjects you will cover and the events of any session will depend on many factors. These include:

The Type of Therapy.

As explained, in short-term therapy you and the therapist spend a brief time working out a specific problem. The therapist will actively center the session around your problem and related subjects. In long-term therapy your entire life is open to study. The therapist probably will take a more "laid back" position and not center the session around a specific topic as much. Instead the therapist mostly will let the subject come from you, then discuss it further.

Stages of Therapy.

If you have just started treatment, your sessions reflect the fact that you and the therapist don't know each other well. The therapist still needs more basic information about you. But you may still be unsure whether you can trust the therapist. In this *early* stage, there's typically a lot of testing by both parties. The therapist gently tries to discover what issues you are comfortable discussing, or what subjects cause you so much pain that they should be left alone. You may be testing to see how firm and fair the therapist is, to discover what won't be permitted, whether the therapist will be offended or critical about your beliefs. There's often a lot of small talk in early sessions about "easy" topics such as baseball, rock music, and current events.

In the *middle* stage of therapy, the relationship that has grown up between you and your therapist allows a freer, deeper discussion of your problems. Less time has to be spent finding out facts about you, less time is needed for you to test the therapist. But the middle stage isn't always so smooth and orderly. Crises arise that make you doubt the therapist again. As you become ready to explore new areas the therapist once again has to get basic "gut" information. Then you may back off and the sessions may return to the earlier pattern for a while, until a crisis has passed, or you feel more confident about opening up.

During the *late* stage of therapy, you and your therapist will have learned each other's language and now understand each other quite well. Many storms will have been passed through together, much information exchanged. There is little need for testing. Sessions may involve going over earlier topics, summing up what you have learned, making plans for your future, discussing your feelings about stopping therapy and, finally, saying good-bye.

The Events in Your Life.

Whatever your stage of treatment, the action of each session is likely to develop chiefly from your talking about what's happened since the last time you've met, things that have upset you (like a family argument), things that have made you happy (like a good time on a date), or just the plain ordinary events of day-to-day living (studying for a test, playing in a basketball game).

You may be surprised to find you get as much, if not more, solid help in understanding yourself through discussing how you respond in everyday situations as you get in discussing how to deal with a crisis. Let's say you are feeling good and nothing particularly is bothering you, so you start talking about a basketball game you played in. As you discuss the game, you might explore your feelings about being a team member, working together with others, tell about who you like or dislike on the team and why, talk about what it's like to win or lose, how you feel about playing in front of a crowd, being booed or cheered.

Sometimes when nothing important is going on in the world outside, the events of your inside life may take the center stage of a session. You may go over a dream you've had last night, or a daydream you had while in class today. You may want to examine your feelings about therapy or the therapist. Actually most of your sessions weave in and out between your inner and outer world as you discuss real events and then explore the ideas and feelings within you these have stirred.

The Therapist's Responses.

Your therapist's responses have a big influence on your session. Depending on the experiences you bring in, and the experiences you have during the session, your therapist will call on the healing experience he or she feels will be most helpful to you. He or she will just listen quietly so you can get something painful off your chest, give you practical advice, or show you how a feeling today is linked to childhood feelings. Knowing the right response, the proper healing experience to emphasize at the right time, is what makes psychotherapy so challenging. Responding isn't mechanical. I don't decide my patient needs reassurance because it says so on page 116 of a psychiatry textbook. My response comes from my heart as well as my head, from my training, from the many hours I've spent with patients, from my feeling for the moment I'm sharing with a teenager here and now. Your therapist's sense of that unique moment may say that you ought to be reassured; on the other hand it may say that dishing out quick reassurance without knowing more of what's been going on may not help you. Perhaps if you are reassured too quickly, you may not get to become more aware of painful feelings you must deal with in order to change.

The Silent Session.

Adolescents are particularly prone to have sessions in which they can't seem to find anything to talk about, and sit in uncomfortable silence. It's possible that your silence stems from strong resentment about being in treatment in the first place. If you are up in arms against the adult world, you may have been expressing your negative feelings elsewhere through pouting. When you bring such angry sulking into your session, I can tell you that you are probably trying to make your therapist out to be just one more dumb grown-up who can't possibly understand you. This is just cutting off your nose to spite your face. Remember you have a *major* part of the responsiblity for making your sessions work. There is no magic power the therapist owns to get you to talk, especially if you are dedicated to proving therapy can't work. If you won't communicate, you cannot expect to get much help in return, and there is *no* point in sticking around.

But it is possible that you *aren't* resentful, you really *do* want to come to your sessions. However, when you do, you find yourself suddenly clamming up. Perhaps your silence is due to sexual thoughts you are ashamed of. Perhaps you are having feelings about the therapist you don't want to reveal. Perhaps, as far as you can see, your mind is just a total blank, for *no* reason.

Faced with continued silences, you may want to leave sessions early, or drop out of treatment altogether. I strongly advise you not to do this. Hang in. When your silence finally does break, even if it's near the end of your session, or several sessions later, you'll be surprised how often good things come out of it.

A good therapist *isn't* going to let you stay silent indefinitely. To help you out of that bind, the therapist may get you to talk about neutral, nonpainful subjects. Sensing you are holding back because you feel ashamed about something, the therapist will try to help you feel more relaxed about sharing uncomfortable thoughts and feelings. If talking to you won't help the silence, the therapist may try to loosen up your session by playing cards, chess, or checkers. Sometimes changing the setting, in or outside the office, will make you feel better able to speak. I've had patients sit in a different chair, or sit in my chair, or go out for an ice cream.

On the other hand, I *do* think that there are times when we therapists put *too* much value on words and *not* enough value in the helpful communication that can happen without words. I've known youngsters who couldn't talk freely with me, but seemed to improve anyway, perhaps because they found something useful in playing cards or taking a walk with an understanding adult who didn't criticize, make demands, or get uptight around them, the way so many others had.

Finally, your silence may *not* be a sign of discomfort, fear, or stubbornness. It may show that you are content and relaxed. A good therapist knows when to let you be quiet in peace. I'll never forget a girl I treated very early in my career. She was the oldest of eight children, and was always being given all kinds of responsibility by her parents for her brothers and sisters. Her sessions were filled with long silences, in which she sat thoughtfully, sometimes knitting, sometimes with her hands folded, just looking ahead. I tried my darndest to get her to talk more, until one day she floored me by saying: "Dr. G., haven't you realized by now how comfortable I am, just being allowed to be quiet here? It's the only place I come to where they leave you alone!"

Ending Your Session.

It would be wonderful if every session had an upbeat Hollywood ending, where the problem you brought in or the issues raised were tied up neatly, and you walked out of the office feeling terrific. There *are* sessions like this, but there are also going to be many others where you won't leave feeling satisfied. You may think nothing has happened, or you may feel you were left hanging when something important wasn't completely resolved. Rarely you may even go out *more* upset than when you went in, and wonder if you should stay in therapy. Please remember that the boring, frustrating, and painful sessions are *all* necessary. A lot more is happening in them than you may be aware of, and it is often out of them that the really good sessions develop later on.

A good psychotherapist will try hard not to leave you terribly upset at the end of a session, although this may happen despite everything the therapist does. On the other hand your therapist may deem it wise to keep an issue up in the air, even if it means ending the session with you feeling somewhat anxious, when he or she doesn't have enough information at the time to say something useful, or if you need a few more days to puzzle the issue over on your own.

Many therapists like to end a session by summarizing what has been discussed, and indicating future areas that might be helpful. Other prefer to stop with a few brief words such as: "That's all we have time for today. Let's see if we can't pick this up next time." You may find it difficult to stop once you have really gotten going in a session, but as you get used to therapy, your ability to stop without feeling frustrated will improve. However, if you are discussing something very important and feel the therapist doesn't appreciate that you need a few more minutes to make a point or complete a story, say so.

15 | *Crises and Semi-Crises*

Most teen-agers go through at least one stormy time while they are in psychotherapy. Most hard times can be handled in your regular sessions. But when you are under special stress, you may need added help from the therapist over the telephone or through extra office sessions, rarely through home visits or placement outside your home.

Just how upset do you have to get before you contact your therapist? There isn't an "uptight scale" to measure the amount of anxiety, depression, or confusion that "deserves" a call. Different people deal with the same amount of stress quite differently. One teen-ager calls his therapist after a quarrel with a teacher over a bad grade; another won't call after being arrested and jailed for marijuana possession.

The average patient in therapy knows enough to contact a therapist in a very serious situation like a bad drug trip. And if you really are "flipped out," chances are someone else will be on hand to call your therapist. Thankfully, emergencies are rare in psychotherapy. What's more common are less serious, yet still painful situations that make you wonder whether to call your therapist or wait until the next session.

To help you decide what to do here, ask yourself how you usually have handled such situations before. Do you tend to overreact and make major crises out of minor troubles? Many patients who call the therapist at the drop of a hat are very dependent and doubt their ability to deal with problems on their own. Sometimes they act first and think later.

Some people who call frequently wish to feel special compared with the rest of the therapist's patients. But plenty of people *don't* call when they should because they are afraid of looking too "sick" or "weak" to handle their problems. They may have given up hope, they may not want to bother the therapist, or they simply don't know that they are supposed to call if they are in bad trouble.

Do you fit any of these descriptions? If so, act accordingly. If you are the overdependent type, do think twice before calling. If you need to be special, you should be talking to your therapist about it *in* your session, not bothering him or her *outside* it. If you are the superindependent type, now may be the time to put aside your pride and reach out for help. It doesn't take away from your real strength to call; in fact it's a sign of maturity to know that you can't handle a difficult problem by yourself.

Ask yourself if your situation is different from past problems that didn't require outside help right away. If it definitely *is* worse and you are very upset, don't hesitate to call. If it isn't, then what's different that makes you want to call the therapist now? Sometimes new patients will call about a situation they've handled well when they weren't in treatment, because they think they're supposed to. But the therapist certainly doesn't want you to lose the independence you've already got.

Ask yourself if you've done everything you can to make your situation better. Would you be more properly helped by talking to someone other than your therapist, someone in or outside your family who's been helpful before during rough times, and might be helpful again? Or would bringing in others only confuse you more and make them needlessly upset? Would going off to a quiet place and trying to think through your problem carefully help? How about just doing *nothing*? Sometimes putting a problem in the back of your mind and going about your business until your next session can be more helpful than puzzling it out. Your mind has a marvelous ability to sort troubles out when your attention is involved with other matters. Have you tried thinking of what advice your therapist would give you if you were to call? By making yourself your own therapist this way, you can often calm down without a call.

Here's a good rule of thumb: If the situation upsetting you is new, or if it's the same sort of situation you've had before, but this time your symptoms and reactions are much worse, if you've tried everything you can think of to help yourself without relief, and if your next appointment is more than a day or two away, then please do contact your therapist.

∎ *The Telephone*

Make sure you find out when you start treatment what your therapist's policies are about phone calls. Some therapists make themselves freely available to speak over the phone between sessions. But most prefer to keep phone contacts as brief as possible except for really important problems or true emergencies.

Most therapists don't like being interrupted by the telephone during a session. They either will take a short message or not answer the phone and let an answering service or a recording machine pick up. A few therapists hold a regular telephone hour, usually near the end of the day, when they can be reached to discuss problems.

If you call and get the therapist's service, leave your full name, your number, state whether you have to be reached right away, and give a couple of times when you can be called back. You don't have to explain at length what your problem is, unless you think there's some special reason for the therapist to know before talking to you.

If you reach your therapist while he or she is working, find out when you can talk freely. Don't get into a long description of why you are calling. It's inconsiderate to take up someone else's time this way. Just think how badly you would feel if the situation were reversed. If your problem is a serious emergency, your therapist may send the patient out of the office to talk with you. This doesn't happen very often, and if it does when *you* are the patient, your therapist should make up the time you missed.

If you have to speak with your therapist at night or over the weekend, the service will tell you where to call or will have the therapist get back to you. Many therapists like to keep their private lives separate from their work, and they won't give out their home number. Other therapists don't care if you know their home number, as long as you don't abuse the privilege.

Once you reach the therapist, he or she will be interested mainly in helping you deal quickly and practically with your trouble. Your therapist will calm you down so that you *both* can understand things better, and give you reassurance, support, and down-to-earth advice about handling your problem. If necessary the therapist will speak with family members over the phone to find out their role in your problem and give them guidance, too. Medicine may be prescribed to get you over a crisis. You may be asked to come in by yourself, or with your family, for an extra session.

Most telephone calls don't require anything more than talking with your therapist alone; it's likely you won't need medicine, or extra sessions, or any further help until your next session. But if you still feel somewhat upset at the end of the call, you may make an arrangement to speak again for a few minutes on the phone before your next visit.

▌ *Parents, Other Outsiders, and Crises*

▌ If parents, guardians, or other outsiders call because they are worried about you, your therapist will find out if a real emergency exists. If not, the therapist will try to get your side of the story, either over the phone or during your regular session, then speak to your parents with your permission to explain what has happened and what should be done. However, most urgent calls from parents concern family disagreements or school problems that may be important, but *aren't* really urgent. Your therapist can handle matters easily on the phone, and will probably end up telling your parents (or having you tell them) that the problem isn't serious enough to see them.

Your therapist will be much more worried when your parents call because there has been a sudden change in your behavior, if you are acting very strangely, seriously threatening to harm yourself or others, or it's been discovered you are involved in criminal activity. These are *truly* emergencies and usually *can't* be handled only over the telephone. Your therapist will still try very hard to get your side of the story even if you are angry and uncooperative. The therapist may ask you and your parents to come directly to the office to deal with the emergency. Rarely, other people you trust may be asked to accompany you if you don't trust your parents.

If you are so upset you won't or can't speak with your therapist, and refuse to come to the office, your therapist may decide to go to your house. In your home the therapist will see you alone and with your family, prescribe medication if required, arrange for hospitalization or some other less serious temporary placement outside your home, such as an overnight stay with a relative. A home visit is a rare event in psychotherapy, but it can really help get you out of a bad emotional state, prevent hospitalization, and strengthen your confidence in your therapist.

If you are suffering from a very serious emotional condition that obviously requires psychiatric hospitalization, or have made a suicide attempt that demands emergency medical attention, a home visit will not be useful, so your therapist will tell your parents to take you directly to a hospital. An ambulance or a police car may be called to get you there, if you are very sick, or very troubled and uncooperative. Please remember that therapists *hate* bringing police or other authorities into patients' lives, and will only do so when physical and emotional health are severely threatened and everything else has failed.

Your parents may call your therapist if you run away from home. When they discover a youngster has left home, parents often want to go straight to the authorities. A therapist generally advises parents to wait, since the average adolescent in treatment will call home pretty quickly to let parents know where he or she is staying, will have someone else call, or will come back home within a day or two.

Rarely, your therapist may be called by friends, relatives, or other outsiders when the outsider has gotten your therapist's number, because you are unable or unwilling to tell your family you are in trouble. Perhaps you are too sick, or are angry at them, afraid of what they'll do when they find out about your trouble, or you want to protect them from blame. This is a tough spot for a therapist. He or she has to reveal just enough about your treatment to make sure you get help while protecting confidentiality. Usually your therapist will ask the involved outsider to get you to your house or to the therapist's office, so that those directly responsible for you can pick up the ball. However, teen-agers can get themselves into some pretty sticky messes, and sometimes a therapist has to take the place of parents or guardians until they can get brought back into the picture.

∎ *Extra Sessions*

You may want extra sessions with your therapist, with or without your family, in the following situations:

(1) Serious crises and emergencies such as suicide attempts, bad drug trips, et cetera.

(2) Family quarrels with causes that aren't clear from your story alone. Bringing you and your family together for a session or two will give your therapist a better picture of what's happening; often the problem will be solved then and there.

(3) Times when you know you'll be undergoing extra stress and think you may temporarily need extra help, such as the hospitalization of a family member for surgery, a rough week of college interviews, et cetera.

(4) Times when your symptoms or problems slowly worsen for no obvious reason. Here your therapist may feel that extra sessions can give both of you a clearer picture of what's upsetting you.

(5) Times when a psychotherapy session has been so upsetting that you shouldn't wait until your next regular session to see if you can calm down.

Since therapy tries to help you solve your problems on your own, your therapist won't give you an extra session lightly. And extra sessions do cost extra money, do take extra time out of your life. Don't expect to have them very often. If you do need extra sessions during a stressful period, you will generally return to your regular schedule as soon as a crisis has passed. However, it sometimes does happen that seeing your therapist more frequently during a rough time proves to be so helpful that you decide to increase the number of regular weekly sessions for a little longer, or for good.

Like so many other issues in psychotherapy, the decision to have extra sessions is a two-way street. If it's your therapist's idea, make sure you understand why, and if you have strong objections to going more often, raise them. On the other hand, there may be times when you feel you need extra help, and your therapist doesn't seem to recognize you're hurting. Here it's up to you to ask.

The "Cover"

When therapists must be away from work because of vacation, conferences, or illness, they leave another therapist to "cover" their practice. You probably will never have to use the cover during the entire time you are in therapy, but it's certainly nice to know that backup help is there. However, if you've been feeling very troubled, and your therapist is going to be away for a long time, your therapist may ask you to see the cover. Depending on the severity of your problem, it may be important for you to see the covering therapist as often as your regular therapist or you may only have to drop by once or twice to make sure you're holding your own. You can expect that the covering therapist will have a general idea of your history and your problem, will know what you've been doing in your therapy, and what, if any, medications you've been taking.

Bringing a new therapist into your treatment can be an upsetting experience, so it won't be recommended unless there's a very good reason. Some people develop the notion that their therapist wants them to see the cover to get rid of them. Put such foolish notions out of your head. The covering therapist should be very careful not to disturb the relationship you have with your own therapist. While the cover can't be a carbon copy of your therapist, he or she will try to follow the same treatment plan you've grown used to.

If you're upset enough to see the cover, it's likely you won't break any new ground or won't be interested in exploring new areas of your personality or your past. The covering therapist's job is to give you whatever simple support or guidance you need until your own therapist gets back.

If you feel a cover is getting into difficult topics you'd rather discuss with your own therapist, say so. If the cover criticizes your therapist, suggests your case hasn't been handled well, tells you he or she can do a better job, I'd advise you to leave immediately and see someone else. You have every right not to trust your care to someone who acts so unprofessionally.

Speaking of vacations, psychotherapists take long ones. Psychotherapy is very tough, demanding work. It requires a long time away from the job so that your therapist can come back rested, with a fresh viewpoint. You probably can expect your therapist to be away on one long summer vacation, usually the month of July or August, as well as a long weekend or week during the rest of the year.

Despite stories you may have heard, most people don't fall apart when a therapist goes away on vacation. In the years I've been practicing, my cover has only received a few calls while I've been away, and I've rarely had to have my patients followed by a cover during my vacation. In fact you may find that you make better use of what you've learned in treatment during the year with the therapist away on vacation. By the time the therapist comes back, don't be surprised to discover you've made important steps forward on your own.

16 || When Therapy Isn't Working

It would be wonderful if every patient could be matched perfectly with the right therapist from the first consultation to the last session. Unfortunately real life isn't always so kind. While most of you will get all the help you need without having to change therapists, it's still important to know certain telltale signs that indicate you won't do well with a therapist from the start, or that previously helpful treatment has stopped working for you.

In psychotherapy as in any other profession there are a few "rotten apples": unethical people who label themselves as therapists but have no, or only the poorest, qualifications to do therapy. This is why you must check out your therapist's background and training. If a therapist flatly refuses to discuss these qualifications without at least telling you where they can be found, or if a therapist's qualifications don't check out, you should *not* start therapy with him or her.

There are also psychotherapists whose personal emotional problems interfere seriously with their work. People who seek training in psychotherapy are usually screened to make sure that they are emotionally stable and have high ethical standards. Still, unethical or troubled individuals do slip by the best screening and get trained. Sometimes their work is poor from the very beginning; more often their troubles show up later on, perhaps after years of good work.

Psychotherapy can be a lonely profession; a therapist spends long hours with patients, and may have little contact with other therapists. When troubled therapists keep trouble to themselves, the private nature of psychotherapy can make it possible for them to keep treating patients while behaving in a confused, strange, or unethical fashion without anyone knowing their problem. Your wish to be cared for by someone strong and wise may make you blind to a sick therapist's difficulties. You may blame a therapist's troubles on your own problems, imagining that you are exaggerating or unreasonably finding fault.

A therapist *is* only human; we all have our off days, times when we're not as sharp as we should be, because of illness or personal problems. Your therapist is entitled to an off session from time to time. But it's a much more serious matter if session after session your therapist is acting quite differently than usual, seems unable to concentrate on what you're saying, can't remember what you've talked about in previous sessions, confuses you with other patients, appears irritable, sad, and unhappy, interrupts to tell you things that don't make sense, appears to be off in a different world.

An emotionally troubled psychotherapist may not return telephone calls, may show up late or not at all without explanation or with lame excuses, neglect to follow through with outside contacts, such as failing to write a report to a court. On the other hand, instead of neglecting your case, a troubled therapist may try to solve personal frustrations by living only for patients, become overinvolved with your life, seeing you too frequently in the office or offering to meet you on the outside. An overconcerned therapist can act as if you were his or her child, not a patient, and may try to take your parents' rightful place by criticizing them frequently, tearing down the good relationship you have with them or other important people.

The behavior of a troubled therapist may be so obviously disturbed and disturbing that you need have no second thoughts about leaving treatment at once. When a therapist makes sexual advances toward you, or smells of alcohol and acts drunk, you should leave immediately. But probably it will be harder for you to tell whether the therapist is really troubled or you are making something out of nothing. The first thing to do is share your concern openly. If the therapist angrily refuses to discuss the situation, or flatly dismisses your feelings as "sick," the chances are quite good that you *are* correct in thinking he or she is troubled, and you should leave treatment.

If your therapist does admit to personal problems, then describes them in embarrassing detail, and keeps bothering you with them afterward, I wouldn't stick around either, for your therapist-patient relationship has been turned upside down. You've become your therapist's therapist, and you're not even getting paid. Don't think you're too young for this to occur. Just as a troubled parent can improperly turn to a child to give adult guidance or support, a sick therapist can improperly lean on an adolescent patient.

When you tell a good therapist about your worries, he or she will explain that you probably are wrong, but will discuss freely why you have worries. A skilled therapist will promise to take a special look at himself or herself to see if there may indeed have been a personal problem affecting your therapy. Possibly he or she will say you are correct, will tell you briefly what the personal difficulty may be in a general way, and will promise to be more on the ball in your sessions. This is a responsible approach; it is worthwhile to stay with this therapist, at least until you can see if things improve. If they don't, then you should think about going elsewhere. And when you are having difficulty with a therapist who you think is troubled, please feel free to break your promise to keep your treatment private, because you may be harmed if you *don't* share your concern with others.

I've previously described the qualities a psychotherapist should have to work well with teen-agers. There are many therapists who are ethical, emotionally healthy, and well trained, but still don't have the right personality to treat adolescents. They may do good work with adults, or young children, but can't grasp what makes teen-agers tick. Yet they treat adolescents because they think they are qualified or because there isn't anyone else available in their area.

It's much harder to tell when therapy isn't working because your therapist doesn't understand adolescents than when the therapist is unethical or troubled. If your therapist floods your sessions with teen-age slang, goes out of the way to show you he or she is "hip" by behavior or dress, doesn't seem to be interested in your *special* qualities and difficulties beyond the fact that you are adolescent, tell him or her to throw out the act and start listening. If you still get the feeling that you're sitting with an overgrown teen-ager instead of a mature grown-up, throw in the towel and see someone else.

On the other hand your therapist may be unhelpful because he or she is too sympathetic with "adultness," too ready to accept the viewpoint of parents, teachers, or other grown-ups over your vision of the world. This kind of therapist is always lecturing you about your responsibilities, is concerned that you behave well, don't get into trouble, get good grades, and don't make waves. Unless you can educate this therapist to remember what it was like to be a teen-ager, you should pack up and move on.

Just as there are a few therapists who shouldn't be treating adolescents, there are adolescents who *shouldn't* be patients. Even though they have serious problems, they aren't sincerely interested, at least for the time being, in getting help. They go through the motions of consulting a therapist just to satisfy someone else. If you have been questioning a therapist's ability or mental health, you should be honest enough to look into your reasons for being in therapy. Ask yourself if you've been fault-finding to give yourself a good excuse to drop out of treatment. You don't need one.

Even when an ethical, well-trained, and skillful therapist treats an adolescent who sincerely wants help, treatment may still never get off the ground. Any relationship between two well-meaning people can fail, without either party being to blame, and psychotherapy is no exception. Experts still aren't sure why some patient-therapist partnerships work out beautifully from the start, while others can't ever seem to get started. When the chemistry or "vibrations" between you and a therapist are all wrong, your therapist may have triggered off strong negative feelings related to another person out of your past. If these bad feelings are strong and deeply rooted, all the exploration in the world won't stop you from feeling uncomfortable. If the therapist develops strong negative feelings about you, that doesn't mean there's something terribly wrong with either of you. A therapist can't like everyone who steps through the door. What's important is that he or she is trained to recognize negative feelings. A wise teacher said that *every* therapist has one blind spot, a certain type of person he or she won't ever feel comfortable with and therefore shouldn't treat. If a therapist is self-aware, he or she will know within a session or two that this has happened, and will refer the patient to a therapist who won't have a negative reaction. It will only be natural for your feelings to be hurt if you are sent to someone else, no matter how gently the situation is handled. But please don't let your hurt prevent you from getting further help. One therapist's blind spot is another's success.

If you dislike a therapist right off the bat, say something *immediately*. When you are completely sure, after discussing the problem, that your dislike is based squarely on things about the therapist's personality that are *not* going to change, your best bet is to seek help elsewhere. If the reason for your negative feelings still isn't clear, you may want to visit the therapist a few more times to see if you like him or her better, or consult with another therapist to see if being with a different person brings out the same bad feelings. When this keeps happening, regardless of what the therapist is like, the problem clearly lies within you and your negative attitudes toward therapy, not the people practicing it. If you want to be in treatment at all, it would probably be a good idea to stick with the first therapist you saw.

Sometimes treatment begins well, you and the therapist like each other, good work gets done for a while, but then you hit a dead end suddenly, or little by little. You start feeling bored and uninterested in your sessions. No new ground is broken in therapy, you go over the same topics again and again, without making any progress. Why is this so?

Perhaps your therapy is drying up because your therapist's approach is *limited*. Some therapists think the best way they can help a young patient is to build a warm, friendly relationship, without exploring the deeper causes of your problem. You might do well with this kind of therapist as long as you just needed a sympathetic ear to pour your troubles into, or a strong shoulder to lean on. But if you really do need a much greater understanding of yourself, this therapist may be unable to help you. Your treatment with a therapist of the opposite sex may do well, until you start discussing sexual issues that make you feel uncomfortable. If you can't work this problem out, it might be better for you to switch to a therapist of the same sex.

If you've been extremely troubled but are now feeling okay due to therapy, you may still consider stopping your treatment with your therapist because he or she reminds you of the time when you were so upset. Saying good-bye and starting afresh with a new therapist may seem like saying good-bye to your child self and hello to a healthier, more grown-up self.

These are only a few of the reasons previously successful therapy may no longer seem to work. It may not be "reasonable" to switch to another therapist because of them, but if your feelings are strong enough the "goodness" or "badness" of your reason won't really matter, and you probably should see someone else without wasting more time. It's possible you won't be able to pinpoint *any* reason for therapy coming to a dead end other than that your relationship with your therapist has run its natural course, just as friendships helpful at one stage of your life are often outgrown and replaced by new ones.

When you and your therapist agree that little progress is being made, you should consider: (1) switching to another therapist right away; (2) consulting with another therapist to see if outside advice can help your treatment; (3) stopping therapy for a while and returning later; (4) continuing therapy for a trial period of a few weeks or months, then changing therapists if you haven't made any progress. Remember, switching when your treatment bogs down *often* isn't necessary; just bringing a problem with therapy into the light may be the *first* step in putting it back on the right track.

17 | *Ending Psychotherapy— and Coming Back*

If you've been in therapy a long time with good results, it's natural to start asking yourself how much better you have to feel or how much knowledge about yourself you have to get before you can stop. Some people won't think of leaving therapy until they are satisfied with themselves in every life area, or until they have reached a very deep level of self-understanding. Others feel good just being able to get through a day without suffering, and won't demand great happiness or self-knowledge in order to stop.

Similarly, there are therapists who believe treatment shouldn't end until you are *completely* aware of what's caused your problems, until you're *completely* free of symptoms, until you are content in every life area. Other therapists won't look for such great improvements. They're satisfied with progress in your most troubled life areas without requiring any bigger changes before you stop.

I do think it's good *not* to expect miracles from psychotherapy. Therapy *won't* give you the answers to all life's problems, no matter *how* long you stay. It can't take away *every* difficulty you may have to face, or change you into a totally different human being. Even if you've been greatly helped with serious depressions or anxiety attacks, you may *still* get a bit depressed or anxious under stress after your treatment is over. Therapy *can* certainly help you live a better life, but it *can't* prevent the accidents, illnesses, and other tragedies that happen just because you are alive. If you are staying in treatment because you are looking for magical solutions or protections, you are doomed to disappointment.

I believe a therapist shouldn't expect miracles either. You shouldn't be kept in therapy because your therapist looks toward further changes that just aren't possible because of who you are, or the stage of life you are at, especially if you are satisfied with your progress and don't want further help.

When you find yourself hesitating about finishing therapy, ask yourself if you really need further treatment, or if you are just hanging on because you are afraid you won't be able to make it on your own. Many people cling to therapy, waiting for one more piece of information, one more explanation that will tie their problems into a neat package. Psychotherapy aims at teaching you to make free choices. If you are secretly using your therapist to make choices that you are now able to make on your own, *your treatment will have turned into the very sickness it was supposed to cure*, a substitute for living independently.

The possibility of becoming too dependent upon therapy is an especially real danger for an adolescent. One of your chief tasks as a teen-ager is separating successfully from your parents and family. If the stresses of separation have created emotional problems, your therapist will help put you back on the path to adulthood. But the last thing in the world you need while you are trying to grow up is to sink into yet *another* unhelpful dependent relationship, this time with your therapist.

A good therapist won't let this happen. He or she may recommend that you stop therapy to have an experience of managing on your own, although you still have unanswered questions, unsolved problems, even a certain amount of mild symptoms. I've found many of my young patients take this action *before* I suggest it, sometimes when I myself felt they weren't ready to leave treatment. I am happy to tell you that most of them have done very well and have frequently told me later that they appreciated my not hanging on to them, even though they weren't 100 percent okay. When things *haven't* worked out, they've been sensible enough to return.

What are the signs you may be ready to end therapy? Improvement of the difficulties that made you seek help is certainly an important sign. But if you *do* feel better, ask yourself if your improvement is *really* that great, and has lasted *long* enough. If the rest of your life was in reasonably good shape before starting therapy, you probably *will* be able to stop treatment after a short time. But if you have been troubled a long time with serious problems before beginning therapy, a real improvement should be measured in weeks and months, *not* hours or days.

Many patients have what's known as a *honeymoon period* right after beginning treatment, when all their difficulties seem to clear up miraculously. The therapy honeymoon is based on relief at finally being able to share your problems with another, on imagining the therapist has magical healing powers, or on a need to prove you've gotten so much better therapy isn't required (especially true for adolescents). But when your honeymoon ends, usually in a few weeks, *all* your original problems will return, possibly even worse than before. It is a *very* big mistake to drop out of treatment during a honeymoon period, at the first sign of feeling a little better. Remember, during therapy people experience ups and downs, times when they feel a little better or worse, when they take a few steps forward or back. A decision to stop therapy never should be based on these up and downs, but only on *real* progress.*

One sure sign of progress is an improved attitude toward your family. A famous writer said that when he was sixteen he thought his father was a fool, but at twenty-six he was amazed to see how much the old man had learned in ten years! Of course the father hadn't gotten much wiser; his son's viewpoint had changed as he had grown. When you become more mature and independent through psychotherapy, you often develop a better appreciation of your parents' strong points and form better relationships with other family members.

Sadly, when the behavior of your parents continues to be very hurtful, or emotional wounds caused by your family go too deep, it may not be possible to have better relationships, at least for a while. But if your therapy has been successful, by the end of treatment you will at least have understood why your parents and family behave hurtfully, how you have let yourself become tangled up in their destructive behavior patterns, and how to avoid getting so involved in the future. With your new understanding, you may also be able to forgive your folks for things they might never have done, had they been more healthy. Before stopping treatment, a seventeen-year-old boy said, "My parents sure do a lot of things that don't make them easy to like. But mostly I love them now despite themselves. Maybe if they had different childhoods, or had been able to get therapy, they would have known how to treat me better."

This balanced attitude is a *true* sign of emotional maturity. Before you reach it, you may often get angry at grown-ups because it seems you are the one who has to do all the changing, while

---

*You should also know that people often have a sudden return of their original problems or symptoms when it nears time to end successful therapy. This period of "falling apart" is usually as brief as the magical improvement of the honeymoon period. It stems from the fear that you won't be able to maintain progress without your therapist. It's as if you were saying to your therapist, "Without you, I just won't make it. Look at how sick I still am. Please don't let me go!"

mended long-term therapy. But *no* amount of therapy can protect you from ever reacting badly to stress again. Therapy always tends to be directed toward issues of greatest concern to you *at the time you are in treatment*. When you are a teen-ager, therapy helps you deal mainly with the problems of being a teen-ager. Therapy may not help you as directly to handle stresses you won't have to face until later on in your life.

Let's say you finish your therapy when you are seventeen, then develop more problems at age twenty-one when you are getting married. At seventeen, if your therapist had spent a lot of extra time exploring what you thought it would be like to be married, not much would have been accomplished because you would have been talking about an imaginary marriage invented by your seventeen-year-old head, not a real marriage with a real person, taking place at twenty-one. So if you were doing well at seventeen, it was better to end therapy then. The therapist *could* point to the future stresses, like marriage, that might be difficult, and might make it necessary for you to come back to treatment.

The return of symptoms after finishing therapy shouldn't make you doubt your therapist's skill, especially if you've done well for some time before things go wrong. Perhaps your problems have returned because of the type or the amount of stress you face now. Perhaps you now need to do further work on issues you and your therapist weren't aware of the first time, or which you weren't ready to deal with. Perhaps you can now accept a different therapy approach, one that was needed but which you didn't want. Earlier you may have only been able or willing to undergo brief therapy with limited goals. Now you may be ready to enter therapy that lasts longer, goes deeper, and is much more effective.

It's also possible that the mental-health profession doesn't know enough yet about your condition to prevent it from coming back. Psychology is a new science. There's a tremendous amount we don't know about how the mind works. Even with the most modern treatment methods, there are still some people who have to be content with less than total improvement, who have to live with the return of their symptoms. The last twenty years also have seen enormous progress, each year more than the year before. New psychotherapy methods, new medications, and other treatment techniques are being developed, old ones being improved. So if you haven't yet been able to lick all your problems, don't give up hope. With the advances being made, there's a good chance that somewhere in the future you'll find the relief you didn't get today.

18 ‖ *Medication*

Within the past forty years a health revolution has taken place because of the development of powerful mind-influencing, or *psychotropic*, drugs. They have brought significant relief to those suffering from the most serious psychological disorders and have helped many people with less serious symptoms as well. Through drug research, investigators also have learned more about the mysterious chemical reactions that take place within the brain in sickness and health.

Drug therapy, however, brings problems as well as benefits. Although most patients can take psychotropic medicine easily, a few have uncomfortable reactions that make treatment difficult or impossible. Drug therapy is sometimes prescribed too quickly by overworked professionals for problems which aren't serious enough to require medicine, or when a person really needs someone to talk to instead of a pill. Experts worry that drugs may be substituted too easily for psychotherapy, which in many cases doesn't give such prompt relief but may offer a better chance for a more long-lasting personality change.

I believe that drug therapy *does* have an important place in the treatment of some adolescent emotional problems. When properly prescribed for the right reasons, drug therapy can help your "talking" psychotherapy by cutting down on symptoms that stand in the way of good communication with your therapist. The chances are great that you probably *won't* need drugs to deal with your problems. For instance, only 10 to 20 percent of the youngsters I treat take medication. But if drug therapy is suggested for you, the following information should answer your questions and, I hope, calm any worries you have.

▌ *When Are Drugs Used?*

Drug therapy is especially helpful in the treatment of severe psychological conditions that seriously cripple your ability to function. These disorders include psychosis, very deep depression, severe anxiety, and phobic and obsessional states. In the past many of these problems, especially psychoses and severe depressions, would require hospital treatment. Drug therapy frequently shortens hospitalization or makes it *completely* unnecessary.

It is harder to decide whether you need drug therapy when your symptoms aren't as serious, and when your ability to function and relate to others isn't as troubled. Often milder symptoms of anxiety and depression can be helped by drugs. Medication may enable you to deal more effectively with realistic life stress such as a divorce or the illness of a parent. Medicine can relieve the emotional strain that's aggravating a psychosomatic problem, such as asthma or an ulcer.

All of these conditions also respond to psychotherapy alone, but perhaps not right away. If your suffering is great enough, you may need the faster relief of medication. The decision to use drugs or not may hinge on how quickly you get a healing relationship started with your therapist. If the symptoms that bring you to a therapist interfere with building a healing relationship, medication may be helpful in smoothing the way; then it will often become unnecessary once you and your therapist know each other better.

Drug therapy is rarely any use in trying to change the basic personality characteristics built up over many years. Behavioral problems such as delinquency and running away aren't usually helped by drugs. Occasionally an episode of delinquent activity due to a concealed depression may respond to medication. But, for the most part, rebellious attitudes, problems with authority, and antisocial actions require a slow and patient process of psychotherapy to uncover their causes. Drug therapy is usually *not* effective in cases of serious dependence on food, alcohol, or other drugs. Indeed, the danger exists that the dependent person may transfer his or her problem to the prescribed drug, so the cure becomes worse than the disease.

Regardless of any other problems you may be having, psychotropic medication may be aimed at helping *one* particular symptom, such as bedwetting or insomnia.

▌ *Who Gives Drugs?*

If you need drug therapy and psychotherapy, it would obviously be best for one person to handle both, but only a medically trained therapist is legally allowed to do this. However, today nonmedical psychotherapists are usually taught about drugs. Although they can't prescribe medications, they do know when they should be used.

If your nonmedical therapist thinks drugs might help, you'll be sent for a consultation with a psychiatrist or other physician, if a psychiatrist isn't available (these days, many medical doctors are quite skilled in the prescription of psychotropic drugs). A consultant won't interfere with your relationship with your therapist. Drug consultation centers mostly around your symptoms, without getting into the deeper issues you discuss in therapy sessions. If it's agreed you need medicine, the consultant first will see you or speak to you on the phone about once a week to regulate your drug. Contact generally will be brief. After your situation is under control, you probably won't have to talk to the consultant more than every few weeks or months unless problems arise. Your consultant and your therapist probably will be speaking with each other. Questions your parents have about drug therapy will be answered by your consultant, your therapist, or both.

▎ *What Kinds of Drugs Are There?*

Researchers have developed different groups of psychotropic drugs. Each is particularly useful in treating certain kinds of emotional problems or symptoms. Thus one group will be better for calming anxiety, another for lifting depression, a third for pulling together disorganized psychotic thinking. In the appendix you'll find the most commonly prescribed drugs within each group below, listed by brand name.

Minor tranquilizers. These are prescribed chiefly in the treatment of free-floating anxiety, tension, and other anxiety symptoms. They are helpful in dealing with anxiety related to outside stress. They also are given to calm the anxiety suffered by alcoholics after a bout of heavy drinking. (They should not be given to most alcoholics on a continuous basis.)

Major tranquilizers. These are sometimes given for mild anxiety and tension conditions, but their most important use is in the treatment of extremely severe anxiety, and to calm the panic and agitation that occur with psychotic conditions such as schizophrenia. These drugs can straighten out the disorganized and peculiar thinking of the psychotic, remove hallucinations and delusions, and calm strange, disturbing behavior. Both minor and major tranquilizers may be prescribed for bad trips brought on by psychedelic drug abuse.

Antidepressants. These are useful in depressive conditions, particularly those serious illnesses marked by weight loss, trouble sleeping and concentrating, withdrawal, and suicidal activity. Antidepressant drugs act slowly and gently to raise your depressed mood. They often take several weeks or months to work, but once they take hold their effects are long lasting. Antidepressants usually *don't* do much for milder depressions. They aren't energizers. They do not speed up your physical reactions, raise your heart beat, or increase your rate of breathing. They do not make you speedy, nor will they elevate your mood if you aren't blue to begin with. Researchers have discovered that antidepressant drugs also can stop bedwetting or improve certain severe panic states, phobias, and obsessions. These effects appear unrelated to antidepressant action.

Stimulants. Drugs know as *stimulants* have a general energizing action on the body as well as the mind, whether you are depressed or not. Stimulants can speed up physical activities like heart rate and breathing. They act quickly, but their effects also wear off quickly. Some stimulants reduce appetite temporarily and therefore have been widely prescribed for weight reduction. Recently experts have seriously questioned this use. Stimulants are sometimes given to combat mild depression, especially when accompanied by fatigue, but they have been largely replaced by the antidepressants, which are safer and more effective. Today stimulants are thought to have real value mostly in the treatment of narcolepsy, a disorder marked by sudden attacks of falling asleep, and in certain cases of childhood overactivity where, for unknown reasons, they produce a *calming* effect instead of a stimulating action.

Lithium. A simple chemical called *lithium* is extremely effective in treating manic-depressive illness, the disorder in which you swing back and forth between the depths of despair and the heights of unreasonable joy. Previously, antidepressants or tranquilizers were used when a manic-depressive was dropping low or flying high. Neither type of medication could do anything to stop the inner merry-go-round that causes the illness. Although it's not clear why, lithium readjusts the disturbed brain chemistry of the manic-depressive person, smoothing out the peaks and valleys, and in many instances restoring people to normal life after years of hospitalization.

Lithium is the closest thing to a real cure in drug therapy. It is the most specific medicine developed so far to be aimed at a particular emotional disorder. The success of lithium increases the hope that one day specific drugs also will be found for illnesses like schizophrenia, so that the basic *cause* of a problem can be medicated instead of its symptoms.

Hypnotic/sedatives. Drugs that belong to the group of *hypnotic/sedatives* are chiefly used to treat sleep problems—trouble falling asleep and staying asleep. They are very widely prescribed, and in the opinion of many experts often *overprescribed*. People with sleep problems may be suffering from deeper emotional problems, which may be treated more effectively with other drugs and psychotherapy. Many sleeping problems can be helped without using drugs at all, through physical exercise and various self-relaxation techniques. If you must use sedatives, it's probably best to take them a short time and then to stop them once your normal sleep pattern has been restored.

Crossovers and combinations. A psychotropic drug may have an extra benefit of helping another kind of symptom associated with your main problem. I've explained that symptoms of anxiety are frequently joined by depression, and depression with anxiety. While they calm anxiety, tranquilizers often "cross over" to help anxiety-related depression. And antidepressants frequently calm depression-related anxiety.

It may be necessary for you to take more than one psychotropic drug. For instance, if you are both extremely depressed and anxious, you may do best on an antidepressant and a tranquilizer. Occasionally a depression will respond better to a combination of two antidepressants than one alone, or a psychosis will improve more quickly on two major tranquilizers. But usually it's safest and simplest to start on one drug that will cover several of your problems, taking other drugs later on if necessary.

▋ *Side Effects and Other Problems*

Drugs are given to produce a particular effect on a particular organ or system of the body. For example, asthma medicine opens blocked breathing passages in the lungs. But since a drug travels throughout the blood stream it can produce side effects on other organs and systems. (A side effect also may stem from the drug having an unhelpful as well as helpful action on the organ it is prescribed for.)

Most side effects are unpleasant, but rarely dangerous. For instance, an antibiotic prescribed for a throat infection can irritate the lining of your stomach and make you feel slightly nauseated. You can usually keep taking the drug despite your stomach upset. In rare cases an antibiotic will interfere with the body's ability to produce the white blood cells that fight infection. This effect is so dangerous you *cannot* keep taking the drug.

Drugs also cause *allergic* reactions. These aren't side effects, but signs that your body's defenses are rejecting the drug. Allergic problems are usually mild—itchiness of the skin, or tearing of the eyes. In rare cases an allergic reaction may be very severe, such as a serious rash over the entire body or a bad asthmatic attack.

Most drug side effects can be handled easily. You learn to live with them, or you take measures to decrease them. The stomach irritation caused by antibiotics can be helped by taking them with meals or by swallowing a liquid coating agent to protect the lining of your stomach. However, most allergic reactions, mild or severe, mean that a drug must be discontinued.

Obviously the best drug for any condition, medical or emotional, would be one that produced no side effects and no allergies. Unfortunately there is *no* such medication. Someone, somewhere, always will respond negatively, even to the safest medicine, including aspirin. The best researchers can do is test a drug very thoroughly before it is marketed to make sure that the majority who take it won't have any side effects or allergies, and that any side effects that do occur will be mild and easily treatable. Under the law, a lengthy testing process supervised by government agencies must take place before any psychotropic drug can be marketed. Thus chances are you won't have many side effects from psychotropic medication. If you do, they will be mild.

Sleepiness, tiredness, and dizziness are the most common side effects of psychotropic drugs, except for stimulants. These problems stem from drug action on your brain and central nervous system—the same targets for helpful drug action.

Sedatives may leave you with a groggy, "hungover" sensation the next morning. Tranquilizers, both major and minor, and antidepressants, may make you feel slowed down and "heavy." Less commonly these drugs produce the opposite effect—restlessness, nervousness, jitteriness.

Because of their action upon other body organs, major tranquilizers and antidepressants can produce problems like dry mouth (*very* common), constipation, and blurring of vision. Increased appetite and weight gain have also been reported, especially in high doses. There are rare sexual side effects in men, including difficulty in having or keeping an erection, and "dry" ejaculations, in which the sensation of orgasm takes place without semen coming out of the penis. These problems most often occur with the major tranquilizer *mellaril*. I mention these unusual effects because adolescent boys who have them are often ashamed to report them and may not know they are due to drug therapy, mistakenly believing they come from some dreadful, mysterious cause that has damaged them forever.

Fortunately none of the above side effects is permanent. Some vanish as your body adjusts to the drug, others can be helped by reducing the dose of drug, or by rearranging the way the drug is given. Rather than take major tranquilizers or antidepressants over twenty-four hours in small doses, a person can often take them safely in one large dose at bedtime. Taking a drug this way may have the added benefit of helping you sleep better. Sleepiness and other unpleasant side effects wear off during the night; the drug then continues to act on your symptoms throughout the next day with few, if any, side effects. Side effects can also be handled by a variety of practical measures and medications—laxatives for drug-caused constipation, sucking on a candy to help you salivate when your mouth gets dry, et cetera.

A small percentage of people who take major tranquilizers develop problems with muscle movement, due to drug effects on parts of the brain that regulate smooth muscular activity. These symptoms usually occur with high doses and include stiffness in the legs and arms, tight sensations in the muscles of the neck, jaw, and throat; shaking or trembling of the hands; small, cramped handwriting; and walking with small steps. Such symptoms often are eliminated by reducing the dose of drug or switching to a different medication. Special drugs known as *anti-Parkinsonian agents* may be prescribed to control muscular problems. (The most frequently used anti-Parkinsonian agents are *artane, cogentin,* and *kemadrin*.)

Side effects of lithium therapy include thirst, nausea, diarrhea, fine trembling of the hands, and weight gain. These usually aren't severe enough to stop lithium, and are controlled by giving medicine at meals for stomach distress, or lowering the dose level if absolutely necessary.

Because of their general energizing action, stimulants can make you jittery, restless, and irritable. A few supersensitive people even get angry and paranoid. Stimulants also cause loss of appetite and weight. Many of these problems fade on lower doses.

Allergic reactions can occur with *any* type of psychotropic drug and, as noted, usually mean you must discontinue your medication. But you can often be switched to a different drug without developing another allergy.

When two psychotropic drugs are combined, an action known as *potentiation* may take place. The two drugs interact to produce good or bad effects *greater* than if either had been given alone. For instance, a dose of tranquilizer that ordinarily might make you feel slightly sleepy might really knock you out if combined with another tranquilizer or antidepressant. To prevent potentiation, lower doses than usual may be prescribed when two drugs are combined.

Alcohol is actually a drug whose sedative properties are potentiated by psychotropic medication. A small amount of beer or whiskey that ordinarily would only make you feel a bit relaxed could knock you off your feet if taken with a major or minor tranquilizer. Many of the drug-related deaths you've read about are actually the result of drinking heavily or even normally, on top of psychotropic medicine. Thus, you should avoid drinking if you are having drug therapy.

Psychotropic drugs may interact badly with medication given for a variety of physical conditions. You must always tell a drug therapist about other drugs you are taking and inform a physician you're seeing for a physical problem that you are taking psychotropic drugs.

Patients and their families often worry about the possibility of addiction to psychotropic drugs. It's possible your folks may object to drug therapy because they fear you will want to keep taking medicine for "kicks" after it's not needed anymore, or worry that using psychotropic drugs might lead to experimentation with dangerous "street" drugs.

These fears are groundless regarding most psychotropic medications. The major tranquilizers, antidepressants, and lithium have just about *no* abuse possibilities. They don't give you "kicks," and they do not produce tolerance or addiction. A few people taking high doses of tranquilizers and antidepressants may develop mild physical discomfort when medication is stopped suddenly, but this problem is easily prevented by coming off the drug in slow, downward steps.

Sedatives (such as barbiturates, doriden, or quaaludes), minor tranquilizers (like valium), and stimulants (like the amphetamines) *are* widely abused. (The sedative/minor-tranquilizer drugs are called *downs* or *downers* in street slang; the stimulants are referred to as *ups* or *uppers*.) These drugs all can cause tolerance, severe physical and/or psychological dependence, and painful, even life-threatening withdrawal symptoms. However, most cases of serious abuse aren't related to taking stimulants or sedatives for a good medical reason, under proper supervision, but occur from experimenting illegally with them, as a result of taking amounts that are far higher than any good physician would ever give. If you are prescribed any of these drugs by a well-trained physician, you will not develop problems with dependency if you follow your doctor's directions *exactly*.

It's thought that individuals with a history of experimenting with alcohol or other drugs may indeed develop a "taste" for sedatives or stimulants prescribed for medical or psychological reasons.

Doctors will try not to give these medications to such patients—if they know who they're dealing with. If you've been taking drugs on the outside, heavily or lightly, you *must* let a doctor who is about to prescribe sedatives or stimulants know about your drug habits. Otherwise you are asking for *very* big trouble. Put aside your fear of exposure or an itch you have for easy kicks, and tell the doctor the truth.

▌ *What Kind of Drug:*
How Much—How Long?

Every group of psychotropic medications contains different drugs, each of which has the same main action but differs somewhat from other members of the group regarding quickness of action, side effects, et cetera. For instance, one antidepressant has more sedative activity than another and might be better for you if your depression is accompanied by insomnia.

Your drug therapist will choose carefully the medication that is best for your particular symptoms and will change drugs if you don't get the help you need. Most patients are able to stay on the drug they begin with; usually the only change needed during therapy is in the *amount*, not the *kind* of medicine.

Each psychotropic drug has a dose level that is effective for the average person. The dose good for you probably will fall within the "ordinary" range. But you may require more or much less medicine depending on your age, weight, and other drugs you are taking. If you are a young teen-ager just starting to grow, you may need less medicine than a larger adult. If you are older, taller, and heavier, you probably will need more medicine. If you have to take medicine for a long time, your dose may have to be increased to take into account the added growth of your adolescence.

Your drug therapist will find the *smallest* dose of medicine needed to help your condition. This is reached by careful upward or downward adjustment, based on how well your symptoms are responding, balanced against any side effects. With some medicines such as lithium it is possible to do a simple blood test that shows if there's enough drug in your body to be helping you.

Just as your therapist aims to give the lowest possible dose of drug that will do the job, you'll always take a drug the shortest time necessary to help you. However, there's no easy way of predicting exactly how long this will be. The time will depend on factors like the nature and the seriousness of your condition, and on how psychotherapy influences your progress.

Drug therapy may only last a few days, as in the treatment of a temporary panic state brought on by LSD. Anxiety related to a specific life crisis may require that you stay on medicine only for as long as the crisis lasts. Certain severe depressions may call for several months of antidepressant drug therapy while you are depressed, and a period of *another* three to six months after symptoms have cleared up, to prevent the depression from returning. Severe psychosis may require major tranquilizers for several years to hold down symptoms like hallucinations and delusions that would otherwise "boil over" and make you sick again. In manic-depressive illness, treatment with lithium may have to continue even longer, just as a chronic medical condition like diabetes would require daily medication indefinitely.

In outpatient drug therapy you usually take medication in capsules (hospitalized people sometimes need medicine in the form of injection, or highly concentrated liquid). As noted earlier, you may be able to take the entire dose of drug prescribed for you at one time, usually before you go to bed. If you can't take one big dose, your medicine will be spread out over the day in smaller doses, at regular intervals, generally at mealtimes.

Psychotropic drugs come in different strengths. When you first start therapy, your doctor may prefer to give you the drug in lower-strength pills because finer adjustments can be made. People who don't understand this often get scared, because they think they are taking too much medicine. Once a good dose is reached, the therapist then will switch you over to a few higher-strength pills that are easier to swallow than a lot of lower-strength pills. For instance, if your nighttime dose of a tranquilizer was 100 mgm., your therapist might switch you from four 25 mgm. tablets to one 100 mgm. tablet.*

▮ *Resistance to Drug Therapy*

Despite the proven effectiveness and safety of modern psychotropic drugs, many people are highly resistant to taking them. Out of fear or stubbornness, they refuse medicine altogether or stop taking it after a while, causing themselves great misery and ruining progress they might make in overcoming their problems.

Why might you avoid drug therapy? Perhaps you believe drugs have been recommended because your case is hopeless, because you can't be helped by ordinary "talking" therapy. In fact drug therapy today *isn't* a last measure, but is prescribed right at the beginning of effective care. As shown, an important reason for using drugs is to make it easier for you to build an effective relationship with your therapist.

Perhaps you imagine you'll become so dependent on drugs you won't ever get off them again. I've indicated that most psychotropic drugs simply aren't abusable, and the ones which might be abused won't hurt you *if* you take them as prescribed. If you are worried about the length of time needed for drug therapy, I'm happy to tell you that it is rare for an adolescent to require psychotropic medicine for longer than six months to a year.

Perhaps you worry that drug therapy will turn you into a zombie or brainwash you, so that you won't be yourself any longer. I can assure you that your basic "you-ness" won't be influenced by psychotropic medication. You won't develop beliefs or actions that run against your basic nature.

Your strong need to prove you are able to manage your

---

*Drug doses are usually calculated in milligrams; a milligram is one/thousandth of a gram (metric measurements).

life without outside interference can make the idea of a chemical crutch even more of a turnoff than psychotherapy. You may be particularly concerned that taking psychotropic drugs will label you as sick or crazy, certainly very different from your peers. If you keep viewing drug therapy as a sign of sickness and dependency, you may overlook the very real benefits you can get from it. Please *try* to think of a drug as just a drug, *not* a label. No one outside your family or your therapist need know you are taking medication, nor should it interfere with your everyday activities.

▌ *Drug Therapy and Psychotherapy*

Drug therapy is as much of a topic for discussion in psychotherapy as anything else in your life. Even if taking medication is a total turnoff, you should at least try to figure out the reasons for your resistance, rather than flatly refusing drugs and dropping the subject.

The question of drug therapy usually is first raised by a therapist rather than an adolescent, but there is no law that says you can't ask if drugs will help your problem. Don't sit back and let your therapist do the deciding about drugs. Ask why he or she feels you should be taking them. You don't have to be a doctor to grasp a simple explanation about the kind of drug being recommended, its side effects, how long you'll be taking it, and what will happen if you choose *not* to take it.

Some therapists shy away from giving information about drugs because they think their clients won't understand or aren't interested in details. You should not let yourself be put off by a therapist who tells you just to take the pills and not to worry. The more realistic information you can get, the less likely you'll be to have unreasonable ideas about psychotropic medicine. Drug therapy really has the best chance of success when you and your therapist are joined in a cooperative effort. Drug therapy also works best when your parents or family aren't afraid of it, so that you don't have to take your medicine along with their worries. If your parents keep bugging you about medication, ask your therapist or your drug consultant to meet with them.

| *The Limits of Drug Therapy.*
| Some people oppose drug therapy because they are so unreasonably afraid. But others welcome and demand drug therapy because they are just as unreasonably hopeful. They expect drugs magically will remove all their problems in the twinkling of an eye, that psychotherapy won't be necessary for them anymore.

While it's true that modern psychotropic medication can be extremely helpful for many patients, drug therapy is *not* the answer for the majority of troubled people. Even if drug therapy might be useful in your case, it alone probably won't solve deep, complicated problems in living. Medicine can help the symptoms that have stopped you from getting in touch with your natural strengths. If you are less phobic, less anxious, less depressed, you're better able to figure out what's caused your problems and where to go with your life. This will take hard, patient work, in psychotherapy or out. Nothing out of a bottle is going to be a substitute for this work.

19 Family, Group, and Other Psychotherapies

Family Therapy

Your adolescence can be stressful for everyone in your family. Your new view of the world may lead you to examine your family life with a very critical eye. Your criticisms can be particularly upsetting to parents who have taken the happiness of their marriage and home for granted. Your adolescence may awaken all sorts of buried problems out of their past (including *their* adolescence), as well as fears about their future. If your parents act out their troubled feelings, you may respond by developing psychological problems where none existed, or may be even more bothered by the conflicts you're already having.

Other children in your family may react to your adolescence by developing problems of their own.

198

Younger siblings get jealous of the new freedoms allowed you. Older children with their adolescence barely over make fun of your "ridiculous" behavior. When bad quarrels go on between you and your parents, your brothers and sisters may get drawn in.

When a family's usual methods for handling its difficulties begin to break down, its discomfort spreads. People outside the home—friends, grandparents, other relatives, clergy—may be called upon for help, or they put their two cents in without being asked. Sometimes outsiders may have already been making problems, which now increase.

Most family members don't understand their role in creating or complicating your problems. When a family with a troubled teen-ager gets into trouble, its members have a way of chalking up all the trouble to the "craziness" of the adolescent. In fact the adolescent labeled as crazy may be the *one* person who realizes how upset the entire family system is. But sadly, the youngster often can express unhappiness about family unhappiness only through alarming symptoms or disturbing behavior that easily gets labeled "crazy."

Experts in the field of *family therapy* believe that your personal problems should be seen as an expression of your family's larger problems. They feel that concentrating on individual therapy gives a limited and sometimes mistaken picture of the way your family functions, and doesn't always offer the strongest chance of changing the family patterns that are making you suffer.

An individual therapist will be constantly reading in between the lines to figure out what *really* goes on in your family from what you report. But no matter *how* objective he or she tries to be, your therapist *can't* have the fullest experience of what being in your family is like for you, because of limited contact with the family. In family therapy there's no need to read in between the lines. For the whole family is brought *right* into the office, so the therapist experiences their problems at first hand and can relay his or her impressions right back to everyone.

When you consult with a family therapist, he or she will meet with every member of your immediate family, both together and separately. Your parents may be seen alone; all your brothers and sisters, including young children, may be interviewed without your parents. You will be seen by yourself, and it is quite likely that other family members may have individual sessions, too. The therapist may decide to consult with important relatives, especially grandparents and favorite aunts and uncles. Sometimes important people who aren't directly related to you may also be included—friends, teachers, et cetera.

Your family therapist will study closely the history of your family through its stages of development, from the time your parents first met and courted until now. The therapist will examine how troubled patterns of relating and communicating in your family have affected you, and find out how your problems have affected the vital balance of your family.

A family therapist has special approaches to understanding what your family is like. He or she may assign your family an imaginary task in a session to see how the family works. If your family is asked to plan an imaginary vacation, how will the decision be made where to go? Who phones to make hotel reservations? Who packs? Who drives? What responsibilities does each family member have during the trip, and who assigns them? Is time set aside for your parents to be alone, and for kids to be off by themselves doing their own thing?

Gradually your family will reveal a great deal about how openly or indirectly members express their feelings and needs, about the sources of power in the family, about its leaders and followers, about who sides with whom, about secret envies, jealousies, attractions and dislikes, about family views on religion, sex, and politics.

Your family therapist may decide to visit your home to see what your life "space" is like, to learn how your family behaves on its own turf. Another excellent method of getting information is recording family sessions on audio- or videotape. Your family may be asked to watch or listen to taped sessions so that they can experience clearly how they relate.

After your consultation is finished, if family therapy is recommended, your therapist will schedule sessions with your family and you in various combinations. The therapist may work separately with you in individual therapy, while also seeing you with your family; or he or she may treat you with your family while another therapist takes you for individual therapy. Less often, family therapy may be your only treatment.*

Family therapy demands great flexibility. The therapist must know who to include in sessions and who to leave out. Depending upon what's going on at home and in therapy, your therapist will shift tactics. He or she may choose to see everyone or to work only with your parents as a couple, to alternate sessions between children and parents, to see you and your parents without older kids present, or to call in your grandparents for one session. The combinations are endless.

In individual therapy there are many times when the therapist sits back and lets you talk for a long time. This doesn't happen often in family therapy. According to the noted psychiatrist Dr. Joel Kovel: "The family therapist has to be actively involved, for it is only the force of his influence that can oppose the weight of the system. . . . He has to introduce new energy into a system that will otherwise roll right along on the path it has carved for itself."

You can expect your family therapist to enter your family's struggles forcefully during a session. The family therapist

---

*Family therapy may be offered as the only treatment because an adolescent or family won't accept anything else. Some therapists think that family therapy alone is the best treatment for many adolescent problems. They believe the family's wholeness should be the main concern in treatment, for if the sick family system is helped, then the emotional difficulties of each member will improve. However, most family therapists combine their work with individual therapy of some type.

energetically exposes family side-taking, mixed-up ways of communicating, and double messages. People are encouraged not to
hide their true feelings behind smoke screens of confusing words or
silence. Your therapist always will respect each family member's
right to privacy, but also will encourage disclosure when the sharing
of secrets has contributed to family problems.

When should family therapy be used? Some experts believe that just about any emotional problem that can be treated with
individual therapy will respond to a family approach. Others think
that family treatment probably will not be very effective if your
symptoms indicate deeply rooted conflicts that at this point have little real connection with everyday family life. Many families certainly
could use family therapy, but may be too resistive to get involved.
Even though a family therapist wants to help, your family may be so
locked into unhealthy behavior patterns that nothing can change
them. When this is the case, it's usually better to leave well enough
alone and concentrate on your individual therapy.

In my own experience, I've found that family therapy
seems to be most helpful to youngsters who are very involved with
their families, and whose problems are obviously related to family
difficulties. Most of these teen-agers are age twelve to sixteen. Family therapy usually isn't necessary for older adolescents who are living away from home or who have a much more limited involvement
with their families while living with them.

It won't help to have family therapy forced upon you
when you don't really want it, even if it's recommended by an expert
for the best possible reasons. If you already are very sensitive about
your family's interfering with your life, resent their butting into
your affairs, and basically want therapy to provide a private place for
exploring your problems, I doubt you will like family therapy. You
might want to attend a few sessions to make sure it isn't good for
you. If you still feel strongly opposed to it, stick to your guns and
stay with individual work. Perhaps if you don't want to attend, your
parents or other family members can go without you. They can still

be helped by a family therapist, without your being there.

Family therapy sessions usually last an hour to an hour and a half, and are scheduled once weekly. Like brief individual psychotherapy, family therapy may last only a few or a set number of sessions. In brief family therapy, specific problems or crises are worked on, and it isn't likely that very deep changes will be made. Instead your family will be returned to its previous level of getting along. In long-term family therapy, treatment may last several years; family life is examined very deeply, and there is a good possibility that very basic, positive changes will take place within the family system.

An interesting approach that grew out of family therapy is called *network therapy*. Your therapist meets with just about every person in your life—the usual family members, plus a wide assortment of outsiders who know you: teachers, friends, clergy. In one case I knew, the grocer, the doorman, and the cop on the beat attended sessions. In network therapy ten or more people actually may be in the office at the same time, while the therapist helps them see the roles they've played in your life, often without each others' knowledge, and shows them how to cooperate better in aiding your problem. Network therapy isn't used too often because of obvious difficulties with time and space, but it has taught researchers a great deal about how people in trouble naturally turn to those around them in trying to solve their troubles.

Family therapy can be practiced by any of the qualified mental-health professionals. The training of psychologists, psychiatrists, and psychiatric social workers today includes course work in family treatment. Many family therapists take advanced training in the field and also have special training in child and adolescent psychotherapy.

The cost of a family therapy session in private practice is likely to be higher than an individual session, since the average family session lasts longer. Family therapy is now also widely available in low-cost clinics.

Group Therapy

It may be hard for you to open up in individual psycho-therapy because you don't believe an adult therapist can appreciate your point of view. You may not wish to have family therapy because you are trying so hard to be separate from your family. Group therapy gets around these difficulties by taking advantage of your natural need to form close relationships with people your own age. In a therapy group you share and compare your experiences with other adolescents who are having problems. An adult therapist is present, but his or her main job is to help all the group members relate better to each other, so that everyone can help one another more effectively. As its members grow together, a group slowly is forged into a powerful tool for healing, larger than the sum of its parts—a living laboratory for studying and improving relationships.

What makes group so special is that the patients themselves do much of the work of solving their emotional problems. You might object to this, and say that people without professional training, with problems of their own, shouldn't be making judgments about your condition. But you don't need a degree in psychology to size up people correctly. You do it every day, without thinking too much about it. Strange as it seems, the fact that you have psychological hang-ups often sharpens your ability to offer sound advice to others in trouble, even though you can't always see your own situation as clearly. The therapy group harnesses the separate abilities of its members to make wise judgments and give guidance to each other, under the professional direction of the therapist. The therapist makes sure that judgments or advice aren't offered to you in a harsh, unfriendly manner, won't let group members keep ganging up on you, and will be there to point out when an opinion about you is wrong.

The Makeup of a Therapy Group.

A typical therapy group consists of about six to eight

members plus the therapist. The members are drawn from the therapist's own practice, or referred by other therapists.

A careful pick of members is very important if a group is going to work well. If the members are too much alike, there won't be a creative mix of many different viewpoints. But if the members are *too* different, they may have trouble finding common ground. It wouldn't be helpful for you to be the only boy or girl in your group. It is often uncomfortable if you are the only person in a group from a very wealthy or very poor background. If you are twelve or thirteen it's likely that you'll have trouble relating to the interests of a group whose members are all in their late teens. A good adolescent group will be properly balanced in the sex of the members, their age, level of maturity, their social backgrounds, and the kinds of problems they have.

Time, Place, Setting.

A group session usually lasts an hour to an hour and a half, and takes place in a therapist's office or clinic. The members sit on chairs or couches arranged in a loose circle. There tends to be a lot more moving around in adolescent groups than in adult groups, perhaps reflecting the higher level of restlessness and energy you bring to your sessions. Thus there's always a certain amount of getting up and sitting down, changing places, leaving the room for a glass of water or to go to the bathroom. Too much activity will make it hard for your group to get its act together, so you should try to control your itchy feet and stay where you are. All sorts of groups, whether a cocktail party or a therapy group, have one common problem: starting on time. Please don't come late, since even a few missing or late members really hurt the group's progress.

What's the Topic?

People new to group therapy wonder what they are supposed to talk about, and who is directing the show. They often have the mistaken notion that a group is like a classroom, where the therapist, like a teacher, calls on you to discuss the lesson of the day. In fact there is no set list of topics to be covered in most sessions, and the therapist rarely will start the ball rolling unless the group stays silent for a while.

Usually group begins as one member describes an experience that happened in his or her life, or makes a comment about the last session. Then other members start to chime in, one at a time, or all together, expressing their feelings about the opening statement, going off on topics of their own, talking more directly and openly to each other as the session unfolds. Some members listen closely, others get distracted and say things off the subject. Sometimes members agree, sometimes they argue; sometimes they express affection and admiration, other times they get angry and argumentative. Whatever goes on, you'll gradually be able to see that there is one theme and thread that often runs through the discussion, no matter what the different members are talking about. One week the group members will be discussing how they cope with angry feelings; the next week everyone will be discussing how it feels to be treated like babies by the grown-ups in their lives.

The "Rules."

Newcomers wonder what the "rules" of a group are, and how they are made. Who gets to talk first? How long should you be allowed to talk? Is it okay to sit on the floor, to smoke, to eat, or to leave the room? What about seeing other members socially, outside the group?

There aren't set rules for many of these issues. For instance, it's up to you whether you want to speak up or keep quiet, whether you want to open a discussion or lay back. If you and another member want to talk about a matter that's just as important to both, then both of you have to work out who is going to get the floor. It is up to the other members, if they choose, to help you talk or shut you up if you hog the group's time. This is how you learn to share and cooperate with others, in and out of the group.

For issues where basic rules may be useful, such as when it's okay to leave a session, a group works best when the members figure out what the policy will be, with a little help from the therapist when needed. Members often look to the therapist to lay down these rules, but it's a much more meaningful experience for you to work them out with your peers, rather than have them handed down from above. There *are* several rules the therapist always will insist upon: not ganging up on someone in a hurtful, abusive fashion; not using physical force, no matter how angry you get; and keeping everything said in group totally confidential. Regarding confidentiality, you should know that if you are in individual therapy with the group therapist or another therapist, nothing will ever be said in group that you've revealed in a private session without your permission.

Some therapists discourage outside contact among group members. I believe that your need for peer relationships is so strong that some outside contact in group is not only expected, but may be useful, as when a member having extra troubles is helped by a phone call or a lunch. But your therapist will probably insist that any outside contact you have with group members should always be shared with the group, so that it won't be undermined by secret alliances. A sexual relationship between group members is *not* tolerated by most therapists, either.

The Group Therapist.

If your individual therapist sees you in group, you'll notice differences in the way you are treated in group versus individual sessions. The group therapist's chief task is to help everyone relate better so that the group becomes stronger and more useful. Therefore the therapist won't be spending a great deal of time with any one member, unless someone is in truly serious distress, or getting deeply into one person's problem will benefit everyone else.

Instead, the group therapist shifts attention from one person to another, asking one, several, or all of the members to comment on their feelings about the issues that are being raised in the group discussion. The therapist may be very active in pointing out poor communication between you and someone else, refereeing an argument, or helping the group to get a quiet member to speak out. The therapist may choose to remain quiet for a long time, allowing the members to speak directly to each other without interruption, when communication is going well.

The therapist is the leader of the group, and one of its members as well; as such he or she should not be hiding important personal feelings. So a group therapist often will be quite open in revealing when he or she is sad, glad, or mad as a result of something that's happened in the group.

▌ Healing Experiences of Group.

The healing experiences that take place in group therapy are like those described in individual treatment. These often have added strength when they occur within the group setting.

Getting things off your chest. At first you usually will find it more difficult to get something troubling off your chest in a group than in an individual session. It's normal for a new member to hold back information on sensitive subjects from a group. Perhaps you feel ashamed, or you just believe that your problem is no one else's business but your own. Once you do become more relaxed and trusting, you will discover that at least one other group member (and often more) will have had similar difficulties. I've told you how lonely it is to have problems; hearing from another teen-ager that he or she is wrestling with the same kind of problem makes you feel you've joined the human race again.

At any moment in the history of your group, there will be members who have gone further in dealing with the kind of trouble you have. Besides being helped by realizing that others share your problem, you will become more hopeful when you see how they have overcome their suffering.

Understanding yourself and your situation better. You are never exactly the same person with everyone you know. Depending on their personalities, different people will bring out different sides of your personality. With one friend you laugh a lot; with another, you are much more serious. But no matter how much of you comes out with close friends or your family, it still is not likely that any one relationship can *ever* bring out *every* part of your emotional makeup.

A therapist can only help you understand the sides of your personality brought out as you respond to him or her in individual therapy. So you may miss understanding an important side of you that doesn't get revealed. But in group therapy, with so many members to react to you and for you to react to, there's a greater chance that more sides of you will show up for people to comment on. In this way, your self-understanding will become that much more complete.

Psychotherapy can help you understand yourself better by making you aware of how you unconsciously carry over unhelpful attitudes related to your family members into outside relationships. This process, called *transference*, may be hard for you to grasp in individual treatment. Let's say your therapist points out that you are having angry feelings toward a popular classmate because he reminds you of your successful older brother. Your therapist can be completely right, yet the explanation still doesn't hit home. You think: The classmate isn't there, the therapist doesn't know him, so how can the therapist be so sure? Perhaps you do agree with the therapist's explanation with your head, but you still don't feel the truth of it in your heart.

Because a therapy group easily becomes a kind of substitute family for you, it can give you a strong, first-hand idea of how you play out your family problems with others. You get a much sharper picture, right then and there, of how unreasonably angry you get at a group member who reminds you of that successful brother, how protective you feel toward another member who reminds you of a baby sister, how rebellious you act toward the therapist who reminds you of your strict father. If you resist acknowledging what's going on, plenty of other people will be there to point it out for you.*

Sometimes you will learn that a group member who seems to resemble someone in your life isn't like that person at all. Sometimes you'll discover that he or she does have a hint of a family member's personality, but you have made this hint the most important thing about him or her, and you haven't acknowledged other parts of his or her personality. You'll also find out what it's like to have other group members treat you not as the person you really are but according to *their* false image of you. You will grow aware of the transferences of others to you, just as they become aware of yours. Eventually each person in the group will appreciate every other person without family "ghosts" getting in the way. Thus you will be helped to see the people you come in contact with *outside* the group just as they are, too.

Support, education, guidance. It's always comforting to know that someone appreciates your view of the world and wishes for your happiness. The more people in your corner, the more supported you feel. Not everyone in your group will approve of everything about you all of the time. In fact you are sure to be called on behavior and attitudes that aren't so great. But whether you are praised or criticized, your group always will give you a strong sense of your basic worth, of your right to be, which can carry you through some very rough times.

A therapy group owns a big pool of information on a wide range of subjects, which is always available to you. Each

---

*No one member of a group will ever be on target about you all of the time. Some members, however, will be right enough more often than not for you to pay special attention to their opinions. When a *majority* of the members have the same opinion about your situation or give you the same advice, the chances are that they are right, and you should listen carefully to what they are saying.

member has had more practical experience in one area o
than someone else in the group. One person may have been
tive sexually, another knows a great deal about finding a jo
be able to learn from people who know things you do
chances are there'll be at least one subject you know enoug
to teach someone else.

People give each other a lot of advice and guic
group, asked for or not. Sometimes it is very helpful to get a
of different opinions about a problem you are having, becau
may be too close to the situation to see all your choices. Son
the group's advice may be confusing or completely wrong.
will be valuable to learn to stick to your own plan of action,
others disagree with it. Often the worth of the advice given i
important as your learning to recognize whether or not the p
offering it really appreciates your needs, or is coming from
place of his or her own that really has very little to do with yo
flood of advice is often a signal that the group members reall
helpless to deal with a problem. Then you may discover the be
in sharing how rough it is *not* to have all the answers.

Role modeling and the corrective emotional experience.
sides identifying with the adult therapist's good personality q
ities, in group you also will identify with the different positive q
ities of the members. You'll take what makes sense to you from v
ous member's characters, and make it part of yourself. You may
one member's good sense of humor to develop a sense of hun
uniquely your own; admiring another member's patience, you m
find yourself becoming more patient.

Every group has a unique set of values. I think a thera
group is like a small democracy, so its members usually come
identify with democratic values, such as respect, tolerance, and u
selfish consideration for the rights and opinions of others. It's po
sible you may not have been treated with respect in your family, o
in other groups you've belonged to. So for many members the goo

treatment received in group represents a powerful *corrective emotional experience*, like having a fresh start with a new family.

If you've been strongly influenced by a group that has criminal, delinquent values, you can have these "rip-off" values turned around by exposure to a therapy group's healthy attitudes. It's been found that a therapy group of delinquent kids often creates stronger pressure for its members to straighten out than an adult therapist can generate alone.

Who Should Have Group?

Group therapy has been used with people of every age and every walk of life, little children and the elderly, ghetto dwellers and the wealthy. It's thought that nearly every condition treated by individual therapy can be helped by group treatment—anxiety, depression, psychoses, psychosomatic illnesses, and delinquency.

The biggest reason for not entering group therapy isn't the nature of your condition, but a strong feeling that group just isn't for you because you're too shy, value your privacy a lot, or simply want a more one-on-one approach. (You may change your mind later on.) No good therapist will plunge you into a group right away. You should be given one or more sessions to explore any doubts and fears you have about group, and to learn more about the group the therapist wants you to join before making up your mind.

Some experts believe group therapy alone can be just as effective as individual therapy. Others agree that group is helpful, but don't think it can go as deeply into the causes of your problems as individual treatment, and recommend that the two approaches be combined. If your problems aren't severe, and you feel that you'll be more comfortable working on them in a group rather than in individual sessions, you may choose a group approach alone at least for the time being.

Length of Treatment.

Group therapy may be brief or long-term, but it usually lasts at least several months. Some people very interested in learning

about their relationships stay in group several years. Sometimes, if you are in combined treatment, you may find it valuable to continue group therapy for a while after stopping your individual work.

Group Turnover.

A therapy group may have the same members from beginning to end, but it is more typical at any time to have one or two new members and another one or two who are in the process of leaving, while the majority have been around for a while and plan to stay on. The rate of turnover of the members may be related to the group's purpose. If a group is set up to give you brief treatment with limited goals, members may come and go rather quickly. But in the most common kind of group, where longer treatment is the aim, the membership is likely to remain the same for long periods.

Special Groups and Special Group Approaches.

In addition to "talking" groups composed of people from a mixture of backgrounds with a mixture of problems, groups with a more specialized makeup or purpose have been used. There are groups composed exclusively of one sex, designed to discuss the particular feelings and problems of members about being male or female. There are groups whose members all have a similar problem—shyness, drug abuse, fear of flying, overweight. Some groups meet at special locations, such as an in-school rap group, where students drop in when they need to talk about problems.

Groups with more than one therapist have been developed. Experts believe that several leaders are often better able to pick up all the complicated interactions that go on in a group than one therapist alone. Having male and female cotherapists can be very useful in an adolescent group, because you get a feeling of a more complete substitute family. With the cotherapists naturally standing in for a mother and father, the members find it easier to work on the problems they're having with their own parents.

Some groups go beyond just talking conversationally about problems. *Encounter* groups stress putting you in better touch with your emotions, getting you to feel your anger, sadness, or joy directly by urging you to shout at group members, cry, stamp your feet, hit a pillow. In *psychodrama* and *role-playing* you act out a scene from your past, present, family, or social life, or even a dream. Group members take part in your scene, playing a mother, a father, a boyfriend or girl friend, or even a part of yourself, like your conscience. The leader helps direct the scene, and may act in it, too.

Some group therapists use these special approaches and techniques all the time, because they believe the plain talking group works too slowly. While I believe many of these techniques are very valuable, especially when a group gets bored and bogged down, I don't think they should replace the natural unfolding of the helpful relationships in group that come about from "just talking."

Who Practices Group?

Like family therapy, group therapy is practiced by many kinds of qualified mental health professionals, including psychiatrists, psychologists, and psychiatric social workers. Medical and nonmedical therapists routinely receive training in group therapy during their education, and may choose to go on to several years of advanced training as well.

The Costs of Group.

Since many patients share the therapist's time in a group, the cost is likely to be lower than an individual session. Privately, group therapy averages about $15 to $30 per session and often clinic group treatment costs even less. Low cost combined with making help available to more patients has played a big part in the rising popularity of group therapy during the past twenty years.

Behavior Therapy

Behavior therapy grew out of research on animal and human learning, which was then applied to the treatment of troubled human behavior. Basically a behavior therapist looks at your symptom or problem as a kind of learned bad habit that has become deeply rooted within you. In a scientific way, the behavior therapist maps out the exact influences and stresses that first create, then strengthen unhelpful psychological habits. Then the therapist sets up a program, using a variety of methods, to "unlearn" your symptoms or problem.

Usually the behavior therapist is not very interested in going into your life history, or finding out as much about your relationships as a therapist consulted for individual talking therapy. Behavior therapy isn't pitched at making you understand all the hidden reasons for your problem. Behavior therapists don't think a deep understanding is really needed to heal many emotional symptoms; they believe your relationships naturally will improve once your problem improves, since emotional difficulties have a way of affecting our relationships for the worse.

So that you can get a better idea of how behavior therapy works, let me describe the approach used to treat a thirteen-year-old girl who came to see me with a bad fear of dogs. She had become phobic after being nipped by an aunt's pet when she was five years old. The bite wasn't serious, and her fear seemed to gradually disappear over the next few years. Her present problem started after a neighbor's German shepherd dog jumped up on her and knocked her down. She wasn't hurt this time either, but her fear of dogs returned even worse than before. Over the next few months she gradually became very afraid of large dogs, then of all dogs, to the point where she actually was beginning to get scared when she left her house. Aside from her dog phobia she was doing well in school, her family and social life was good, and she had no other psychological symptoms. She told me quite openly that she was very turned off to the idea of coming in every week to talk to a shrink and wanted relief from her problem as quickly as possible. I therefore decided to send her to a friend who practices behavior therapy.

My friend agreed with me that she had never really forgotten being bitten as a child. She had continued to worry about dogs throughout her life, especially during stressful times. He noted that she was a middle child, who felt she didn't get as much attention from her parents as an older brother and younger sister. Her parents grew greatly concerned each time they saw her getting a-fraid of a dog, and spent a lot of time reassuring her. The behavior therapist thought that without realizing it, the parents were helping her fear remain rooted, by *rewarding* her with the attention paid to her symptom. (In behavioral language this is called *reinforcing* a piece of behavior or attitude.)

The behavior therapist's program to help the girl with her phobia began by teaching her *deep relaxation*. His method—there are a number of them—was to have her lie down on a couch, close her eyes, and let her muscles go loose, progressing slowly from the bottom of her feet to the top of her head. After she had learned this, the therapist mapped out a series of imaginary scenes involving dogs, beginning with one that created very little fear—imagining she was standing on the doorstep of her house and seeing a man walking far down the block with a small dog on the leash—then moving up through scenes that would ordinarily make her feel more afraid—imagining a middle-size dog trotting right past her—then to the scariest scenes she could think of—imagining petting a dog or having a big dog like the German shepherd jump up on her.

In a series of sessions, each taking an hour, the therapist had the girl relax deeply, then ask her to picture these scenes, starting with the least scary one and staying with it until she could see it clearly in her mind's eye without getting upset; then she passed on to the next scene until she wasn't afraid of it, and so on up the ladder, until at the end of treatment she could imagine all the dog-related activities she was previously afraid of without getting anxious.

As the girl grew less afraid in the imaginary scenes, the therapist encouraged her to put herself into real situations involving dogs, but never in ones that were too scary for her to handle. (Some behavior therapists actually will bring the feared object or animal into the office, or will go with you into the situation you're scared of; this wasn't necessary here.)

The method used to treat this girl's dog phobia is called *desensitization*; it is the best-known technique in behavior therapy. When the girl told the therapist about her successes, he praised her highly, which made her feel even more encouraged to try harder. Here the therapist used another approach called *positive reinforcement*, rewarding the patient's efforts with praise to increase the effectiveness of her desensitization work.

The therapist also met with the girl's parents, and advised them to stop reinforcing her phobia by having them pay as little attention as possible to it. He directed them to pay strong attention to her achievement in school or in Girl Scout activities instead. This change in the direction of reinforcement helped the desensitization work to go even more quickly. By the end of two months the girl was no longer afraid of dogs and could leave her house easily.

Behavior therapy, also called *behavioral modification*, at first was used chiefly to treat such simple phobias. Over the years desensitization, reinforcement, and a wide range of other techniques have been called upon to treat many other problems, including obsessions, compulsions, eating disorders, speech difficulties, bed wetting, and poor study habits. You may want behavior therapy if, like the girl, your problem isn't too complicated, you aren't interested in deep exploration of your problems, or if individual therapy just doesn't appeal to you for some other reason.

You should know that there's always been some disagreement between individual therapists and behavior therapists about behavior modification methods. Some behavior therapists have argued that their treatment should replace ordinary talking therapy altogether, even for complicated, serious conditions. They maintain that behavior therapy is easier to do, takes less time, and is therefore cheaper (although individual behavioral sessions often will cost as much as an individual therapy, from $30 to $70 or more privately). Therapists who believe strongly in an individual talking approach argue back that behavior therapy is too mechanical, treats people like laboratory animals, doesn't pay enough attention to your rich inner life or your outside relationships, only helps surface symptoms or behavior, and leaves deeper personality problems untouched.

Actually, behavior and individual therapists recently have been discovering they have a lot more in common and a lot more to teach each other than was first thought. Behaviorists, for instance, *do* explore your relationships, but from a somewhat different point of view, examining what in them particularly makes you form fixed emotional patterns. And talking therapists *do* spend a lot of time reinforcing positive behavior or discouraging negative attitudes. So the two branches of therapy have become closer. Today there are therapists who will treat your problems with a combination of a behavioral and a talking approach. For some patients, undergoing individual and behavior therapy with two different therapists may be more useful.

Behavior therapy was originated by clinical psychologists, and most specialists in the field are still psychologists. However, this is beginning to change as other mental-health professionals have grown interested in the behavioral approach.

▌ *Biofeedback Therapy*

Just as your mind can be taught unhelpful emotional symptoms from unpleasant, stressful experiences, the organs and tissues of your body can be taught or conditioned by life stress to respond with unhelpful physical reactions like high blood pressure or headaches. Behavior therapy aims at unlearning psychological symptoms. Biofeedback therapy, an offshoot of behavior modification, has proven helpful in unlearning physical problems linked to emotional stress.

Machines used in this approach actually feed back to you a continuous measurement of physical reactions such as skin temperature, pulse rate, level of muscular tension, or brain-wave activity. With a combination of feedback and the relaxation techniques already mentioned, you are taught how to change these physical reactions until you reach a peaceful state of mind in which symptoms decrease or even disappear.

Here's how biofeedback would be used to treat the common problem of the tension headache. Tension headaches are related to tensing of the muscles of the jaws, neck, and forehead. One particular forehead muscle, the *frontalis*, is known to be an extremely sensitive indicator of your tension level. It's easy (and totally painless) to measure the electrical activity of this muscle. Electrical impulses from the frontalis are sent from a pad placed over your forehead through a wire into a biofeedback machine, which changes the impulses into sounds—musical tones or clicks. A lot of electrical activity, signaling you have a lot of tension, will make the machine give off a high-pitched tone or frequent clicks. As the frontalis activity decreases, signaling your tension level is dropping the machine's tone gets progressively lower, or the clicks slow down.

To help your tension headache you are first taught a deep relaxation technique. Then you relax yourself while you are hooked up to the biofeedback machine. You actually hear the message from the machine telling you when you are reaching a more relaxed state. This message, the lower tone or fewer clicks, signals that you are at a "good place," physically and emotionally. It serves as a reward, or *reinforcement*, for the effort you have put in getting there. You continue to practice your relaxation exercise several times a day away from the machine. By repeating the process over and over again, on and off the machine, you eventually get control over your level of muscle tension. When you get a tension headache, you know how to drop your tension level and decrease your symptom. Eventually you will not need the machine anymore to do this. Using similar approaches, you can be taught how to lower your blood pressure, return an abnormal heart rhythm back to normal, and help other physical difficulties related to stress.

Biofeedback therapy has become more popular as its machines have been made simpler, smaller, and cheaper. Now biofeedback techniques are used to treat psychosomatic disorders such as stomach ulcer, to deal with purely emotional problems such as anxiety states, and to promote a peaceful state of mind even if you don't have any problems.

Biofeedback therapy is practiced mostly by psychologists, psychiatrists, and other physicians. A biofeedback therapist will often set up your program with you, and then have you come into the office to practice it with a technician. You may even be able to take a biofeedback machine home to work with.

A biofeedback session lasts about a half hour to an hour, and costs anywhere between $25 to $70 privately. Learning a biobeedback program takes usually between ten and twenty sessions. As with other types of behavior therapy, you may want to come in for a refresher session or two after you have successfully completed your program in order to reinforce what you've learned.

Hypnosis

Hypnosis! The word has a mysterious, even scary ring. It makes you think of Count Dracula, luring his victims to their doom with his piercing stare. While there *is* much that's still mysterious about hypnosis, there's nothing supernatural or scary about it. It was used in primitive rituals, then by all sorts of fakes, quacks, and entertainers, until it began to be studied seriously by doctors two hundred years ago. Sigmund Freud, the father of modern psychotherapy, used hypnosis to further pioneer studies into the hidden depths of the mind, at the turn of the century. Interest in it then died out, but recently new scientific research has reawakened its use in physical and psychological medicine. Hypnosis eliminates pain during surgery, dental work, and the delivery of babies. By itself, or combined with other psychotherapies, it has proven helpful in treating a number of emotional conditions.

We now know that being hypnotized is *not* the same as being asleep, although it may look the same. Under the hypnotist's guidance, you enter into a unusually strong state of mental concentration called *deep trance*. Your awareness of the outside world drops away, to be replaced by attention to the hypnotist's commands. You become very suggestible, follow directions while you are in trance, and even after you awaken. However, you *cannot* be forced into hurting yourself or anyone else, or into doing anything that is criminal or basically against your own ethical beliefs.

In order for you to be hypnotized, the hypnotist establishes an atmosphere of kindness and trust, tells you in a quiet, soothing voice that you will be put into a deep, comfortable sleep. Step by step you are directed into the trance state. The hypnotist may help you along by having you count slowly backward, stare at a slowly moving object like a pen or coin, or listen closely to a loudly ticking clock. Your eyelids get heavier and heavier—they seem to drop like weights—and then you are in the hypnotic state.

Waking up reverses the process that put you under. The hypnotist tells you that your eyelids are getting lighter and lighter, that you are feeling less and less sleepy, and that you will awaken at the end of a count to three.

Since in deep trance you aren't very aware of your surroundings, a good hypnotist will always make sure that you don't accidentally hurt yourself and will also determine that you are fully awake when you come out of your trance, so that you don't leave the office in a daze.

If you're like most people, you have a 70 percent chance of being hypnotizable. How deep your trance is and how easily you respond to the hypnotist's directions differs widely. Some people are naturally more suggestible than others.

Here are some of the uses of hypnosis in the treatment of emotional difficulties:

(1) To remove a symptom completely. Example: telling a girl with a dog phobia during trance that she will no longer be a-afraid after she awakens.

(2) To change the nature or the location of a symptom, thereby making a person feel less ashamed and more comfortable with the "new" symptom. Example: A boy with a severe tic of his

eyelids and cheeks is told under hypnosis that the tic has been switched to his little toe.

(3) To change unhealthy attitudes or driven, addictive behavior. Example: A two-pack-a-day smoker is told to smoke an imaginary cigarette while hypnotized; as he inhales, the hypnotist says he is drawing a deadly poison into his lungs that make him cough; the man is then told that after he awakens, he will feel like coughing out the poison anytime he smokes.

(4) To promote relaxation in tension states. The hypnotist teaches you to enter into a light trance in which you feel more relaxed, but still remain aware of your surroundings. This technique may be used to help you unwind, or to promote sleep when tension causes insomnia. Hypnotic relaxation is one of the techniques used by behavior therapists in desensitization programs.

(5) To help remember forgotten painful experiences. The hypnotist can help you relive hurtful past events you've forced out of your consciousness, which are now causing emotional problems. Hypnosis has been particularly used for this purpose since World War I in treating psychological casualties of combat.

Example: An eighteen-year-old infantryman and his best friend were on patrol in Vietnam when they were surprised by a Vietcong soldier coming down the trail. The friend and the enemy soldier were both killed in an exchange of gunfire. Afterward the infantryman could remember almost nothing about the patrol, but he started drinking heavily, grew extremely depressed, and threatened to kill himself. He was seen by an army psychiatrist, who hypnotized him, then helped him relive the experience. The infantryman described seeing the enemy soldier on the trail stumble upon him and his buddy, step back, and raise his gun. For a second the infantryman froze, and in that second the Vietcong soldier got off the burst of fire that killed his friend. Consciously he had forgotten the frozen moment, but revealed in the trance that he continued to blame himself for not reacting more quickly. The psychiatrist told him he would remember the entire patrol and woke him up. The psychiatrist then pointed out his fine record, told him strongly he was neither a coward nor a goof-up, and said that what had happened to him on that trail could have happened to anyone. It was only a stroke of luck that he had lived and that his friend had received the burst of fire that killed him. Much of his emotional pain came from guilt at having survived. With his pride restored the infantryman quickly recovered from his suicidal depression to feel a more natural sadness at the loss of his friend.

Hypnosis was used in the early days of psychotherapy to recover painful past memories, especially buried childhood events linked to later problems, just as the soldier's depression was related to his forgotten frozen moment. It was then discovered that treatment was more effective for most patients if buried memories were recovered by longer talking therapy while awake, instead of using hypnosis as a shortcut. The issue of hypnotherapy versus talking psychotherapy isn't completely settled today, but in practice hypnosis is used *least* often to understand your past, and most often for the other purposes listed above.

Hypnotic sessions last about an hour, and can be quite expensive—$100 or more. The high cost is balanced by the fewer sessions needed for symptom removal or behavioral change. In some cases as few as one or two sessions will bring relief. Like any other form of psychotherapy, hypnosis doesn't always work. Even when it does, your problems may come back.

Hypnosis is performed by psychiatrists, other physicians, dentists, psychologists, and nonmedical therapists who have received training at a recognized teaching program.

Running and Meditation

It's been known for a long time that regular running can be excellent for improving your general health and helping your heart and circulatory system do a better job. In addition, running, jogging, or brisk walking can help you feel calmer and more cheerful. I've found that swimming laps at a pool, weight lifting, tennis, and other sports produce the same emotional effects for a smaller number of people. I often recommend a half-hour or so of daily jogging or walking to many of my patients who suffer from anxiety and depression. If you've never run before, you'll need some basic facts about the right sort of shoes to wear, stretching exercises before and after running, and health and diet measures to follow while on a running program. For further information I suggest you read *The Complete Book of Running*, by Dr. James Fixx.

Thousands of years before psychotherapy came along, wise men of the Eastern world had perfected powerful meditation techniques for calming unpeaceful thoughts and troubled feelings. Today many of these ancient practices are used in the West, combined with standard psychotherapy to treat a variety of physical and emotional difficulties. To meditate you may sit in a quiet place with your eyes closed, count your breathing, or repeat a word or phrase over and over again while you empty your mind of everything else. Since I don't have the space to describe meditation methods in greater detail, I recommend an excellent, easy-to-follow book called *How to Meditate*, by Dr. Lawrence LeShan. Yoga is a system of physical and mental exercises developed in India thousands of years ago. A powerful tool for promoting a peaceful mind in a healthy body, yoga is quite popular in the West today. Many Y's and community centers offer yoga classes.

▮ *Taking a Stand on "New" Therapies*

▮ You may want to try a new form of psychotherapy because the ordinary individual approach just doesn't make sense to you, or because talking psychotherapy isn't working out. If you aren't satisfied with your treatment, don't hesitate to discuss a change of approaches. Most psychotherapists today know about the newer methods, and should be open to discussing their advantages and disadvantages without an ax to grind. It *is* still possible that your therapist may object strongly to *any* new therapy. Some individual therapists who believe deeply in their work may tell you it's worthwhile to keep plugging away even when treatment isn't going well, rather than run to an easy cure like behavior modification, biofeedback, or hypnosis. You also can find therapists practicing the newer methods who are just as outspoken in recommending their brand of treatment over individual treatment.

Whatever a therapist thinks is the best approach, remember that *you* are the consumer. You, and only you, have the final right to decide what method seems best suited to your particular personality, problem, and amount of patience. And you certainly *should* look into a new treatment if you've been in individual therapy a long time without making much progress.

A Word of Caution

You should be especially careful to check out the background and training of a therapist working in newer fields. It would be best to see someone with a great deal of training and experience. This isn't always possible since these new approaches haven't been around as long as individual therapy, and there aren't as many programs for training therapists in their use. Not everyone who practices a new method will have an advanced degree.

Nevertheless, your therapist should have either (1) received some training in the special field while becoming a recognized health or mental-health professional; (2) taken courses in the special field after graduating from professional training at a recognized hospital, medical school, college, or clinic; or (3) had practical experience learning under the supervision of therapists who are highly qualified in the special field. It's also okay to have therapy with someone who's training in a new treatment approach, as long as your therapist is under close supervision at a recognized teaching program.

20 Psychiatric Hospitalization and Other Out-of-Home Placements

Because of your need for good family relationships during adolescence, a psychotherapist always will try to treat your problem while you live at home. However, this isn't always possible. Your home may be too troubled for your therapy to succeed. Or your condition may be too serious to be helped by outpatient therapy. If you are one of the few patients who will do better living away from home, for a short or long time, a number of possible placements may be suggested. In this chapter I'll mostly discuss psychiatric hospitalization because there is so much fear and ignorance surrounding it. I'll also say a bit about other kinds of placements.

▮ The Psychiatric Hospital

Psychiatric hospitalization is available on special floors in private or public medical hospitals and in hospitals that treat psychiatric problems only. If you live in a small town without a psychiatric hospital program, and/or your problem doesn't require close supervision, you may be treated by a therapist on an ordinary hospital ward, rather than traveling further from home. It is an aim of modern hospital treatment to keep you as close to your family as possible.

▮ When Is Hospital Care Necessary?

A therapist will try to avoid hospitalizing you whenever possible because hospitalization means a serious interruption in your normal activities. Even after hospitalization has helped a lot, some people still feel that they must be terribly damaged emotionally because they were ill enough to be hospitalized. Others like being in the hospital so much they become too dependent on it; they get the idea a hospital always will be an automatic solution to life's problems. Furthermore, our society hasn't reached the point where a person who's been psychiatrically hospitalized is treated as fairly as someone hospitalized for a medical condition. While matters are improving with regard to getting a good job or being admitted to a good school after psychiatric hospitalization, we still have a long way to go before such discrimination ends. It's still hard, with a history of hospitalization, to enter military service or to hold an important political post.

As important as it is to keep you out of a hospital, it's equally vital to know when hospitalization is the only possible way to deal with your situation—when you are crying out that there is no way for you to stay at home, and no other place to get the care you need.

Emergency psychiatric hospitalization may be recommended when you are so disturbed by symptoms, so out of touch with reality, so suicidal, such a threat to others, or so heavily dependent upon substances like drugs or alcohol that you cannot be treated at home or in a less protected place. The seriousness of your condition isn't the only reason for hospitalizing you quickly. Some very troubled people could be managed at home, except that their families aren't calm enough during a crisis. And sometimes, when immediate treatment is needed away from home, no other place is as readily available as a hospital.

Nonemergency psychiatric hospitalization may be advised if you have a psychological problem that is serious and baffling, one which requires a great deal of concentrated study and close observation by trained professionals.

Resistance to Hospitalization.

Most adolescents are even more resistant about entering a psychiatric hospital than starting outpatient psychotherapy. Your parents may have strong objections, too, even though they recognize you are troubled. The fear of psychiatric hospitalization is related mostly to old-fashioned notions of what a hospital is like. Even though great progress has been made in psychiatric hospital treatment, it's amazing how many people still think a hospital is a place where you are dragged against your will by men in white suits, to be locked away, put in a straitjacket, knocked out with medicine, and forced to have weird treatments administered by mad doctors. Here are the realities of how you enter a psychiatric hospital, and what goes on once you are there.

Admission to the Hospital.

The *majority* of patients today enter a psychiatric hospital of their own free will, *voluntarily*. In most of the United States permission of your parent or guardian is needed for hospital treatment if you are underage, but this does not mean you have no control over hospitalization. If you are troubled but still in good touch with reality, a therapist will explain carefully to you why he or she thinks hospitalization is necessary, but will not force hospitalization upon you until you are ready to accept it. On the rare occasion where you are too troubled to recognize the need for your hospital- · ization, and are in serious danger of hurting yourself or others, you can be admitted to a hospital against your will by your parents, or by hospital authorities taking responsibility for your admission. But you *cannot* be kept in the hospital a long time against your will.

In recent years legal authorities have become very concerned with guarding the civil rights of psychiatric patients, including children and adolescents. Many hospitals now have court-appointed lawyers who protect a patient's rights, including the right to manage your financial affairs and to be discharged from the hospital when you want. Soon after entering the hospital you are entitled to see a lawyer, who will seek to win your release if your mind is clear enough for you to understand what is going on, and your condition doesn't make you a threat to society or yourself.

Even if it would be unwise for you to leave, even when your doctors and your parents strongly urge that you stay in the hospital for good reasons, even if your lawyer believes you should stay, he or she will still defend your rights if you insist, because American law maintains that it's more important for you to keep the right to make a wrong decision than to have the right decision made for you by someone else.

Despite what you may have seen in the movies or on TV, most people aren't brought to a psychiatric hospital in an ambulance or by police, but come with their relatives, in their own transportation. Your therapist usually will tell your parents or other family members to go with you to the hospital, since the presence of people you know often lessens anxiety about hospitalization. Whether a therapist has been treating you for a while, or is seeing you for the first time in a crisis, he or she may decide to go with you to the hospital to make admission easier.

If you are so troubled that nobody can convince you to enter a hospital voluntarily, and outsiders such as police or an emergency squad must be called in, it's likely they'll have received special training in dealing with troubled people, and will always try to use words rather than force.

Admission to a psychiatric hospital may not be easy. There are *more* people who need hospitalization in the average community than places to treat them. Lack of hospital space is especially a problem for troubled adolescents. The quickest way for you to get into a psychiatric hospital is to have a psychiatrist arrange for admission to the private psychiatric hospital he or she is connected with. But there aren't that many private hospitals, and they tend to be small and very expensive. So most people in need of urgent psychiatric care are seen in the emergency room of a public hospital, by a staff psychiatrist or a team of mental-health professionals.

Since you may have doubts about going to a public hospital run by your city or state, you should know that public institutions now offer much better psychiatric care than in the past. The quality of services at a public mental hospital may be as good or better than at a private hospital, particularly when the public psychiatric program is connected with a medical school or university.

When you are brought to the psychiatric emergency room, the admitting psychiatric or mental-health worker will talk to you and your relatives, and will often consult with your therapist if you have one. Public hospitals may be under even more pressure to admit patients than private hospitals, and even more short of space. Overcrowding of psychiatric units hurts the quality of care, so you may be sent home, under close supervision, to wait for a space to open up for you. If your family has the funds to handle private hospitalization, but no private space is available and your condition is very serious, you may be admitted for a few days to a public hospital and then transferred when the bed opens up.

Hospitalization and Your Outside Therapist.

If you are already in psychotherapy, it is a good idea for your therapist to continue treating you while you are in the hospital, especially if you will be able to go back home after a short stay. Unfortunately this isn't always possible. Your therapist may not choose to do hospital work, may live too far from the hospital to make regular visits practical, or may not be on the staff of the hospital you are admittted to. However, if your outside therapist can't see you frequently, he or she will usually keep in touch with you by phone, or drop by occasionally to say hello, so that you won't feel abandoned.

The Psychiatric Milieu.

Originally, individual psychotherapy was the most important feature of psychiatric hospitalization. The therapist, usually a psychiatrist, was the most important person in the patient's hospital treatment plan. Nonmedical mental health professionals mainly were supposed to help the therapist by seeing family members, conducting psychological tests, giving out medication, et cetera. The importance of other forms of therapy and of the patient's relationships with other staff members beside the individual therapist wasn't stressed. The therapist made all the principal decisions about medication, visitors, passes, and discharge. Staff carried out orders with little room for discussion.

This kind of hospital care is still available, and you certainly can be helped by it. However, a different approach has been developed in recent years called *milieu* therapy (*milieu* is a French word for "surroundings" or "environment"), which many experts rate the most advanced and effective form of hospital treatment.

Milieu therapy gives you a total therapeutic world in which every staff member on the unit has a say in helping you. Patients themselves join in and play a big part in making the milieu a good place to live and get well. Individual therapy still is an important feature of treatment, but it is fitted into an overall program in which the importance of other new therapies (such as group and family work) and other relationships between staff and patients are fully recognized.

Every group of people living together develops disagreements, but if you're troubled enough to be hospitalized, it's likely that you've had more than your share of difficulties in getting along with others. Every day in the milieu brings plenty of conflicts over a wide range of issues, some directly involving you and others in which you are only indirectly involved.

How do you handle your roommate's accusations that you've stolen his watch, when you haven't? What do you do when Louise asks you to take sides in a quarrel she's having with Sarah, and you think that Sarah is right? What do you say when everyone on the ward wants to watch *Dallas* during the evening recreation period, but you want to see the basketball game? If you've learned unhelpful ways of dealing with people on the outside, you'll have a tremendous number of opportunities in the psychiatric milieu to understand your unhelpful reactions and to develop more healthy behavior by dealing with such issues. Your new knowledge and improved behavior will be applied to similar outside situations when you leave the milieu.

Free and open communication between everyone is emphasized in milieu therapy. Decisions about your treatment by staff aren't simply handed down from above, made only by the individual therapist. Instead management of your situation is based on frequent discussions between all the people who work with you in other therapeutic areas besides individual psychotherapy. This pooling of information gives the staff a much better picture of the progress you're making and means better care for you. You and your fellow patients also may become involved in making decisions about the welfare of particular patients, and general ward policies.

In the old kind of adolescent psychiatric hospital program, every staff member pretty much stuck to one job. The psychiatrist ran the ward and concentrated on individual therapy. Nurses nursed. Teachers taught. In a modern psychiatric milieu a staff member's job is not so narrowly defined. The ward may be run by a psychologist. Mental-health workers other than psychiatrists practice psychotherapy. All staff members are encouraged to take part in additional therapeutic tasks besides their main jobs. A nurse and teacher will colead an adolescent therapy group under a psychiatrist's supervision. More service is given to you, and staff members have a chance to learn new skills.

Adolescent Milieu Therapy.

At one time psychiatric hospitals treated adolescents just like adults. With the growing appreciation of the special problems and needs of adolescence, specialized approaches to the hospital treatment of teen-agers were blended with modern milieu therapy. Today it's common for there to be a separate milieu for adolescents in the psychiatric hospital. When teen-agers are placed in the same milieu as adults, they are provided with their own separate programs and treatment experiences, staffed by mental health professionals trained to work with adolescents.

A modern adolescent psychiatric hospital program or adolescent milieu offers the following treatment experiences:

Individual psychotherapy. This may be performed by your outside therapist, or a member of the milieu staff. You'll probably be seen two to three times a week in individual sessions. Your therapist will chat with you informally every day or so for a few moments, to see how you are getting along, and will often be present if a crisis arises.

Medication. Most people troubled enough to require psychiatric hospitalization usually need some form of medication at some point during their stay, perhaps throughout their stay, and after they leave. Although a psychiatrist prescribes medication, other staff members know about it, and their opinions frequently will be sought in regulating your drugs.

Family guidance and therapy. Early, active involvement of your family in your hospitalization is often the key to successful treatment. Your parents and other important family members will be interviewed at your admission, to get their picture of your problems. Afterward they will be kept up to date about your progress. Their opinions will be carefully considered in making important decisions. If necessary, counseling of family members or family therapy will be provided.

Group therapy and other group experiences. Milieu therapy is really one big, continuous experience in group living. More special group experiences also will be offered. There are *adolescent therapy groups* composed of about six to eight of your fellow patients, led by one or two staff members, run like outpatient adolescent groups. Here you share your problems on the outside as well as your experiences in the hospital. In *unit meetings* the entire ward staff and patients meet in a large group to air gripes, discuss scheduling of activities, and work through issues of daily unit life. In many milieus there is one long unit meeting every week, and a shorter meeting every morning to discuss the day's program.

Tests. All the tests described earlier in this book usually can be performed in a quick, concentrated fashion in the hospital. You'll routinely get a complete physical examination—some basic blood tests, analysis of your urine, and perhaps a brain-wave study (EEG) and X ray of your skull—to make sure your problems are purely emotional. You may have psychological testing as well. More specialized tests will be ordered as your condition requires.

School. Most adolescent milieus that treat you longer than a few days now have schoolroom facilities, with one or more teachers trained to educate troubled teen-agers. The unit school allows a vital part of your normal outside life to continue. Class size is likely to be very small, with individual attention to your educational needs. Your milieu teachers observe first-hand how your emotional problems have affected your school performance outside. They can pick up special learning problems such as a reading disability. If necessary your unit teach will contact your school, get reports on how you were doing before hospitalization, and work out a good educational program for you after your discharge.

Vocational guidance and therapy. Many milieus, especially those with older adolescent patients, now offer vocational guidance to find out the sort of work you are best suited for, and to arrange job training and placement with outside agencies during or after your hospitalization.

Activity therapy. The activity program fights a universal problem of the psychiatric hospital—*boredom.* Activities provide you with outlets for your natural energy, encourage you to express yourself artistically and through movement, and help you become better related to others through cooperative tasks.

Activity therapists organize your participation in dancing, sports, arts, and crafts. They teach practical living skills such as cooking and sewing. Day trips off the unit to movies and museums are often provided. Even overnight trips to activities further away, like camping and fishing, may be planned.

Psychiatric nursing. The special caring experiences described above couldn't get off the ground if it weren't for the psychiatric nursing staff, which includes nurses with special training in psychiatry and aides or attendants who have received on-the-job training. The nursing staff attends to your basic living needs on the ward, sees that you get to bed and awaken at a reasonable time, makes sure you are properly fed, washed, clothed, medicated, and sent to scheduled activities on time. There are usually three shifts of nursing staff—day, evening, and night.

Of all the milieu members, it's nursing personnel who spend the most time in direct contact with you—including listening to gripes and managing crises big and small, such as a suicide attempt, a fistfight, and a lonely kid waking up in tears from a bad dream at three in the morning. If you ask most teen-agers who helped them in the hospital, you'll be surprised to find that instead of naming the therapist, they'll mention a nursing staff member.

Living Conditions.

The typical psychiatric hospital milieu or unit has about fifteen to thirty patients of both sexes living together. When adults and adolescents are mixed together, about a third of the patients will be teen-agers. Whenever possible the milieu will duplicate healthy living conditions on the outside. For instance, instead of pajamas and gowns, you'll dress in your everyday clothes. Staff members often wear street clothes, too, with name tags to identify them.

Many milieus are kept unlocked throughout the day (quite often twenty-four hours a day), so that the ward will not seem like a prison, and you will have a greater sense of freedom and self-respect. It's been found that keeping the psychiatric unit open often *stops* people from running away because running away doesn't seem like such a challenge.

Having a living space you can call your own in the hospital is very important for a teen-ager. Some hospitals are able to give you a private room with shower and toilet facilities. But it's more common, and perhaps more helpful in learning how to get along with others, for several patients to share one room, with separate beds, closets, or lockers. Showers and toilet facilities usually are located elsewhere on the ward. Often the ward living spaces will be divided so that men live on one side and women on the other.

To give you a greater feeling of responsibility for living conditions in the milieu, you'll be asked to keep your own room tidy; you may also be requested to do simple chores around the unit such as cleaning up ashtrays. Most hospitals have a housekeeping staff to do heavier cleaning, but some milieus have even experimented successfully with having staff and patients do *all* the tasks necessary to keep the unit comfortable.

Most psychiatric milieus have the following living and working areas:

The nursing station. This is a centrally located area where medication is given out and records are kept. A nursing station has a lot of clear window space so that staff can keep track easily of what's going on in the ward. It's a natural place for nursing staff to meet informally with each other and with other staff members, and for patients to come with their problems.

The dining area. Your meals will be brought from a central kitchen located elsewhere in the hospital, or prepared on the ward itself. Food usually is served cafeteria fashion by kitchen staff or nursing staff. People eat informally, at tables that seat two to four. In some milieus patients and staff eat at the same time and in the same place. Everyone generally eats the same food, and the selection isn't always that great (the biggest complaint I've heard in hospital work is not about therapy, but about food). A dietician may·be available to set up diets for patients with special nutritional problems—overweight, underweight, diabetes, et cetera.

Between meals and at nighttime snacks such as juice and cookies will be served. Your relatives also will be allowed to bring you snacks, as long as this doesn't get out of hand (the wealthy parents of one girl I treated brought her a whole sliced turkey because they were afraid the hospital wasn't giving her enough to eat). Most hospitals have canteens, coffee shops, or food machines where you can use your own money for treats. In many adolescent milieus you are given a weekly allowance out of your own funds for food, cigarettes (if smoking is allowed), and other small items. Less fortunate youngsters receive money from ward funds for their needs.

The day room. This is a large, comfortable area with many couches and chairs, where you socialize with other patients, staff, and your relatives during visiting hours. The day room contains items like a TV set, a phonograph, and a Ping-Pong table. On larger units there may also be a room for recreational equipment.

The quiet room. This is a place set aside for you if you become very troubled, upset, or angry, when you have made such a disturbance in normal ward activity that other people can't go about their business, or when normal ward activity seems to be making you very upset. A quiet room is *not* a dungeon cell where staff members dump you, lock the door, and throw away the key. You'll only be asked to go there when every other method has failed to calm you down. The least amount of physical persuasion will be used to get you there, in line with the hands-off approach typical of a modern psychiatric unit. Today restraints of any sort are rarely used in psychiatric hospitals. Staff only uses force when nothing else works, and there's a serious danger of someone being harmed. And staff members usually have received training in special techniques for restraining people without hurting them.

Some people do better left alone in a quiet room, and will even request that they be put there and left alone for a while. Others pull together faster when a staff member can sit with them. The quiet room will be used mostly for brief periods, with the idea of returning you to social contact quickly. Locking the door of a quiet room is discouraged—in fact in many states it's *illegal*. There is usually only a mattress or a soft chair in the quiet room, so that no one can get hurt.

Offices. Doctors' and other therapists' offices; school-rooms; conference rooms; craft, occupational, and music therapy rooms may be located on your unit or elsewhere in the hospital.

Recreational areas. Many hospitals provide some sort of space on or off the milieu where you can exercise, play, dance, and generally let off steam. I believe the lack of good recreational facilities is still one of the biggest problems in hospital treatment. Some hospitals do have a gym, an outside playing field, even a swimming pool, but these facilities aren't nearly as available as they should be, especially in public psychiatric programs.

Laundry room. Rather than have your folks lug your dirty laundry back and forth, many psychiatric milieus now provide their own washers and dryers which you are encouraged to use.

▌ *Your Treatment Plan.*

Just as in outpatient psychotherapy, the people taking care of you in the hospital will work out, with your help, a treatment plan geared to your special needs and difficulties, covering the type of therapy you'll receive, medication you'll be taking, the visitors you'll be allowed to see, and your ward passes and privileges.

Basic Expectations.

Even though you may be very troubled, a basic level of reasonable behavior will *still* be expected, concerning things like your grooming, your sleeping and eating habits, and your general ward behavior. It's been found that a *big* factor in your getting better in the hospital is the clear expectation by staff *and* other patients that you can get your act together.

An example of how healthy expectations help a patient get well was the case of a fourteen-year-old obsessive-compulsive boy who quickly found he wasn't making himself popular with other kids on the ward by keeping them waiting for a trip while he washed his hands fifty times. At home he had had almost no friends, had been increasingly afraid to go outside, and his parents had let his compulsions run their lives. On the ward, with healthy feedback from his peers about his behavior, he soon began making his first serious efforts to control the handwashing compulsion. Then his other compulsions began to improve, too.

Rules and Regulations.

In order to get its job done, a psychiatric milieu must have guidelines and rules. Some rules are very clear-cut: no drugs allowed on the unit, no physical violence. Others are more open to question and change. Your ward staff will be flexible about many guidelines and will be ready to stretch rules covering situations that aren't clear-cut and suspend rules that don't make sense anymore. However, the staff will be firm when important rules are broken. Penalties can range from a temporary loss of canteen privileges if you are caught smoking in a nonsmoking area, to being sent off the unit permanently for doing something cruel to another patient (this happens rarely).

Whether setting limits or enforcing rules, staff reacts

firmly but *not* angrily. Limits are being laid down not because staff is angry at you, out to get you, or likes to throw its weight around, but so that you will learn that your behavior is unhelpful, unsocial, or downright wrong.

Restrictions and suspensions of privileges aren't required just because you've acted up. You may need to have your activity limited when you become too upset to leave the unit. Sometimes a weekend pass will have to be canceled through no fault of your own because your family is in bad shape. It's hard here not to feel punished or rejected, but please recognize that these things are being done *for* you, not against you.

Since you have to live according to unit rules, many experts believe it's fair that you and your fellow patients should play a part in making and enforcing them. Your milieu may have a committee of patients who meet regularly with staff for this purpose. In some advanced psychiatric milieus, patients form their own ward government whose members are chosen by secret vote. With limited help from staff, the patient government sets various ward policies and penalties for breaking rules, assigns chores, and settles differences. Outsiders find it hard to believe that troubled people can still be healthy enough to govern themselves, but experience has shown that patient government works, and is in itself an effective form of therapy. It teaches you to deal with differing points of view, to handle responsibility, and to recognize the rights of others.

Progress in the Hospital.

When you enter the hospital, you may have limits on your movement off the ward if you're very suicidal, seriously out of touch with reality, or are behaving aggressively. You also may need such limits simply because you aren't known very well to the staff. As you improve and staff knows you better, you'll have more freedom, including passes to go elsewhere in the hospital with or without a staff member, to canteen, religious services, et cetera. When your condition permits, you'll be given passes to go home during the day, overnight, and over weekends. Home passes maintain your surrounding for a year or longer, in some cases even for the rest of their teens. Conditions that may require a very long hospital stay include serious cases of schizophrenia or other psychoses; deep, suicidal depressions; crippling, widespread phobias and obsessions; or life-threatening illnesses such as anorexia nervosa.

A long-term, private psychiatric hospital that offers the services described above is just too expensive for most people. A few private psychiatric hospital milieus in America do provide adolescents this kind of care for $50,000 or more per year. Most youngsters in such hospitals come from well-to-do families, although a few may be treated with scholarship funds. Thus if you do need long-term hospital care, the chances are you will get it at a public psychiatric hospital run by your state.

In the past state hospitals often were described as snake pits, huge, cold-looking places, located far from cities, with too many patients, too few therapists, and very limited treatment. I'm happy to tell you that conditions really have improved at many state institutions, because the greater interest in mental health since World War II has led to more public money being funded to state hospitals. Over the past thirty years the quality of care has been upgraded in older hospitals, while newer hospitals are being built that are smaller, homier, and easier to reach. Things are still far from perfect, but many state hospitals do offer long-term adolescent treatment programs with a reasonable quality of treatment.

▮ *The Residential Treatment Center*

This institution treats adolescents with serious emotional problems for a year or much longer, and provides many of the healing experiences of the psychiatric hospital (psychotherapy, special schooling, recreational programs), but with more open living arrangements than in a hospital. There are fewer limits and restrictions on your activities, especially after you have been living at a

family relationships, and give the staff a chance to see how you get along in outside situations that may have caused you trouble before.

Because of your strong natural recovery powers and the wide range of effective treatment methods, chances are your time in the hospital will be short. The average stay in my experience with most hospitalized adolescents is a week to a month. At various times in your stay, and especially around the time you are ready to leave, your case probably will be presented to a *staff conference*. The staff who've been working with you will review your history, your progress, and discuss future plans. At the conference you may be interviewed by a specialist in adolescent psychology from the outside, the therapist who is treating you, the person who runs the ward, or another staff member. Your family may be asked to attend, too.

It can be kind of scary talking about yourself in public, but you'll know most of the people at the conference already, and care will be taken not to get into topics embarrassing to you. Your opinions about your problems and about your stay in the hospital will be asked, and if any decisions are made at the conference, you will be told about them. You don't have to attend a planning conference if you don't want to, and you can leave anytime you want if you feel upset. I've found most youngsters *do* want to attend, stay the whole time, and find the conference useful.

▮ *Easing Out.*

If you've been doing well but it isn't certain that you're ready to be discharged, the hospital may ease you back into everyday life by having you go back to regular school or other outside activities during the day, then return to the ward each night. Your weekend passes at home may be stretched out to several days to see how you get along before discharge. If there's no question about your improvement, you'll be discharged without easing out.

▮ *Follow-up.*

Whether you've been in treatment before or not, it's frequently a vital part of your care to have good follow-up, either privately or through a clinic. If hospitalization has interrupted outside psychotherapy, the milieu will keep in touch with your therapist and make sure he or she is ready to resume treatment before discharging you, or will arrange for another private therapist to see you if your former therapist can't pick up the ball.

Perhaps psychiatric hospitalization is the beginning of your treatment, for the crisis you've passed through may indicate you and your family will need more help. Some hospitals offer their own follow-up, and you may even be treated by the same therapist who saw you in the hospital. Others can't offer their own follow-up, but will help you find it elsewhere. Teen-agers often need additional services besides psychotherapy after hospitalization (special schools, reading therapy, vocational training)—and a good adolescent milieu will set up these services for you before your discharge.

Day Hospitalization.

In recent years many psychiatric hospitals have developed day treatment programs that provide the services described above with one *big* difference: You continue to live at home and attend the hospital program, much the way you would go to school.

A day program allows you to get the intensive care you need when you are very troubled, while keeping up your natural outside ties, which isn't as easy to do when you have to be away from home twenty-four hours a day. With day hospitalization you don't feel so different, you aren't as likely to think of youself as sick when you can go back home at the end of every day. Your parents also appreciate having you home, and therefore may find it easier to follow various treatment suggestions.

Day hospital treatment may be recommended for you in these situations:

(1) When it is very difficult for you to participate in your ordinary activities but your condition isn't quite serious enough to make hospitalization a must. Your family should be strong enough for you to stay at home.

(2) When you need to be in a hospital, but you[ ] raises such strong objections that the only way to get tr[ ] started is to give day hospitalization a trial.

(3) When you've been hospitalized for a while, a[ ] ready to live at home, but still cannot return to regular a[ ] outside your home.

Day treatment may be worked into a regular ad[ ] psychiatric milieu, so that you attend the same activities as you[ ] who live in the hospital all the time. A day program may be[ ] elsewhere in the hospital, or in a location away from the h[ ] like a clinic or community center. Day hospitalization may b[ ] but some seriously troubled youngsters require it for several[ ]

Day programs are extremely effective. Experts agr[ ] if more of them were available, a lot of people wouldn't hav[ ] hospitalized in the first place, or wouldn't have to stay in a h[ ] as long. Unfortunately, there aren't nearly enough day hospi[ ] they are particuarly hard to find in smaller cities and towns.

Cost of Hospital Care.

Overnight psychiatric hospitalization is *extremely* [ ] sive (another point in favor of day hospitalization, becaus[ ] cheaper). Even in a public hospital care costs several hundre[ ] lars a day, and the figure is even higher for private hospitals. I[ ] most health insurance programs do cover almost all of the co[ ] several weeks or months of inpatient hospitalization, which is[ ] the time most teen-agers need to recover from their problems[ ]

Long-term Psychiatric Hospitalization

Ideally, hospitalization should take place close to [ ] you live, and last a brief time. You should return quickly to[ ] home, community, and everyday activities. But even with the[ ] up-to-date methods, there still are some adolescents whose [ ] lems are so severe that they have to remain in a protected h[ ]

center for a while. You assume more responsibility in managing your life than you would in a hospital. You spend much more time outside and are freer to come and go.

Less medication or none at all is given at a residental center. Although the center usually is directed by a psychiatrist, therapy is often practiced by nonmedical therapists. Residential treatment centers tend to be located in the country and look like a collection of small houses or cottages. The atmosphere is homey. You live with a small group of people on a floor or in a cottage, and deal with the same staff and patients for a long time. Staff lives nearby or at the center itself. Many staff may not be nurses, but people who after graduating high school or college have had some sort of special training in dealing with troubled adolescents.

A residential treatment center is meant to be a home away from home; visits with your family take place less frequently than during hospitalization. Your family may come to see you or you may go home to them every few weeks or months. Toward the end of your stay, you go on home visits more often, as you ease back into your regular life again.

If you've been hospitalized, have improved to the point where you no longer need close observation, but still have serious problems remaining that require long-term care, a residential treatment center may be the best place for you, especially if your family has so many of its own problems it can't begin to handle yours. Residential treatment also has proven useful in the treatment of delinquents, who don't do well in a standard psychiatric hospital They resent being put in the same place with more obviously troubled people, and they act up and ruin other patients' care. But living with kids like themselves in a center staffed by skilled people who know how to be both tough and kind, they have a much better chance of developing healthier behavior patterns.

Residential treatment centers are run privately, as well as by public, community, and religious agencies. Staying at a private residential center is very expensive, but many nonprivate centers do provide for treatment at low or no cost. The main problem with getting into residential treatment isn't the expense involved, but the lack of centers compared with the many young people who need them.

As with other placements described in this chapter, you may be referred to a residential treatment by a private or clinic psychotherapist, by a social or community agency, by another institution you're already staying at, or by a judge of the juvenile court.

▌ *The Drug House*

A drug house is a special residential treatment center for the heavy drug abuser—the head whose life is totally centered around drugs and the drug scene. Like a delinquent, a heavy drug abuser often doesn't do well in a psychiatric hospital. A hospital may help withdraw a head safely from drugs (detoxification), or straighten out the head's head after a bad drug trip, but it is rarely the right place to help the serious personality problems that caused drug abuse in the first place. Heavy abusers don't do well in outpatient therapy either, because their involvement with the drug scene is more important than anything else, including getting to a therapy session.

A drug house program aims at treating the very behavior problems other approaches fail with. The house is run very tightly, even more tightly than many hospitals. The rules for getting up, going to bed, and going outside are very strictly enforced, because heads lack the inner discipline to set their own limits and manage their own lives well. Youngsters who break the rules repeatedly are quickly asked to leave the house.

A drug house follows a *level system* (which also has been used by other institutions). At the beginning of your stay you are placed at the lowest level, with many limits on your activities and privileges. You then move up the ladder to higher levels, as you show increasing responsibility both in your behavior toward others, and in the performance of the tasks assigned to you. If you break the rules or don't handle new responsibilities easily, you are moved down to a lower level until you improve again.

A drug house staff often includes ex-abusers (who have themselves been through a drug house program), working under the supervision of mental health professionals. Group therapy is more important than individual counseling. A forceful group approach seems to be the most effective method for getting drug abusers to stop running away from everyday life stress through drugs (many of the special group encounter techniques mentioned earlier were developed from work with drug addicts and alcoholics at places like Synanon). Vocational training is heavily stressed because of the great difficulty abusers have handling steady work. Drug houses are sometimes called *drug-free programs* because the use of *any* medication to calm anxiety is frowned upon.

▌ *Placement for Teen-agers with Family Problems*

▌ The following placements are recommended when it's not wise for you to stay at home because your family is troubled by physical or emotional illness, or because it can't function as a family due to parental abandonment, death, or divorce. You may be able to get some psychotherapy in these placements, but their chief aim is to provide you with a secure, comfortable place for your adolescence to unfold normally.

▌ *Living with Relatives or Friends.*

▌ Staying with relatives or friends looks as though it should be a good arrangement for living away from home, because you are staying with people who at least know you instead of total strangers, and in a family setting instead of an institution. But it can turn out to be a disaster if friends or relatives are emotionally troubled, don't have a clear picture of what they're getting into, take you in because of anger toward your parents, or *really* don't want you but can't admit it.

You must remember that living with others will cause a stress for you and your substitute family. Because you feel grateful for being taken in, you may find yourself acting extra "good," and then feeling frustrated when you can't let off steam and express yourself openly. Because people may be trying extra hard to treat you better than you were treated at home, they may not set proper limits for you. Or out of a belief that your parents have been *too* soft, they may exercise unfair strictness. Natural children may react badly to you, get jealous, pick fights, or simply act as if you aren't there. You may find the way your new family runs is so totally different from your own family that you can't adjust, no matter how hard you try.

Over the years I have seen too many well-meaning people offer their homes to adolescents, then back down from their agreement once trouble began. The teen-ager was forced to leave, and his or her situation became even more difficult than before. Of course this may never happen to you. But with all the things that can go wrong, I'd think twice about living with relatives or friends. I strongly suggest that if you are planning such a step, you and your family consult with a mental health professional (if you aren't in therapy already). Perhaps a therapist should even meet with the people you're thinking of living with to see what they're like, clarify their reasons for wanting you, and help them adjust to the change if you decide to move in.

The Foster Home.

Foster care means living with people who take in other peoples' children because of their emotional and/or financial needs. Foster placement offers many of the same good possibilities as living with relatives or friends. You grow up in a family atmosphere instead of an institution. The fact that foster parents usually don't know you beforehand may work in your favor. Because they aren't personally involved with your family, foster parents may be less likely to bear your parents a grudge, or feel they have anything to prove about how their care will compare with the care you've received. They may form a clearer picture of your situation than someone who is already close to you, and hopefully won't spoil you or be improperly strict.

Unfortunately you may find the *same* problems in a foster home as you would in the home of a relative or friend, plus some *new* ones. Just because you *are* living with complete strangers, they may not feel as sympathetic to your situation as someone who knows you better. Many foster parents do an excellent job but, sad to say, some are just interested in the money they get every month from the agency that's placed you. Or they may be too emotionally troubled to give an adolescent from a troubled home a healthy growth experience. There are foster parents who are good at raising little kids, but who just can't adjust to having a teen-ager around. In fact most foster parents don't like dealing with teen-age problems, so it's harder to find a foster home for adolescents than for children.

Relationships between foster and natural children often are more strained than between children who have some blood relationship. A foster child may feel like the Cinderella of the family, the one blamed for everything that goes wrong, the one who has to do all of the dirty work.

Problems may even arise when foster placement goes well. Sometimes natural parents grow jealous of strong ties between their child and foster parents. They may demand the child be returned to them, which they usually have a legal right to do. It's then terribly painful to return to your old family when you've felt for a long time that your new family is your *real* family. And think of the pain foster parents feel about losing someone they've grown to love.

I'm against foster placement for most teen-agers, because

I think it raises more problems than it solves. I've seen too many kids have their adolescence ruined by being passed from one foster home to another, or being forced to return to parents they didn't really want to live with anymore. Unless you have a strong possibility of going to foster parents who have the very special ability to raise other peoples' children, you'd better look into other placements.

The Group Home.

Many experts in adolescent development have always maintained that group living is better for teen-agers than foster-home placement, and perhaps even better than living with relatives. A lot of the tension that builds up in a family placement doesn't get generated in a larger group setting, or else it seems to blow over more easily. These days it's more likely that an institution called a *group home* will be recommended to you rather than foster care.

At a group home you live with other teen-agers in a pleasant, reasonably supervised setting, attend regular school and other activities which may be located in or outside the home, and do various chores around the home. A group home serves anywhere from twenty to several hundred youngsters who stay in smaller groups in cottages or dormitories.

Group homes are sponsored by social, community, and religious agencies. They are located in cities or in more countrified settings. Staff members often live near or at the home, especially when it is run by members of religious orders such as Catholic nuns or brothers. Instead of working in shifts, staff frequently will be available around the clock, much as adults would be in a regular family. The relationships you make with staff and other kids can be as close as those at home. These people become another family for you if you stay with them long enough.

A group home isn't really the right place for someone with extremely serious emotional problems. You probably will have a social worker or some other staff member assigned to you who will help you with your financial needs, medical care, contact with family members, and plans for job or school after leaving the home. You may be able to get psychotherapy, too, either with a mental health professional who visits the home, or through an outside clinic or private therapist.

While life is supervised at a group home, the controls and limits aren't as strict as a hospital or a residential treatment center. You have an evening curfew time, but as you get older you'll be given increasing freedom to come and go as you please, to school, after-school jobs, sports events, even dates.

It's not unusual to stay at a group home for several years, sometimes into your mid- or late teens. Many group homes are prepared to care for you throughout your adolescence, and after graduating high school youngsters can go directly from the home to college, military service, or to a job and living on their own.

While a group home isn't cheap to run, staying at one is not as expensive as a hospital or residential center. Most group homes receive some kind of public or charitable support, which allows many teen-agers to be taken care of at low or no cost to their families.

The Boarding School.

A boarding school is a live-in educational institution, usually located in a country or small town setting fairly far away from your home if you come from a big city. Boarding schools sometimes are called *preparatory* or *prep* schools, a name that comes from the days when the majority of youngsters went out into the world after high school, except for the few fortunate enough to get a private education to prepare them for college. The purpose of today's boarding school is *still* to give you a good high-school education before college. Most boarding schools are especially big on athletics and other extra-curricular activities, too.

You live on the grounds of a boarding school in dormitories or cottages, with one or more roommates. Many schools today are coeducational. Your life is supervised by teaching staff and administrative staff, many of whom live at or near the school. You go home over several short vacations during the year, and have a long summer vacation. Limits and discipline differ greatly from one boarding school to another. Some schools are run very strictly, while others are quite relaxed. In general the more advanced your school year, the more freedom you'll be given to come and go.

A few boarding schools do specialize in educating and caring for kids with emotional problems, and may even have psychotherapists nearby to give treatment. However, most boarding schools are interested in teaching you, *not* treating you, and most students aren't there to get away from troubled homes. They attend because they and their families believe a boarding school is a good way to combine a first-rate education with a healthy growth experience. But if you're reasonably secure emotionally, have been doing fairly well in ordinary school, and are having serious family problems, a regular boarding school may be a very good answer to your difficulties.

If you're already in treatment at home, a big factor to consider before you go away to a boarding school is that you'll have to stop seeing your therapist regularly, and it probably won't be easy to find an adolescent psychotherapist near your school. On the other hand being away from your family may take enough pressure off you so you no longer need therapy. Over the years I've sent a number of kids I've been treating to boarding school, and have been pleasantly surprised at how well they did. Frequently they didn't need further therapy, or were able to get along with a couple of sessions during vacations.

Boarding school costs anywhere between $3,000 and $10,000 a year, so your family will have to be fairly well off to afford it. Some scholarship help is usually available for students from less wealthy backgrounds. Boarding schools specializing in adolescents with emotional problems may receive public or charitable funds, allowing them to take in more youngsters from lower-income families.

Military School.

A military school is a boarding school run like a service academy, along the lines of West Point or Annapolis. Discipline is very strict. You must obey your superiors—teachers, the administrators of the school, many of whom are retired military officers, and upperclassmen as well. You will wear a uniform and have a rank. In addition to your regular class work you will study military subjects like history of war, and perform military duties like having your room inspected, marching, standing guard duty, and going on maneuvers.

Unfortunately some parents of youngsters with behavioral, delinquent, or other emotional problems may be advised to send their child to a military school to "get straightened out with a little old-fashioned discipline." I think military school is the *last* thing troubled teen-agers need. Instead of straightening out, many adolescents feel terribly rejected and punished by being packed off to a military school. Usually they wind up doing even worse there than at home. Even if they look as though they've adjusted, they are probably quietly hating the school and their parents for sending them there.

I believe that the *only* reason you should go to military school is if you are interested in a military career, for it *will* give you a fine preparation for entering a service academy.

Placements When You're in Trouble with the Law

If you've gotten into trouble with the law, and you are underage (in most states underage is sixteen years and less for boys, eighteen and less for girls), your case probably will be referred to the Youth Division of your city or state court. You'll have a special Youth Division juvenile officer assigned who'll interview you and your family, and speak with anyone bringing a charge against you.

The officer will arrange for an interview with a court psychiatrist if necessary, set up other required psychological or medical tests, and then prepare a report for the judge of the juvenile court.

Most offenses committed by teen-agers do not go to jury trial, unless an offense is very serious and you are old enough to be considered adult by your state. In fact, what brings most adolescents into court isn't real crimes but difficulties like running away from home a lot, truancy, or unwillingness to obey parental discipline.

Whatever your problem, you'll probably have a hearing before a judge instead of a trial. Your side of the case will be argued by a lawyer appointed by the court or chosen by your family. A lawyer from the state or local district attorney's office will present the case against you if there is one. Because of increasing concern about protecting legal rights of adolescents, a judge may appoint a lawyer to act in your behalf even in noncriminal matters such as running away. You have the right to ask for your own lawyer if the judge neglects to appoint one, or if your wishes about your situation are opposed by your parents or guardian.

The judge listens to the evidence presented, goes over the juvenile officer's report, and then decides what to do right away, or after further hearings. In a criminal matter both your attorney and the opposing attorney already may have agreed on a recommendation before the hearing begins, which they will present to the judge. But sometimes they cannot agree. Since the judge's decision is what finally counts, it's very important that he or she be completely fair and unprejudiced. If you feel a judge's decision has not been right, you may ask your lawyer to *appeal* it to a higher court.

Whenever possible a judge will try to keep an adolescent living at home. In noncriminal juvenile problems or less serious criminal offenses, the judge will usually recommend some kind of outpatient approach—individual psychotherapy, family therapy, or continued outside supervision by the juvenile officer for a set time. In many states it's possible to have a record of minor juvenile crimes legally erased after a year or two so that your future isn't affected.

If a judge decides that you and your family are too troubled, or your offense is too serious to allow you to stay at home, any of the away-from-home placements mentioned above may be recommended. If a proper placement isn't available right away and you can't stay at home to wait for one, a judge may order you to go to a juvenile hall, youth shelter, or a group home run by your local government for temporary placement. Many of these institutions have good services, with their own schools and recreational programs. Some aren't very good. In my experience the problem with all of them is that they often aren't so temporary. Sadly, because of the shortage of proper placements, you can spend many weeks waiting at a youth shelter for the right placement.

If you are guilty of a serious criminal offense (and even in some states if your offense is minor or noncrminal), it's possible that a judge won't allow you to stay at home, and won't send you to an ordinary placement. Instead you may be sent to a special institution known as a reform school, training school, or juvenile detention or correctional facility. Your stay there if you are underage may range from several months to years, depending on the nature of your crime and your state's policy on sentencing adolescents. No matter what fancy name these correctional institutions are given, they're really like jails. Many have bars and guards, and they are run with the same harsh discipline found in an adult jail. Many have the same problems as adult jails, too—overcrowding, poor recreational and educational facilities, fighting, and homosexual assaults.

Most adolescent offenders have serious emotional problems aside from their criminal activity. I wish I could say that as much progress has been made in the care offered by correctional institutions as in the hospital treatment of adolescents, but I can't. There are a few places, a very few, that are secure, escape-proof, and give care to youthful offenders similar to the treatment provided by a psychiatric hospital milieu or a residential treatment center. But the average adolescent correctional institution today still offers little, if any, treatment beyond a school, a gym, an exercise yard, and shops to learn simple trades. Very few young people get reformed at a reform school. Frequently they come back into society more emotionally crippled than before. Instead of being straightened out, they've actually learned more ways to act antisocially, and are now set up for a career in crime, with the strong possibility that they will spend most of their adult lives behind bars.

Afterword

In the bibliography that follows I've listed other books about psychotherapy and teen-age emotional problems. If you want more information about where to go to get help for yourself or your family, you'll find the names and addresses of national organizations concerned with mental health which can furnish you with the addresses and phone numbers of their local branches near you. You may also write to me, if you wish, % Four Winds Press, 730 Broadway, New York, NY 10003.

During the terrible depression of the 1930s, President Franklin D. Roosevelt brought hope to millions of Americans with bold new programs for economic recovery. In a famous speech at that time he said: "We have nothing to fear but fear itself." I've shown you how it's possible to overcome the despair and suffering of psychological illness through psychotherapy and other new treatments. But in order to get help you first will have to look your fears about treatment squarely in the eye, and make up your mind not to let them stand in your way. Remember, when it comes to getting the help you need, you, too, have nothing to fear but fear itself.

Bibliography

Berry, James R. *Kids on the Run: The Stories of Seven Teen-age Runaways*. New York: Four Winds Press, 1978.
Runaways explore their motives for leaving home.

Boekman, Charles. *Surviving Your Parents' Divorce*. New York: Franklin Watts, 1980.
How to cope, how to share feelings, et cetera.

Carlson, Dale Bick. *Boys Have Feelings Too: Growing Up Male for Boys*. New York: Atheneum, 1980.
Freeing oneself from macho myths.

_____. *Loving Sex for Both Sexes: Straight Talk for Teen-agers*. New York: Franklin Watts, 1979.
Feelings, attitudes, and decisions about sex that affect our lives.

Casewit, Curtis W. *The Stop Smoking Book for Teens*. New York: Julian Messner, 1980.
Why people smoke, why and how to quit.

Coles, Robert; Brenner, Joseph H.; and Meagher, Dermot. *Drugs and Youth: Medical, Psychiatric, and Legal Facts*. New York: Liveright, 1970.

Although some information is outdated, an excellent general discussion of how the whole issue of drugs relates to the problems of coming of age in our society today.

Corsaro, Maria, and Korzeniowsky, Carole. *STD: A Commonsense Guide*. New York: St. Martin's Press, 1980.
Symptoms and treatment of sexually transmitted diseases.

Eagan, Andrea Boroff. *Why Am I So Miserable if These Are the Best Years of My Life?: A Survival Guide for the Young Woman*. New York: Avon Books, 1979.
A guide to help the teen-age girl learn who she is, what she wants, and how to make decisions.

259

Fayerweather Street School. *The Kids' Book of Divorce By, For and About Kids*. Edited by Eric E. Rofes. Lewis, 1981.

How divorce affects children—by twenty young people.

Fixx, James F. *The Complete Book of Running*. New York: Random House, 1977.

Everything you always wanted to know . . . physical, mental, and emotional aspects of running.

Gilbert, Sara D. *Feeling Good: A Book about You and Your Body*. New York: Four Winds Press, 1979.

Physical, emotional, and mental changes that occur during adolescence.

_____. *Trouble at Home*. New York: Lothrop, Lee & Shepard, 1981.

How to deal with divorce, child abuse, illness, death, et cetera.

Gordon, Sol. *The Teenage Survival Book: The Complete, Revised, Updated Edition of YOU*. Alexandria, Va.: Time-Life Books, 1981.

Enables teen-agers to examine themselves as persons.

Greenberg, Harvey R. *What You Must Know about Drugs and Drug Abuse*. New York: Four Winds Press, 1972.

Overview of drugs and drug-related problems by the author of this book. Out of print, but available in many libraries.

Horvath, Joan. *What Girls Want to Know about Boys: What Boys Want to Know about Girls*. New York: Elsevier-Dutton, 1976.

Ideas, desires, thoughts, and feelings by and about the opposite sex.

Hoyt, Patricia. *How to Get Started When You Don't Know Where to Begin*. New York: Harcourt Brace Jovanovich, 1980.

Getting a job, an apartment, et cetera.

Janeczek, Curtis L. *Marijuana: Time for a Closer Look*. Healthstar Publications, 1980.

Social, medical, and scientific aspects of smoking pot.

Johnson, Eric W. *Love and Sex in Plain Language*. New York: Harper & Row, 1977.

Intercourse, pregnancy, birth, homosexuality, masturbation, et cetera.

Jones, Kenneth L. *Drugs and Alcohol*. New York: Harper & Row, 1979.

Basic information on the use and abuse of drugs and alcohol.

Kovel, Joel. *A Complete Guide to Therapy: From Psychoanalysis to Behavior Modification*. New York: Pantheon Books, 1977.

Different approaches to therapy.

Krementz, Jill. *How It Feels When a Parent Dies*. New York: Alfred A. Knopf, 1981.
Eighteen children tell in their own words about the death of a parent.

Laiken, Deidre S., and Schneider, Alan J. *Listen to Me, I'm Angry*. New York: Lothrop, Lee & Shepard, 1980.
How to deal with anger.

Landau, Elaine. *Death: Everyone's Heritage*. New York: Julian Messner, 1976.
How people accept it.

————. *Teen Guide to Dating*. New York: Julian Messner, 1980.
Meeting new people, going steady, marrying young, et cetera.

Langone, John. *Bombed, Buzzed, Smashed or . . . Sober: A Book about Alcohol*. New York: Avon Books, 1979.
The history, use, abuse, causes, and effects of drinking.

————. *Death Is a Noun: A View of the End of Life*. Boston: Little, Brown & Co., 1972.
Its meanings and forms.

————. *Like, Love, Lust: A View of Sex and Sexuality*. New York: Avon Books, 1981.
A view of friendship, love, and sex.

LeShan, Eda J. *You and Your Feelings*. New York: Macmillan, 1975.
A guide to understanding feelings and relationships with others.

LeShan, Lawrence. *How to Meditate: A Guide to Self-Discovery*. New York: Bantam Books, 1975.
Easy-to-read discussion of meditation and a wide range of meditative methods suitable for the beginner.

McCoy, Kathy, and Wibbelsman, Charles. *The Teenage Body Book*. New York: Pocket Books, 1979.
Questions and answers about health and sexuality.

McGough, Elizabeth. *Who Are You?: A Teenager's Guide to Self-Understanding*. New York: William Morrow, 1976.
Problems and changes of adolescence—dating, decision making, et cetera.

Marks, Jane. *HELP: A Guide to Counseling and Therapy without a Hassle*. New York: Julian Messner, 1976.
Advice on choosing professional help.

Moore, Bob. *You Can Be President (or Anything Else)*. Gretna, La.: Pelican, 1980.
The power of positive thinking—how to be "president" of your own life.

Richards, Arlene Kramer, and Willis, Irene. *Boy Friends, Girl Friends, Just Friends*. New York: Atheneum, 1979.
Making, keeping, and losing friends.

————. *How to Get It Together When Your Parents Are Coming Apart*. New York: David McKay, 1976.
How to deal with parents' marital problems—getting through the pain and fear.

————. *Leaving Home*. New York: Atheneum, 1980.
Breaking ties, temporarily and permanently.

Schowalter, J. E., and Anyan, Walter R. *The Family Handbook of Adolescence: A Comprehensive Medically Oriented Guide to the Years from Puberty to Adulthood*. New York: Alfred A. Knopf, 1981.
Excellent description of common physical and emotional problems of adolescence, as well as information on normal adolescence. Aimed a bit more at parents than teen-agers.

Whelan, Elizabeth M. *Sex and Sensibility: A New Look at Being a Woman*. New York: McGraw-Hill, 1974.
Love and sexuality.

Winship, Elizabeth C. *Ask Beth: You Can't Ask Your Mother*. Boston: Houghton Mifflin, 1976.
Selections from her syndicated column, dealing with sex, depression, drugs, et cetera.

Zimbardo, Philip G. *Shyness: What It Is, What to Do about It*. Reading, Mass.: Addison-Wesley, 1977.
Overcoming shyness.

▌ National Organizations

American Psychiatric Association
1700 18th Street, NW, Washington, D.C. 20009
(202) 797-4900

American Psychological Association
1200 17th Street, NW
Washington, D. C. 20036

American Society for Adolescent Psychiatry
24 Green Valley Road, Wallingford, Pennsylvania 19086
(215) 566-1054

National Association of Social Workers
1425 E Street, NW
Washington D. C. 20005

Alcoholics Anonymous World Services
P. O. Box 459, Grand Central Station, New York, New York 10163
(212) 686-1100

(*For relatives and families of alcoholics*)
Al-Anon Family Group Headquarters
1 Park Avenue, New York, New York 10016
(212) 481-6565

(*To combat sexual abuse of children*)
National Committee for the Prevention of Child Abuse
332 S. Michigan Avenue, Suite 1250, Chicago, Illinois 60604
(312) 565-1100
or
Parents United
P. O. Box 952, San Jose, California 95108
(405) 280-5055

(*For divorced parents*)
International Youth Council of Parents without Partners
7910 Woodmont Avenue, Suite 1000, Washington, D.C. 20014
(301) 654-8850

(*For troubled families*)
Families Anonymous
P. O. Box 344, Torrance, California 90501
(213) 775-3211

National Legal Aid and Defender Association
1625 K Street, N.W., 8th floor, Washington, D.C. 20006
(202) 452-0620

National Association on Drug Abuse Problems
355 Lexington Avenue, New York, New York 10017
(212) 986-1170

National Runaway Switchboard
2210 No. Halsted, Chicago, Illinois 60614
(312) 929-5854
Toll-free number 800-621-4000
or
Runaway Hotline
P. O. Box 52896, Houston, Texas 77052
Toll-free number 800-231-6946

International Association for Suicide Prevention
%Charlott P. Ross, Suicide Prevention Crisis Center,
1811 Trousdale Drive, Burlingame, California 94010
(415) 877-5604
or
National Save-A-Life League
815 2nd Avenue, Suite 409, New York, New York 10017
(212) 736-6191

(To help youth develop goals in life)
National Youth Development Foundation
3460 Hollenberg, Suite A, Bridgeton, Missouri 63044
(314) 291-1423
or
(Multi-purpose programs, e.g., group homes, counseling centers, hotlines, et cetera)
National Youth Work Alliance
1346 Connecticut Avenue, NW, Washington, D.C. 20036
(202) 785-0764
or
(Supportive alternatives for youth in crisis)
Special Approaches to Juvenile Assistance
1743 18 Street, NW, Washington, D.C. 20009
(202) 483-7252

▌ *Appendix–Drugs*

Type or Purpose of Drug	Brand Name	
"MINOR" TRANQUILIZERS OR ANTIANXIETY AGENTS*	Librium Valium Ativan Serax Equanil (also known as Miltown)	Loxitane Tranxene Atarax
"MAJOR" TRANQUILIZERS	Thorazine Mellaril Stelazine Trilafon Prolixin Haldol	Taractan Navane Loxitane Moban Serentil
ANTIDEPRESSANTS	Elavil Tofranil Parnate Nardil Marplan Norpramine (also sold as Pertofrane) Vivactil (also sold as Aventyl)	Deprol Sinequan Surmontil Asendin
ANTIDEPRESSANT/ TRANQUILIZER COMBINATIONS	Triavil Limbitrol Etrafon	

MANIC-DEPRESSIVE OR "BIPOLAR" ILLNESS	Lithium	
SEDATIVES*	Barbiturates (include Amytal, Nembutal, Seconal, Butisol, Tuinal)	
	Dalmane	Chloral Hydrate
	Noludar	Doriden
	Quaalude	Placidyl
STIMULANTS (Also used for hyperactivity in childhood)	Amphetamines (Benzedrine, Desoxyn, Dexedrine) Ritalin	

*To a certain extent, "minor" tranquilizers and sedatives may be interchanged; in some cases, minor tranquilizers may be useful when given in the evening to combat sleeplessness; sedatives can occasionally be effective in low doses for anxiety and tension.

‖ Index

616.89 Greenberg, Harvey
GRE   R.

Hanging in

21,325